# FIRESIDE PAPERS

# FIRESIDE PAPERS

BY

FREDERIC ROWLAND MARVIN

I have sought repose everywhere, and have found it only in a little corner with a little book.
—*St. Francis de Sales.*

When evening has arrived I return home and go into my study. I pass into the antique courts of ancient men, where, welcomed lovingly by them, I feed upon the food which is my own, and for which I was born. For hours together the miseries of life no longer annoy me; I forget every vexation; I do not fear poverty; for I have altogether transferred myself to those with whom I hold converse.
—*Machiavelli.*

*Essay Index Reprint Series*

## BOOKS FOR LIBRARIES PRESS
### FREEPORT, NEW YORK

First Published 1915
Reprinted 1968

LIBRARY OF CONGRESS CATALOG CARD NUMBER:

68-8482

PRINTED IN THE UNITED STATES OF AMERICA

*These pages are dedicated with tender love
and great gladness of heart to my dear wife*

PERSIS

When gaily o'er the fields she tripped,
The flowers they burst aflame;
My heart, that was a worthless weed,
A crimson rose became.

Pray thee, take care, that thou tak'st my book in
    hand
To read it well, that is to understand.
                     — *Ben Jonson.*

# PREFACE

Books are a perpetual friendship. The library wherein they are stored is not only a depository of literary treasures, but also the meeting place of kindred minds. The man who is at home in my library is something more than a transient guest — he is my friend. If my books delight him, we have much in common. My neighbor I respect as a good man. He enters my home, and I enter his. We are interested in each other's welfare, and would do much to further good-will between us. But the companion who makes with me a willing escape from that world of which Wordsworth warns us, and which he tells us "is too much with us," is surely my friend. When I shut the door and go apart by myself, my friend is not wholly excluded. "Getting and spending," which "lay waste our powers," are for the time put aside. I leave behind me the troubles and vexations of life, I thrust from me the little fears that destroy peace of mind, and I pass with glad heart into Machiavelli's "antique courts of ancient men, where, welcomed lovingly by them, I feed upon the food which is my own, and for which I was born." The man of books finds his happiest hours in his library. There he is at home as he is at home nowhere else.

# PREFACE

When one is sick at heart, and all that is beautiful has faded from one's life in dull drab; when radiant hopes have suffered sad eclipse, and the days seem to hold little of worth; when trouble and disappointment gather in dark clouds around one, and the very air seems lonely and charged with death; when all the springs of comfort and strength are dry,— then it is that the lover of books turns to them for the companionship that he is sure he can find nowhere else. Blessed, thrice blessed, is the man who in seasons of trouble and disaster can forget himself and his own little field of misfortune in the larger world of literature. In that bright wonder-world there is medicine for the soul, friendship, pleasure, and new strength for achievement and duty.

These "Fireside Papers" are all the flying years have left me of many happy hours. In them linger the thoughts, hopes, and remembrances of evenings gladdened by the sweet fellowship of friends that age not with the failing strength of those who have loved them and who will always love them. The ancients called all good books a "Treasury of Remedies for the Mind," but they are more than that, for in them gather what is best in every age and land. The philosophers, poets, and teachers of all time are with us still. When they were on earth, as we are at the present moment, they were called living men and women; and now that we see them no more with the natural eye, we think of them as dead. Nevertheless they are not dead, but live

# PREFACE

and breathe and have their being in many books of priceless value. Were Homer materially present in the world, but few could enjoy his society. I could not hope to entertain by my fireside one upon whose companionship the entire literary world would make such great demands. But all that would make the Greek poet so enthusiastically sought were he dwelling now in any of our cities, he has left with us in those marvelous poems that all men may read. The glorious genius that exalted Homer and Shakespeare above other men may find a ready place by my fireside. I know those two immortal poets far better than the people of their own times knew them. My firelight may fall brightly upon the upturned face of the " thousand-souled " poet of old England, as fell the light of long age upon his noble features. Whatever is best in ages and lands is mine, and over them all I write with grateful heart, " *Mash Allah* "— the Gift of God.

# CONTENTS

# I

## THE LONELINESS OF GENIUS

Σοφὸς ὁ πολ-
λὰ εἰδὼς φυᾶ·
μαθόντες δὲ, λάβροι
παγγλωσσίᾳ, κόρακες ὣς,
ἄκραντα γαρυέμεν,
διὸς πρὸς ὄρνιχα θεῖον.
*— Pindar.*

The light of genius is sometimes only the light of
a falling star.
*— Maudsley.*

So lonely 'twas that God himself
Scarce seemèd there to be.
*— Coleridge.*

# THE LONELINESS OF GENIUS

IT is commonly believed that men of genius are sad. It is true that there would be no great difficulty in naming a number of men distinguished in professional circles, and endowed with rare intellectual gifts, who have known much of the brighter side of life; and yet it is nevertheless a fact that those who possess what we call creative ability, which is the ability peculiar to poet, musician, and artist, are, for all in all, men of depressed spirit who inhabit a twilight-world and live amid its shadows. Their depression is partly due to a peculiar cast of mind and partly to a certain acuteness of perception which in some measure all the sons of genius possess. They see much of the distress of mind and physical hardship incident to man's life on earth, while those who have less penetration not only do not see, but do not even know of many of the more sorrowful experiences of our race. It is both the fortune and misfortune of men of genius that they see below the surface of things. The German *Welt-Schmerz*, with which the common man troubles himself little, lies open to the finer vision of the man of genius. He perceives the vastness of the terrible problem involved in human sorrow, distress, and wrongdoing, and he appreciates the extent of the evil which it entails. And the sensitiveness of his nature, which reinforces the acuteness of his per-

1

ception, makes the world-sorrow to be for him in truth *Selbst-Schmerz.*

Still further, the man of genius is aware of the significance of sorrow. He sees in sorrow what others fail of discerning,— the ceaseless tragedy of man's life on earth. It is the sight of this that sunders him from his kind. His is the loneliness of an experience all his own. He shares it with so few that the isolation often seems well-nigh complete. Into the gayeties that so delight the thoughtless multitude he finds himself unable to enter, for his vision penetrates to the waiting sorrow beneath.

Nature is very much what we make it. The green hills and fertile valleys, ocean, forest, and prairie, these are, all of them, in themselves, apart from man's creative vision, nothing more than natural variations or irregularities in the surface of the earth. Only in so far as we view these things through the eye of the mind are they anything more than physical peculiarities devoid of wonder and charm. The desert may mean suffering and death to one who, deprived of water, is perishing upon its level floor of glass-like sand beneath the insufferable heat of a burning sky. But let the poet's eye, or the eye of the artist, relieved of all distress, rest upon those arid wastes, and they are at once transformed. The appalling expanse, . trackless and lifeless, takes on marvelous beauty. Nature is what we make it to be. The commonplace, unimaginative man lives in one world, while the artist and poet live in another and different world. Man is the creator of his own visible universe. To all intents and purposes there would be no universe were there no intelligent beings to view it.

To the eye of genius all things are fluid. " Solidity," wrote a New England author, " is an illusion of the senses. To faith, nothing is solid; the nature of the soul renders such fact impossible." Fabre d'Olivet held that the outward universe was wholly dependent upon the individual mind, and that our world would be as it should be were men only as good as they should be. He even held himself personally responsible for the obliquity of the axis of the earth. He was sure that if he could only attain to the right spiritual state, he should be able to look on outward nature and say: " I snow, I rain." Without indorsing extreme idealism, we may say that the universe is to us what it appears to be. What it is in itself, apart from our observation and experience, we can never know. It stands related to us and is a part of us as we are a part of it. George Herbert was a poet and not a philosopher, but he knew of this close connection of man with his environment when he wrote:

> " Man is all symmetrie,
> Full of proportions, one limbe to another,
>     And all to all the world besides;
>     Each part may call the farthest, brother;
> For head with foot hath private amitie,
>     And both with moons and tides.

" Nothing hath got so farre
But Man hath caught and kept it as his prey.
His eyes dismount the highest starre;
He is in little all the sphere.
Herbs gladly cure our flesh, because that they
Find their acquaintance there.

" For us the windes do blow;
The earth doth rest, heav'n move, and foun-
    tains flow.
Nothing we see, but means our good.
As our delight, or as our treasure;
The whole is either our cupboard of food,
    Or cabinet of pleasure."

The good man sees around him a world of divine beauty ; he sees as well a world of opportunity, and he feels within him a desire to improve
still more the world as it presents itself to his
mind. The evil man beholds a world full of base
and worthless things that please his evil mind,
and he proceeds at once to make it still worse.
The loneliness of the desert is a poetical conception formed in the human mind. The traveler,
standing on the edge of the Libyan waste, is
overcome by the sense of solitude; but the Arab
pitches his tent far out in the rainless region,
and lies down at night beneath the silent stars
with no thought of discomfort. The two men
inhabit different worlds and each has created for
himself the world in which he lives.

Algot Lange, who was lost in the interminable
forests that surround the headwaters of the

Amazon, told me how, having seen his little party die, one after another, from fever and snake-bite, until he was left alone in the vast jungle, he came face to face with a horror that neither language nor art can depict. It was the opening of his eyes to the terror of his situation. He was not overcome by the fear of death, for neither he nor his men were afraid of death at any time during the journey. It was not privation, for they were inured to that. It was an absolutely unique experience that came with a vision of the loneliness of his situation. A sudden internal experience changed for him in a few moments the entire appearance of so much of the world as at that time concerned him. But the South American Indians inhabiting that part of the continent saw nothing in the landscape to terrify or distress them. Geographically they were not far away, but though only a dozen miles, it may be, separated them from Lange, they and the explorer were, nevertheless, dwelling in entirely different worlds.

But the desolations of nature are not greater than those of the human mind. They do not so effectually separate a man from his fellows, neither do they have within them that sense of mystery which adds loneliness and apprehension to the problems presented. Our dread of the unseen world is only a dread of mystery, as is also the child's fear of the dark. A man once said that he would be more terrified by the presence of the disembodied spirit of his dearest friend than

by the presence of his most implacable foe in the
flesh.  Our Saviour, after his resurrection, appeared to the disciples.  Instead of receiving him
with gladness of heart, they were alarmed.  They
loved him as devoutly as ever, but they were
afraid of the dead.  It is largely the mystery
in death that gives to the last hour its power
to alarm the human mind.  When our Saviour
had overcome that sense of mystery by eating in
their presence, the disciples recovered their self-
possession and calmness of mind.  Death and all
supreme hours are lonely.  Before them we stand
with bowed head and in reverent silence.

But the loneliness of genius is unlike all other
kinds of loneliness.  It is a loneliness centering
in the man himself.  Wherever he goes there goes
with him a sense of separation.  This isolation
has been called " the loneliness of the laurelled,"
but that is a description that does not describe.
Some of the most gifted of mankind have had
little to do with laurel.  The world did not appreciate them.  No doubt there are to-day men
of genius and learning who fail of obtaining
recognition.  Some are crushed beneath the
weight of their own poverty; some are driven by
their timidity and modesty into an undeserved
obscurity; some are made the butt of ridicule
because they refuse to pander to the rude vulgarity of the crowd.  " Mute inglorious Mil-
tons " there are in every land and age.  These
go all unlaurelled to forgotten graves.  It is a
coarse world we live in.  To contend successfully

with it one must have the hide of a rhinoceros.

Galileo was certainly one of the greatest of men, but his own age despised him. He died in 1642, with little or no recognition. What thoughts rise in the mind of the pilgrim as he stands in the Torre del Gallo where the philosopher studied! It was there Milton visited him in 1638, and it was in that observatory he made some of his most valuable discoveries. With a very poor telescope of his own construction he discovered four satellites of Jupiter, the phases of Venus, the starry nature of the Milky Way, the hills and valleys of the moon, and the spots on the solar disk from the motion of which he inferred the rotation of the sun. Twice he was persecuted by the Inquisition because of the support he gave the Copernican system. To his other discoveries he added that of the gravity of the air. Surely he was a very great man, but he was not among the " laurelled." There were in Italy ignorant ecclesiastics who basked in popular praise and favor while he was viewed with aversion because of his great discoveries.

It has always been the ill fortune of men not in close sympathy with their age to endure its opposition. There are now idle women of wealth who do nothing all day but count their diamonds and gaze through latticed windows upon the toiling crowds that hurry by on their way to places of useful labor. Upon the busy crowds they look with condescension or, it may be, with open contempt. Yet in the street below are the makers of much of our true wealth and real glory. The world could spare the " four hundred " and be none the worse for so trifling a loss; but it can ill afford to lose the sons of genius who, it may be all unnoticed, are laying the enduring foundations of true greatness.

Mediocrity will never suffer for want of company, but the men and women of commanding ability are few. And they must remain alone because genius in a measure excludes those who possess that treasure from the larger but commonplace intimacies of the world. And, in fact, they are not so dependent upon the society of ordinary men and women as is the average man. They do not feel so keenly the need of companionship, for they find society in their work, and as well in those dreams and visions which they ever strive to realize in actual life. How much companionship did Erasmus have in his day? He had a friend in Ammonius and in the few scholars living at that time in remote lands, with whom he corresponded. His way was for the most part a lonely one, and yet the isolation did not distress him because of the large intellectual resources at his command. Like Michael Angelo, he could say, " I have need of but few friends." His solitude was not desolation.

It is not long ago that eccentricity was supposed to be a distinctive mark of genius. Dryden was so sure of the soundness of Seneca's dictum, " There is no great genius without a tincture of madness," that he paraphrased it and so gave it a wonderful currency. Lombroso is of the same mind, for he holds in his book, " The Man of Genius," that well nigh all the great poets, musicians, artists, and men of exceptional ability are, if not stark mad, at least in the borderland of derangement and in imminent peril of a writ *de lunatico inquirendo.*

If the reader insists upon inquiring into the nature of genius, I must confess in all frankness that I do not know how to define that mysterious and scintillant word. It has been insisted upon by more than one author that it stands for nothing beyond " an infinite capacity for taking pains." But no such meaning can be attached to the word. Putting aside all objection to the misuse of the expression " infinite," which cannot be applied to anything human, it may be said that the description is too commonplace, too dull and " humdrum," for a word, and much more for a thing, the entire force and significance of which are in the direction of the exceptional. Think of describing the genius of Shakespeare as a " capacity for taking pains." Is it to pains or effort only that we owe the charm and beauty, the wealth of wisdom, the wit and eloquence, of " Hamlet," " The Merchant of Venice," " Julius Cæsar," and all the rest of those marvelous plays that make their author's name immortal? Then indeed is genius a thing so cheap that no one need despair of possessing it. One has only to persist and it is his.

The " capacity for taking pains " is by no

means a difficult thing. Marshall Field, who at
the time of his death had the largest wholesale
and retail dry-goods business in the world, was
a man of immense persistency. He may have
taken more pains with his business than Shakespeare ever thought of taking with any or all of
his deathless dramas. I doubt not he possessed
a more resolute purpose, and brought to bear
upon his enterprise a more tireless energy than
the greatest of writers ever dreamed of. If the
comparison be wholly in the field of letters, shall
we say that the " capacity for taking pains "
was greater in Shakespeare than in many of his
fellow writers, who, with better opportunity, for
want of that something we call genius, failed
where he succeeded? No, genius is vastly more
than the " capacity for taking pains."

Yet Disraeli believed in the patience-theory.
He said as much in his " Contarini Fleming."
No doubt patience is worth much to the man of
genius, as it is to all who would play their part
well in whatever circle their labor and duty may
lie; but it is not even the thing Disraeli calls it,—
" a necessary ingredient of genius." There have
been those who wrote their names in large characters upon the roll of fame and were yet neither
patient nor strong of will. Genius is a thing in
itself, a peculiar thing, and the possession of but
few of the sons and daughters of our race. We
are born with it if we have it at all.

Lowell, in his essay on Rousseau, distinguishes
between talent and genius. The former, he tells

us, is " that which is in a man's power," while
the latter is " that in the power of which a man
is."   Genius, according to Lowell, is of the nature of inspiration, and, at the same time it is
the normal faculty or endowment of certain
minds — normal, because in the course of nature.
Inspiration, which it resembles, is a thing from
without; it is a direct and special endowment of
God.   Lowell helps us, but he leaves us as far
away from a precise definition as we were at the
beginning of our paper.

No man can be a great poet or a great artist
without some measure of genius.   It is the faculty, or capacity, or whatever you choose to call
it, that gives objective reality to those subjective and illusory dreams that come only to peculiar minds.   While leaving the man free, it still
exerts a certain compulsion of which he is not
aware so long as he yields to its requirements,
but of which he is sometimes painfully aware
when he refuses to comply with its demands.   It
may be that the poet knew something of its nature when he wrote,

> " I do but sing because I must,
> And pipe but as the linnets sing."

There you have compulsion in perfect freedom.
One who sings as the birds sing does so both because he would and because he must.   " Poetry,"
wrote John Wesley, " is a gift of nature."   Natural gifts are of all gifts those that most demand
expression.   What we acquire we may put aside,

but what we are we must remain. Without in any way approving the use of opium save as a medicine, I yet believe that some idea of the nature of genius may be obtained for certain minds by small doses of the drug. The revelation is brief, and the punishment, in most cases, severe, for a slavery quite unlike the wholesome compulsion of genius is easily entailed. Yet the disclosure is, while it lasts, interesting if nothing more. It awakens the dream as a subjective experience, but it, in most cases, does nothing more. It gives the dream no expression. Very few things of any real worth have been written, and perhaps no work of art has been executed, under the influence of any drug in any form. I know it has been said that we owe " Christabel " and " The Ancient Mariner " to the unfortunate use their author made of the juice of the white poppy. I do not believe it. The poems named are, to my thinking, fragments of what might have been written by Coleridge had he dallied less with the drug that enslaved his will and impeded the natural working of his mind. It must be remembered that Coleridge was a man of genius in and of himself, and apart from all external adjuvants. His writings are mostly fragmentary and of very unequal value, all of which inequality was in large measure, I believe, due to his confirmed opium habit. He was " a magnificent dreamer." Wordsworth wrote, " He was the only wonderful man I ever knew." Yet it has been said: " All that he did excellently might be bound up in twenty pages, but it should be bound in pure gold." Well, that would depend somewhat upon the size of the pages. They would indeed have to be very large to cover all that Coleridge " did excellently " in both prose and verse, but larger still would they be had he trusted his genius more and his drug less.

De Quincey also was a man of genius whose output would have been larger and better had his indulgence in opium been restrained. The faint vision of what genius may be in itself, subjectively, is not worth the cost. If one has the desire to follow this subject further, but from an entirely different point of view, it may not be wholly a waste of time to read a little pamphlet called " The Anæsthetic Revelation and the Gist of Philosophy " by Benjamin Paul Blood, privately printed at Amsterdam, New York. From most of Blood's conclusions we wholly dissent, but none the less are we interested in his novel views and still more novel results.

Chopin was a man of rare fineness of temper and great delicacy of feeling, a man of remarkable genius, a musician of enduring fame. But one does not have to read far into the story of his life to discover how sad was his spirit. His was a sadness that distressed not himself alone, but others as well, for his kindness was such that others could not but sympathize with him. He was a man of fine courtesy and delicate perception. Music, of which he was one of the great masters, was the supreme outlet through which he gave graceful expression to his sadness. He has been called a tone-poet, so poetical were his musical compositions. They are as fresh and delightful to-day as they were when first given to an astonished world. They will always possess indescribable charm.

Beethoven was another great musician, a man of supreme genius. No doubt the unjust severity of the critical attacks to which he was subjected in the early part of his career had much to do with the gloom that settled down upon his spirit and colored many of his productions. He said: "I was nigh taking my life with my own hands. But Art held me back. I could not leave the world until I had revealed what lay within me." Of him Mr. Alger said: "He was poor, deaf, solitary, restless, proud, and sad; sometimes almost cursing his existence, sometimes ineffably glad and grateful; subject now to the softest yearnings of melancholy and sympathy, now to tempestuous outbreaks of wrath and woe. Shut up in himself, he lived alone, rambled alone, created alone." His last words were, some say, "I go to meet death with joy. Farewell, and do not quite forget me after I am dead." Others give his last words thus: "I shall hear in heaven."

How tender and gracious was the spirit of the saint and mystic, Eugénie de Guerin, whose posthumous letters and journal revealed to the world one of the most beautiful of characters. For the few days of gladness that brightened her gifted life she was profoundly grateful. " God be praised," she said upon one occasion, " for this day spent without sadness. Such are so rare in my life. A word, a memory, a tone of voice, a sad expression of face, a nameless nothing, will disturb the serenity of my spirit — small sky that the lightest clouds can tarnish."

The literary history of Petrarch is too well known to call for comment. If some of his lines seem effeminate and his praise of Laura exaggerated, especially in view of the fact that no love on his part could be honorably returned by her, it should be remembered that his melancholy was at times dangerously near self-destruction. His genius was of a melancholy cast and darkened all his life. Much of his literary work, in which we find so great a satisfaction, gave him no pleasure whatever, but rather added to his distress.

Dante was a man of austere habit and severe manners. He was a man of strong will, and, though one of the greatest of poets, he was nevertheless a fearless defender of what he believed to be right. He was of heroic build. His marriage was not a happy one. Had Gemma Donati been all she should have been, it was still not in him to make such a husband as a woman would be likely to desire. Had Beatrice been his wife, things would, no doubt, have been even worse. Stern, sad, and lonely, with determined purpose, and a genius towering above, not his

own age alone, but other ages as well, he walked
the earth in a solitude upon which no companionship could have made any impression.   It is recorded of him that one wild and stormy night he
came to Corvo, where he was blessed by one of
the friars, who, not knowing who he was, asked
what he sought.   Upon a quiet night, very unlike
the one that brought our poet to the ancient monastery, I wrote in my library, just before retiring,
the following lines in which the question asked
by the friar is answered as Dante is said to have
answered it:

### DANTE AT CORVO

His hand the Benedictine laid
    Upon the brow of him
Who craved alone the gift of peace,
    With weary mind and limb.

And, as beneath sweet Corvo's shade
    The stranger sank to rest,
The droning friars guessed not who
    Preferred that strange request.

'Twas not within their power to give
    The boom he fondly sought,—
Peace, gentle peace, where grief
    Her bitter work had wrought.

War he had waged till every nerve
    Within him burned like fire;
They knew not Heaven and Hell had joined,
    That stranger to inspire;

Nor that the world should long revere,
  Beyond all sense of wrong,
In him the master of immortal verse,
  The pride of Tuscan song;

That he should live, divinely clear,
  Serene, and strong, and brave,
When their poor songs, to memory lost,
  Sleep with them in the grave.

Ah, little dreamed they that brief night
  Of fame that should abide,
That 'neath their sacred roof-tree slept
  Their country's hope and pride.

They only thought a stranger craved
  What they could not bestow,
Peace,— that sweet gift a whole world seeks,
  And few may ever know.

Great master of immortal song,
  Whose dust Ravenna holds,
Death brought thee what she hath for all,—
  The peace that Life withholds.

Life must always be lonely to one who thinks.
Thinking is a process of separation. It sunders
man from man, and gives to the mind a separate
life and an aim different from that which controls
the surrounding world. It is surprising how
large a part of our common existence is carried
on with little thought, and how much of that little thought is automatic, subconscious, and hap-
hazard. I do not know how much of the depres-

sion that enters so surely into the mind of the
man who thinks apart from the conventional be-
liefs and opinions of his fellows, is due to the
isolation that must in the very nature of the case
follow; but certain it is that men who blaze new
trails must learn to draw their strength from
within and not from without.    Social habits and
commonplace opinions provide an easier road for
the ordinary traveler, and there can be no good
reason why he should not remain in that road to
the end of his days, in association with agreeable
companions.    But there will always remain those
who find other roads more to their liking; those
who are willing to forego fellowship and joint
interests of every kind if only they may come
upon unfrequented ways and break into undiscov-
ered worlds.    To such travelers the commonplace
route, though safer and less difficult, is dull and
unattractive.    The highway is well graded and
leads straight ahead, with few turns to right or
left; but one must take chances in strange paths
and in districts wherein there are no paths at all.
In lonely roads there are lonely experiences, and
such experiences are never far removed from the
sadness that surrounds us all, whether we know it
or not.    The more isolated the way, the more
intrusive and persistent the sadness.    A mournful spirit breathes through all human experiences, of whatever kind.    One does not have to
turn to the pages of Schopenhauer if he would
learn how vast is the loneliness of our human

life.   One has but to think, and at once the process of disillusionment commences.

I have in my home a little bird that hops all
the long day from perch to perch in its wire cage.
It appears happy in the degree possible to its
animal existence.   To open the door of the cage
and give that creature freedom would be to kill it.
And yet nevertheless the unvarying monotony of
its dull life, in which one day is as another, can
produce in me only a sense of melancholy.   Is
not the man who commiserates the narrow and
restricted life of the bird himself very like that
little bundle of yellow feathers?   How limited is
the sympathy my bird enjoys!   The cat, for
the mere pleasure of killing a living creature,
would improve the first opportunity that might
come in its way to catch and destroy my di-
minutive pet.   The vivisector would care nothing for its momentary distress if by plunging
into it a scalpel he could see some physiological
peculiarity.   Were the creature freed from its
confinement, permitted to roost upon some tree,
the first boy who might happen by with a shot-
gun would ask no better fun than to send it in
agony to the earth.   Were its plumage worth
the having, how willingly would yonder fine lady
now passing my door transfix the little creature
and fasten it to her bonnet as an Indian chief
would tie a scalp to his girdle.   There is not a
taxidermist in all the land who would not kill
that bird and stuff it for a few shillings.   Noth-

ing but my fondness for the bird stands between
it and a painful death.

Is the case different in the matter of man's
treatment of his fellow?  Is it not true that

> " Man's inhumanity to man
> Makes countless thousands mourn "?

Would a young and beautiful woman be safe a
quarter of an hour in any city park, to say
nothing of a lonely country road, after dark?
Would you count yourself secure at night if it
were known that you had in your home a considerable sum of money?  Do you not encoun-
ter upon the street every day men who would
cut your throat for a few dollars?  Range these
questions, and include them if you will under
the head of Pessimism,— what does it matter?
Names go for nothing; it is the thing that
counts.  The man who inveighs against these
views and insists upon it that his fellows are, all
of them, at heart good, is just as careful to lock
his money in the burglar-proof chest he calls his
safe when he returns home at the end of the day
as is the person who professes less faith in a
general distribution of righteousness.  There
does not seem to be a very decided and wide-
spread confidence in the spotless integrity of our
officials, or indeed in that of politicians in general.
All these things, when one sees them clearly,
have a decided tendency to congeal sympathy,
create suspicion, and increase the loneliness of
life.

I am not a victim of agaraphobia, or of that dread of the ocean which physicians name thalassophobia; and yet long distances, when I stop to think of them, produce in my mind a decided sense of loneliness, and, as well, a feeling of depression. Vast stretches of space isolate and appal the mind. They make man and all his affairs seem unimportant and even insignificant. Our universe, which is but one of many millions of universes, contains countless stars compared with many of which our earth is as a pin's point for size. Our own sun weighs three hundred and thirty times as much as the planet upon which we live. The two little words, " No end," seem to have in them the sound of doom even when they guarantee pleasure. The thought of that which never began and can never end is too great a thought for the finite mind. Only when it brings with it the even greater thought of the infinite love of an eternal God can it be endured by one who is awake to its meaning. The idea of infinite space, numberless stars, unbroken and endless duration, involves a loneliness that language is powerless to describe. All supreme hours and experiences are companionless. And, as a matter of fact, our closest associations are more seeming than real. It has been shown by men of science that no two particles of matter touch each other. We ourselves are like those particles. There are unbridged spaces between my soul and that of my dearest friend. We touch only at points. Society is composed of

social atoms, each atom being a human personality. We think we know each other, but the
isolation is complete. Surely ours is a lonely
world when once we give it due consideration.
So thought the poet when he wrote:

> "We are spirits clad in veils;
>     Man by man was never seen;
> All our deep communing fails
>     To remove the shadowy screen.
>
> "Heart to heart was never known;
>     Mind with mind did never meet;
> We are columns left alone
>     Of a temple once complete."

There dwelt not long ago in the woods of
Maine a woman who, in a little hut far removed
from village life, acquired many unusual languages. She was a woman of fine mind and of
great learning. She read Greek as some of us
read English. She knew many strange things,
and was always kind and courteous to those who
called upon her. Yet few cared for the intellectual treasures she had to bestow. Had she
been in the habit of distributing coins to her
callers she would, no doubt, have received more
attention than she would have cared for.

It was only toward the end of his life that
De Quincey was called a great author. No one
had thought of the Opium-Eater as an unusual
writer. Carlyle said of him:

" He was a pretty little creature, full of wire-drawn ingenuities, bankrupt pride, with the finest silver-toned low voice, and most elaborate, gently winding courtesies and ingenuities in conversation. What wouldn't one give to have him in a box, and take him out to talk. A bright, ready, and melodious talker, but in the end inconclusive and long-winded. One of the smallest man-figures I ever saw; shaped like a pair of tongs, and hardly above five feet in all. When he was seated, you would have taken him, by candle-light, for the beautifulest little child,— blue-eyed, sparkling face,— had there not been a something, too, which said, ' *Eccovi* — this child has been in hell.' "

How little did Carlyle understand the lonely mind of that marvelous child of genius whose imagination drew for himself and his readers the great picture of " The Flight of a Tartar Tribe "! Alas! gifted, himself, with a rare spirit of mystery and power, he yet was unable to comprehend the loneliness of De Quincey's genius.

The woman who dwelt alone in the Maine woods, when asked how many persons visited her upon a certain day, said, " Only one." " But," said the questioner, " I thought I counted eight." The hermit replied, " Eight persons entered my hut, but only one even remotely approached me." Her experience was that of Thoreau who wrote in his home on the shore of Walden Pond :

" Society is commonly too cheap. We meet at very short intervals, not having had time to acquire

any new value for each other. We meet at meals
three times a day, and give each other a new taste
of that old musty cheese that we are. We have had
to agree on a certain set of rules, called etiquette
and politeness, to make this frequent meeting tol-
erable, and that we need not come to open war."

When Thoreau came to think it over, he wondered why there should be any attempt at the
artificial meeting of minds separated from each
other by something more spacious than statute
miles and degrees of latitude. In "Walden" he
inquires:

"What sort of space is that which separates a
man from his fellows and makes him solitary? I
have found that no exertion of legs can bring two
minds much nearer to one another. What do we
want to dwell near to? Not to many men surely,
the depot, the post-office, the bar-room, the meeting-
house, the school-house, the grocery, Beacon Hill,
or the Five Points, where men most congregate, but
to the perennial source of our life, whence in all
our experience we have found that to issue, as the
willow stands near the water and sends out its roots
in that direction. This will vary with different
natures, but this is the place where a wise man will
dig his cellar."

> "Wisdom divides, and they who know
> Whence forever the far winds blow
> And the swift tides unceasing flow,
> Are sundered by those winds and tides
> From other minds. Wisdom divides."

As has been said, the man of genius does not always win recognition and substantial reward. In the lack of recognition may be discovered a very potent source of loneliness. He sees common men praised and rewarded for inferior work, and the sense of injustice operates as a dividing element separating him from his kind. Doubtless it should not so operate, but human nature is what it is, and no man takes kindly to lack of appreciation and neglect. Publishers are responsible, in the case of authors, for much of this. They are as mercenary to-day as they were a hundred years ago. Chatterton wanted for even the common necessities of life. Sénancour rests undisturbed in his tomb beneath the willows of Sèvres, and few are the pilgrims of sentiment who seek his lonely grave. He died, a broken-hearted old man, after a long life passed in fruitless endeavor. Later, Matthew Arnold celebrated his " Obermann," but the crowd cannot even now tell you what it was that Arnold found in the writings of that solitary recluse to interest him so greatly. George Sand and Sainte-Beuve recognized his genius, but even they could find no publisher who thought his compositions worth printing.

The advice that an old author gave a young writer, though pitiful enough, is not without force. " If you want a publisher," said the experienced man of letters, "blow your trumpet vigorously. It matters little whether the trumpet

be of tin or of some better material so long as the
wind holds out and the trumpet holds together."
Not infrequently a poor poem, once started on
its round, goes from anthology to anthology, re-
newing its foolish youth with every passing year,
while much better lines, for lack of "the
trumpet," sink out of sight and perish utterly.
I could from my own personal acquaintance with
authors construct without difficulty a substantial
list of men of unusual ability, and in some cases
of marked genius, who, because of modesty, self-
respect, and even more unfortunate impecunios-
ity, perished in neglect.

The publishers tell us that they are looking
for good books, and that a valuable manuscript
is never allowed to escape them unless it be by
some rare mistake.  It is not true.  Publishers,
like merchants and others, are out gunning for
the nimble shekels, and it is the shekel-hitting book
they want.  For that alone I do not blame them.
If the author may write for money, why may not
the publisher put his wares upon the market with
the same end in view?  I blame them for their intensely mercenary spirit, and for their discourse
about "good books."  It is the stolen halo that
stirs my wrath.

There is an artificial loneliness of a purely
æsthetic kind that men of an imaginative and
poetical turn of mind enjoy.  It is not real.
The best thing about it is the fact that it may be
put aside when there is the will to do so.  It is
of a sickly nature and has in it little that is

noble and manly. Those who have a measure of taste for verse, painting, or something else of the kind, and yet possess no real artistic genius, affect this sort of loneliness. It is, as has been said, not a genuine thing, but only a paste that a little experience will enable one to distinguish from the true gem. It is an imitation of the loneliness of genius. Those who sorrow thus " swim about in their own tears," and enjoy the soothing bath.

## II

## PHILOSOPHERS AND PATRIOTISM

Ἀλλὰ κἀκεῖνο, δεῖ σε ἐνθυμεῖσθαι, ὅτι ἕκαστος ἡμῶν
οὐχ αὑτῷ μόνον γέγονεν, ἀλλὰ τῆς γενέσεως ἡμῶν τὸ μέν
τι ἡ πατρὶς μερίζεται, τὸ δὲ τι οἱ γεννήσαντες, τὸ δὲ οἱ
λοιποὶ φίλοι.

— *Plato.*

Was Goethe a patriot? If to join the army,
toss one's cap in air, shout and sing for liberty,
and bellow about national honor,— if to do these
things constitutes one a patriot, then the poet and
philosopher, the pride and glory of the German
people, was no patriot. If, on the other hand, to
live for one's fellow men a worthy and useful life,
if to use every power of a great mind in the service
of one's country,— if thus to help one's native land
constitutes one a patriot, then Goethe was of all men
an illustrious and noble-minded patriot.

— *Archæologia.*

# PHILOSOPHERS AND PATRIOTISM

IT is commonly charged against philosophers that they have little patriotism. It does not occur to those who prefer the charge that philosophers may have something better about which to concern themselves. Thoreau said in one of his essays, " To a philosopher all news, as it is called, is gossip." There you have the secret of much of the serene indifference with which men of studious and contemplative mind view the political arena. The news of the day that so interests the ordinary man is beyond all doubt nothing more than gossip. The Germans denounced Goethe because he pursued his studies and continued his literary work while his country was at war with implacable and determined enemies. But Germany had hundreds and thousands of able-bodied men to fight her battles, while she had few indeed who were qualified and disposed to do her thinking. She had one Goethe and only one, and he knew his worth to the fatherland and to the great world of many fatherlands. He knew his place and his mission, and he was faithful to both. The news that fired the German heart seemed to him nothing more than a larger kind of gossip. True, it was not the foolish gossip in which elderly matrons indulge over their teacups; but it was the scarcely less inconsequent chatter of lords and ladies, of soldiers and a sovereign.

31

Goethe had work to do for his country and the world, and it was work that called for a tranquil mind undisturbed by the excitement of the hour. Against the reproaches of his countrymen who charged him with indifference, he defended himself in a memorable paragraph in " Eckermann's Conversations with Goethe." To those who called him to account for not having taken part in the War of Liberation he said: " How could I take up arms without being impelled thereto by hatred? And how could I hate at my age? War is foreign to me, and I am without military ambition." Still further, he pointed out to Eckermann why he could not become enthusiastic over war. He said frankly and without hesitation:

" I have never written love songs except when I loved; how, then, could I have written songs of hatred without hating? Between ourselves, I never hated the French, although I thanked God when we were rid of them. How could I, to whom the question of culture and barbarism alone is all-important, hate a nation which is among the most cultured of the world, and to which I owe so great a part of my own culture? National hatred is indeed a peculiar thing. It is always found more pronounced and violent where civilization is lowest; but there is a stage of culture where it vanishes altogether, where one stands, so to say, above all nations, and feels the happiness and the sorrows of a neighboring people as much as if they were a part of one's own."

Goethe was wrong in thinking hatred essential to a liking for war. Some of the ablest commanders have entertained neither bitterness nor dislike.

No one who knows anything about the glory and worth of patriotism will wish to belittle that love of country which lies at the foundation of civil government, but there are nobler sentiments than that of ordinary love of country. The love a man may cherish for his race is far greater and more blessed than that he may cherish for a comparatively small number of men and women who live in one place and speak the same language. And glorious beyond all other loves is the love of God that may even lead us to refuse aid to the land of our birth when that land has ranged itself against the cause that we believe to be worthy of our support. " My country, right or wrong " is an evil motto, and unconditional loyalty is disloyalty to God because it exalts one's country above its Creator and the Creator of all lands and of the whole world.

Fichte was a philosopher, and one of marked ability. He held himself in trust for the entire world, and for truth above all. He was by no means wanting in patriotism, for he gave his life in defense of his country. But I think few will at this late day justify his sacrifice of himself. His work was worth more to Germany than was his life. By connecting himself with the army he unintentionally robbed his own land. These are his words:

" To this I am called — to bear witness to the Truth: my life, my fortunes are of little moment; the results of my life are of infinite moment.  I am a priest of truth: I am in her pay; I have bound myself to do all things, to venture all things, to suffer all things, for her.  If I should be hated and persecuted for her sake, if I should even meet death in her service, what wonderful thing is it I shall have done — what but that which I clearly ought to do."

Did he really serve truth when he went into the German army?  No, his country should have known better; it should have refused the disastrous sacrifice.  Any ordinary peasant was then and would be now of more value to the army than a dozen philosophers; but Fichte in his lecture-room, stimulating and instructing the minds of the German youths, was worth more to his country than can be easily determined.  No country can afford to endanger the genius, learning, and literary and artistic training over which it has control.  Authors, artists, musicians of distinguished ability, and men of science should be not only exempt from military service, but disqualified and prohibited from enlisting.  Was it well that Koerner gave his inspired life to a service others could have rendered?  How his songs, ringing like a battle-cry through the German land, thrilled the hearts of his countrymen and fired the spirit of the soldiers!  His verses were worth more to Germany than ten thousand men-at-arms could by any possibility have been.  Yet

in the fierce conflict at Leipsic all that increasing
wealth of martial enthusiasm was allowed to perish.  Was Koerner's example worth so much to
his country?  Was his sacrifice of himself so
helpful to his cause?  " The Lyre and Sword "
was worth more; and what greater service might
still have been rendered can never be known.
Everything should be done to encourage genius
and learning.  The glory of a nation is not so
much in its possessions as in its achievements, and
these are for the most part the work of its great
men.  Civilization itself is the gift of the few
to the many.  Only while the gifted, trained, and
qualified few are in control is the land safe and
its prosperity assured.  It is not denied that the
trained few may prove recreant to their trust,
and may become wholly unworthy of confidence,
but that in no wise alters the fact that no country is long prosperous when deprived of the wisdom and guidance of its great men.

The philosopher should be something of a poet
in his sympathy and tastes.  The world is full of
beauty, but one must have eyes with which to see
it.  In these days men make little of poetry, and
in some cases they even affect to despise it.  But
poetry, like music, is an open door to some of
the most marvelous beauties in the great world
of nature.  Dr. Johnson did not like music, and
who that is familiar with his life does not see
that the dislike was a limitation of his nature?
Happily for him that limitation was offset, and
in a way corrected, by his fondness for poetry.

Indeed, the love of poetry is that of music as well, and so it came to pass that the " colossus of letters " was, without his knowing it, something of a lover of music after all. True poetry has in it some measure of music. Its words are singing words. A subtle enchantment works in all its lines, and by that enchantment even Dr. Johnson was influenced, though he would have developed a towering rage had any daring person ventured to enlighten him upon the subject. " Music," said Plato, " is a moral law. It gives a soul to the universe, wings to the mind, flight to the imagination, a charm to sadness, gayety and life to everything." If we are to trust the Greek philosopher, music is an essential part of the intellectual universe, and he who despises or even neglects it is hardly a philosopher in the better sense of the word. Carlyle knew well the meaning of music when he called all minstrelsy " a kind of inarticulate, unfathomable speech which leads us to the edge of the infinite, and lets us for moments gaze into it."

Goethe and the Greek philosophers who lived and wrote long centuries before he saw the light viewed this matter in very much the same way. It is related of Anaxagoras, who was falsely accused of impiety and condemned to death, though the sentence was commuted, that he was censured by his friends for what they called a want of patriotism. He repelled the charge with more warmth than was his wont. Pointing to the stars, he said, " I have the greatest affection for my country.". After a moment of silence, during which he still gazed at the heavens, he resumed his study of astronomy and natural science. He believed that he was serving his country by the use he made of his learning in a way much better than that in which those who criticized him thought it his duty to serve it.

It is to the arts and learning, with the benign influence of our Christian faith, that we are to look for the final abolition of war. Tolstoy and writers who sympathize with him in this matter hate war, and desire above all things to create in the hearts of men a like detestation and abhorrence of everything resembling an appeal to arms. They endeavor to expose its brutality and futility. Seldom does war lead to a permanent settlement of any dispute. The vanquished nation will not rest until the decison arrived at by its defeat is reversed in some later and more fortunate conflict. Each new year brings with it a still more deadly explosive of one kind or another. The men who kill their fellow men and who must themselves die in battle are always from the same social level. They have nothing to gain and much to lose. In most cases they do not know the nature of the quarrel they are called to arbitrate with their blood. The so-called upper classes, the gentlefolk, are seldom seen in the ranks that are so soon to be ploughed with shot and shell. The men of birth and breeding are either superior officers or stay-at-homes who not infrequently accumulate fortunes hard to acquire in times of peace. It is always the ignorant, befooled, and, it may be, the coerced workingmen who pay for the fracas with their lives.

In Russia war is a business, and the government is never far from a semi-belligerent attitude. The men who fight have no bitterness of spirit. Why should they have? The quarrel is in no sense of the word theirs. The only thing they hate, when they hate anything, is war itself. They are none the worse fighters for that. The old belief that hate increases the efficiency of armies is a thing of the past. Mr. Jane, the distinguished English naval critic, thinks the Japanese defeated the Russians because they hated them, and were only anxious to kill them, while the Russian soldiers felt no bitterness and simply acted as machines against their " antlike foes." In my humble opinion Mr. Jane is in error. In the first place, the English were the real antagonists with whom Russia had to contend. They financed the war for Japan, and they gave that land every possible encouragement. In the second place, the Japanese were moved by a profoundly patriotic spirit,— an unthinking, unreasoning spirit, it is true, but still a patriotic one. Mr. Jane's theory is that of the Great Britain of a century or more ago — a theory inherited from half-civilized ancestors.

The best fighters are the men of cool head and determined purpose. They are not the men who are anxious to kill, but those who are resolved to conquer. It has been said, " The best lovers are the greatest haters," but a truer saying is the line from a song by Bayard Taylor, " The loving are the daring." It is neither hate nor recklessness that tells with greatest effect on the field of battle. Kipling still holds Mr. Jane's worn-out theory, but it is a theory that does little honor to human nature and that contributes nothing toward bringing in that bright day so eagerly desired when " they shall beat their swords into ploughshares, and their spears into pruning-hooks." Koerner did not hate his enemies whose aim it was to subjugate Prussia. Goethe was too much of a philosopher to interest himself greatly in war from any point of view. Fichte was less of a philosopher for the enthusiasm which drove him from a chair of learning in a German university and led him to play a less worthy part as a soldier. Men of ideal purpose, of poetic genius, artistic feeling and achievement, and scientific accomplishments, should have nothing to do with those vulgar, inartistic, unscientific, and inhuman cataclysmic upheavals that turn the world upside-down for no good reason whatever. Think how these upheavals endanger the world's priceless treasures of art and learning. Think for one moment what it means to bombard a city holding within its walls the Venus de Milo, that miracle of beauty in marble:

" Venus triumphant! so serene and tender
  In thy calm after-bloom of life and love,

More fair than when of old thy sea-born splendor
  Surprised the senses of Olympian Jove."

Think of shelling a city to the keeping of which
is entrusted the Madonna di San Sisto, the most
wonderful of all Raphael's creations.   Think of
endangering a city over which falls the shadow
of the Parthenon.   Once that "finest edifice on
the finest site in the world" was damaged by
a Venetian shell; and again, in 1827, it was
slightly injured by an invading host.   Think of
offering violence to a city that treasures for all
the world Westminster Abbey.   These gifts of
genius to our human race are worth more than
many victories.   Of what sacrilege were the German troops guilty when they destroyed the beautiful city of Louvain, and when, with ruthless
hand and savage instincts, they made of the
Cathedral of Notre Dame at Rheims a target for
their shells.   Men who commit such outrages are
the enemies of civilization.   The cathedral, dat-
ing from the thirteenth century, was, because
both of its age and of its architectural excellence,
the joy and pride of an entire world.

The more one sees of war the more one realizes
its iniquity.   It is a crime against mankind.
We do not for a moment question the right of
every nation to defend its own territory against
the invader; but when that necessity arises, war
is still a calamity, and the aggressor is to be accounted an enemy of all good men.   As such he
is to be dealt with by every civilized nation.

" Blessed are the peacemakers." Another has well said:

" Blessed are the peace-dreamers; for they shall be called the poets of mankind.
" Blessed are the peace-shouters; for they shall be called the orators of the common weal.
" Blessed are the peace-schemers; for they shall be called the diplomatists of the modern world.
" Blessed are the peace-makers; for they shall be called the Sons of God."

War will become a thing of the past when the common men of all lands refuse to leave farm and shop, and say to governments of every kind, " We will not fight." All must refuse if the movement is to succeed. If a few hold back and refuse to defend their country, they must be accounted guilty of treason. The movement must cease to be treasonable by becoming general. No single nation can disarm. If the German Empire can spend forty years in preparing to subjugate Europe, then Europe must spend those same forty years in preparing to prevent that subjugation. The common people in all lands must act together. When they do so act, there will be no more war. The common men are the men that are killed in battle. Most of those who enlist and nearly all who are drafted are from the humbler walks of life. That is because most of the men and women in all lands are born and live in the lowly homes and occupations of the world. The few are educated, and still fewer may be trusted with the care of property and the great enterprises of this world, all of which render them far too valuable to be wasted in a bloody battle. Their education enables them to avoid in many ways the common conscription. Knowing more than the average men and women of the world, they know the various ways of escaping duties and dangers that others must face with what courage they may. There is a way of escaping almost everything if you only know the way. Educated men know many ways and many things of which the uneducated are ignorant.

It is said that most of the taxes are paid by the poor. There is much truth in the saying. There are various ways of avoiding taxation. Some of those ways are dishonest, and some of them involve no breaking of law. Education helps a man here as elsewhere. The professional classes, as a general thing, do not go to the war. They are of less use in the army than are men of affairs. When men of cultivated mind do go, they are usually commissioned officers, chaplains, surgeons, or engineers, and as such are not wanted on the firing line. They also may resign if they wish. The dangers, burdens, and hardships of war fall to common men, whilst the emoluments and advantages go to the privileged few. It would be a blessed thing if the common men of all nations could combine and refuse to fight. We have already learned not to waste men of genius and of exceptional ability upon war; how long will it be before we learn that common men have a value, and are not to be wasted on shot and shell!

The rights of common men will not be respected so long as the military idea prevails. German Imperialism is opposed to both modern civilization and the rights of ordinary men. Civilization rests upon the people, while Imperialism looks to the army. The German Emperor said, " The army is the foundation of the social structure of the Empire. . . . The soldier and the army, not parliamentary majorities and decisions, have welded together the German Empire. My confidence is in the army; — as my grandfather said at Coblenz, ' These are the gentlemen on whom I can rely.' "

What the Emperor thinks of the people may be learned from one of his addresses as reported by a German professor, the distinguished Dr. Ludwig Gurlitt. This is what the Emperor said: " The masses are children not yet of age. The government alone is competent to prescribe the course of their social and cultural development." The Emperor is Germany. It is his prerogative to govern alone, with no responsibility of any kind. His word is law. Of course that means despotism pure and simple. The common man can have no rights under such a system.

In order to carry out the German program it is necessary to shut off criticism. The light must be extinguished. It is a rule with the English royal family that no member of it, from the King himself down to the least important person connected with him, is ever to bring an action for libel, no matter how vile the slander may be. The German Emperor takes a more drastic method of procedure. All criticism of the sovereign is *lèse majesté*, no matter how just and wholesome it may be. If you say anything about the Emperor of which he does not approve, he may send you to prison. The man who is placed above criticism is also placed above responsibility. You cannot call him to account for anything. Under such a system neither the common man nor any other kind of a man can have any guaranty that his rights will be protected. He has no rights to protect.

All absolutists hate free institutions. Thus Bismarck did not like the United States. He was born under an absolute monarchy and he was a believer in militarism, and it grieved him to see German boys emigrate to our American Republic. Why should they wish to leave the Fatherland and live all their days under a constitutional government? He could not see, or rather he would not see, that only under free governments like those of England and America the common man possesses rights that must be respected by all.

# III

## THE PHILOSOPHIC TEMPER

Be mine a philosopher's life in the quiet woodland
    ways,
Where if I cannot be gay let a passionless peace be
    my lot.

                        *— Tennyson.*

Years that bring the philosophic mind.
                        *— Wordsworth.*

How charming is divine philosophy!
Not harsh and crabbed, as dull fools suppose,
But musical as is Apollo's lute.
                        *— Milton.*

# THE PHILOSOPHIC TEMPER

IT is the shame of the age in which we live that it has in large measure lost the ancient delight in nature that filled with overflowing gladness the Greek mind and heart, and that has always been associated with true culture. Our fathers read poetry. They did not count the literature of imagination worthless. With neglect of the ideal elements in life comes a dense vulgarity that degrades whatever it touches. Beautiful pictures are viewed only as ornaments. Art loses its ethical significance and becomes merely decorative. Faith languishes and dies deserted, where once she spoke with authority, and had for all the world a vision of angels.

In Charles Darwin, the greatest interpreter of the physical side of nature our world has ever known, we have an illustration of the benumbing influence of natural science when wholly separated from moral and spiritual forces and ideals. In his early life Darwin was fond of music and poetry. He once thought of entering the Christian ministry. Later he gave himself up to the study of natural history, and became so absorbed in that branch of learning that he put aside all refining influences. The taste for beauty died within him. Physical truth, the facts of science, the laws of the material universe,— these took entire possession of his mind. Toward the end of

life he remembered with sadness his lost treasures.
He wrote:

" If I had to live my life again, I would make it
a rule to read some poetry and listen to some music
at least once every week; for perhaps the parts of
my brain now atrophied would be kept active
through use.  The loss of these tastes is a loss of
happiness, and may possibly be injurious to the intellect, and more probably to the moral character,
by enfeebling the emotional part of our nature."

In the same way religious feeling faded from
the mind of the great naturalist.  He wrote in
his journal:

" I well remember my conviction that there is
more in man than the mere breath of his body, and
I so expressed myself, standing in the midst of the
grandeur of a Brazilian forest.  But now the
grandest scenes would not cause any such convic-
tions and feelings to rise in my mind.  It may be
truly said that I am like a man who has become
color-blind. . . . Disbelief crept over me at a
very slow rate; but was at last complete.  The
rate was so slow that I felt no distress."

No man can afford to do what Darwin did,
much less can he afford to range himself with
Buchner, Vogt, and Haeckel.  We must keep all
the windows of the soul open to the beautiful,—
the beautiful in both art and ethics.

" A pagan, kissing, for a step of Pan,
The wild-goat's hoof-print on the loamy down,

Exceeds our modern thinker who turns back
The strata-granite, limestone, coal, and clay,
Concluding coldly with, ' Here's law!   Where's
    God?' "

It may do us good to remember that for the
poorest nature, unless the mind be actually deranged, our world is crowded with opportunities
which no man can afford to despise, and any one
of which might lead on to fortune.   In other
words, the philosophic temper implies hope.   It
is astonishing how easily we relax our hold upon
hope.   Every year hundreds of men and women
resort to suicide who have or should have many
reasons for wishing to live.   Among those who
committed suicide in the United States in 1907,
there were one hundred and ten persons of dis-
tinction and education, such as clergymen, physicians, teachers, bankers, artists, capitalists,
merchants, officials, and manufacturers.   Some
of these may have been insane, but the large majority we must account to have been of sound
mind, unless we hold suicide to be always in itself
conclusive evidence of mental derangement.   The
most distressing thing connected with the statistics of suicide is the increasing number of children who take their own lives.   Dr. Samuel Mc-
Comb, in his book, " Religion and Medicine," attributes the self-murder of little children to dis-
illusion,— that is to say, to the loss of the ideal.
The fairy world dissolves, and the naked matter-
of-fact life of commonplace experience crowds

out from the delicate child-mind the early romance and tender faith which, once lost, never
return.

Not long ago I received through the mail a
pamphlet setting forth the great advantage to
be derived from a union of all Christian churches
under a single denominational standard. Of
course the standard was to be that under which
the author of the pamphlet was already enrolled.
I once heard a man describe in glowing colors
the republic of the future that was to unite all
nations in common devotion to popular institutions, one flag, and one language. Of course the
republic was to have its capitol somewhere in
the District of Columbia, its flag was to be
abundantly supplied with stars and stripes, and
its language was to be that in which the orator
was declaiming. When election time approaches, a thousand wigwams and town halls
spout fire, and we are assured upon every hand
that the Kingdom of Heaven is about to be in-
augurated. But after the election is over, and
the banners have been taken down, the Kingdom
of Heaven seems to be about as far away as it
ever was. Quack doctors and reformers have
their panaceas, and all kinds of nostrums are
prescribed, but somehow popular ills continue.
The Socialist is sure that, could he have his way,
the world would be made over at once into a
Garden of Eden.

When will men learn that life is in large measure what they make it, and that a hundred differ-

ent men, with as many different dispositions and temperaments, must forever make a variety and inequality in both church and state that nothing can reduce to a common level? It is not true that all men are born free and equal. Money, education, health, intellectual gifts, unforeseen circumstances, and much besides, render equality nothing but an iridescent dream of the visionary. One man is born with a silver spoon in his mouth, and another is born with his teeth set on edge. We cannot have all the prosperity we want, nor can we all succeed in what we undertake. Thousands covet the wealth of Crœsus, the fame of Alexander, and the genius of Shakespeare, but for all their coveting they get nothing but disappointment.

Inequality is the rule of life, and the sooner we make up our minds to take things as they come, turning them to the best account for ourselves and others, the larger will be our field of usefulness and the greater will be our reward. We should all of us cultivate a philosophic temper that refuses to brood over troubles, break its heart over trifles, and contend against the inevitable. We must adapt ourselves to circumstances, and remember that the wise man " stoops to conquer." The forces of nature become our willing servants only when we learn to obey them. The key to every situation is found in surrender. The man who most vigorously asserts his personal independence is most likely the very man who knows the least of true liberty. Any fool

may fire a gun and wave a flag, but he is the true
patriot who obeys the law, minds his own business, practices virtue, and subordinates his personal interests to the public good.

We shall find it impossible to cultivate a
philosophic temper unless we learn to extract
pleasure from the common things of life. The
world is full of beauty, but only the poet's eye
discerns it. A lady visited Turner's studio,
where she saw a picture of wood and field that
she had often seen. Long she gazed at the can-
vas, and then exclaimed, " Mr. Turner, I have
been under those trees and by that meadow brook
many times, but I could never see what you have
put into that landscape." " Well, madame," replied Turner, " but don't you wish you could
see it? "

The ability to see makes all the world ours.
The poet's eye, even though we may not have the
poet's gift of utterance, is essential to the
philosophic temper, for surely we cannot take
the world for what it is unless we know it to be
good; and we cannot be satisfied with what it
offers unless in it all we discern the beauty. The
gardener turns the sod, but his dull eyes perceive
not

> " The pomp of poppied meadows,
> The revel of June roses."

The philosophic temper dispels in a measure
the fear of death,— that dreadful fear so hard to
overcome, and which, unless we do overcome it,

must inevitably deprive life of its sweetness and delight. To the men and women of a generation or two ago thanatophobia, or dread of death, was a perpetual distress. A modern poet has written lines which, save for their unbelief, belong to the time of Cromwell rather than to the period in which we live; and yet I fear there are many even now who find those lines true to their own experience.

" I am afraid to think about my death,—
When it shall be, and whether in great pain
I shall rise up and fight the air for breath,
Or calmly wait the bursting of my brain.

" I am no coward who could seek in fear
A folklore solace of sweet Indian tales;
I know dead men are deaf, and cannot hear
The singing of a thousand nightingales.

" I know dead men are blind, and cannot see
The friend that shuts in horror their big eyes;
And they are witless,— oh, I'd rather be
A living mouse than dead as a man dies."

I never before heard of a man who could wish to be a living mouse rather than a dead human being, but I knew of one who said he would much prefer to be a live dog that fears no future than the man he was, facing day after day a destiny that he could not understand and that caused him only terror. Death makes miserable cowards of many of us. An experience that is universal should not be so greatly dreaded. The author of the foregoing lines seems to view death as the end of all things. I understand him to mean by the "folklore solace of sweet Indian tales," in which he sees nothing more than race-fables and legends, that heavenly home, the blessed anticipation which gives the Christian peace and gladness of heart. If I am right in my interpretation, the author must find some other solace, or face alone the great future, without hope.

I do not wonder that men who believe in no other world than this look forward to death with mournful foreboding and, in many cases, with fear. Strange it is, those who hold that there is nothing behind the veil to awaken apprehension, still approach that veil with anxiety. It would seem to indicate that after all they are not so sure of personal extinction as they profess to be. Still, it is to be remembered that annihilation is to some a more dreadful thing than death, unless death be viewed as preliminary to an existence of great distress. Professor Huxley a short time before his last sickness wrote to John Morley: "It is a curious thing that I find my dislike to the thought of extinction increasing as I get older, and nearer the goal. It flashes across me at times with a sort of horror that in 1900 I shall probably know no more of what is going on than I did in 1800."

Professor George J. Romanes went as far in agnosticism as did Huxley. He was the en-

thusiastic pupil, and later the friend, of Charles
Darwin, for whom he retained to the end of his
life the most profound reverence.  Darwin was
always a frank and honorable antagonist, who
sought, not victory, but truth.  He could see
even better than could Romanes the other side of
an argument.  One day during the period of
Romanes' unbelief,— a period during which he
was in substantial agreement with Darwin,— the
former published an essay against Theism.
Soon after the publication of that essay, Darwin, recognizing the difficulties of unbelief, addressed a letter to Romanes, in which he said that
he could see no way in which a scientific man
could prove that force and matter possessed necessarily, and apart from God, the attributes they
now have, and that they had had them from all
past eternity.

But Romanes could not rest in unbelief with
that indifference which seemed so natural to the
author of " The Origin of Species."  Like John
Fiske, he began new investigations with a view
to the discovery of some substantial foundation
for religious faith.  He had a great love for
certainties; more than that, he had within him a
deep longing for spiritual rest.  Little by little,
with hard fighting and no lack of distress, he laid
what he believed to be a solid foundation for
faith.  It certainly sustained him in life and
comforted him in death.

Darwin was in every respect a man of science.
His entire life centered in those branches of

physical science to which in early life he gave
his entire mind and, indeed, his whole being.
Romanes was also a man of great scientific at-
tainment, but he was alive in every direction.
He possessed both the religious and the philosophic temper.   He could not leave matters of
such great importance where Darwin left them,
to live or die as the case might be.   His habits
of physical investigation and his scientific training were neither of them had at the fearful cost
of spiritual suicide.

Dr. C. A. Stephens has spent much time in his
laboratory at Norway Lake, in Maine, demon-
strating to himself that " death ends all."   I
never heard that the demonstration convinced
any one but himself.   On the strength of his inconclusive experiments, he publishes from time
to time certain books of despair.   If the human
race is doomed, can it help any one to know of
that doom?   Shall we be made stronger by an-
ticipating our approaching defeat?   I thank
God that faith has a better foundation and a
more hopeful outlook.

Among adults loss of spiritual hope is often
the impelling cause of self-destruction.   Severe
Calvinistic views of destiny, the fear of Divine
Justice, and an inward sense of guilt, are causes
that operate in mature minds.   There can be no
doubt that the Roman Catholic confessional has
been the means of saving hundreds, if not thousands, of human lives.   It has enabled remorse-
ful souls to unburden conscience.   Even Prot-

estant ministers are called upon to hear the di-
vulgements of guilt-oppressed men and women.
Whatever destroys ideal and spiritual elements in
human life tends to suicide. Whatever strains
those elements conducts to the same end. Weininger, in his book, " Sex and Character," deprived man of every ideal element, and left him
nothing but an animal, and not a first-class animal at that. The world was not surprised when
Weininger took his own life.

The philosophic temper kindles hope. It says
to every man, " Fortune smiles upon thousands
around you — your turn may come next. Why
throw away your chance? " It lights up the
ideal world. It breathes the name of God. It
whispers, " Wait." It also suggests to the soul
that what it most fears may not be so bad after
all, and that many things coveted are not so good
as they appear. It brings to mind the old
maxim, " Never cross a bridge before you come
to it,"— that is to say, do not anticipate troubles. It takes short views of life. The future
we dread may never come to us. Many things
that we fear, we should not fear did we know them
better.

The philosophic temper avoids extreme views
and opinions. It uses the good things of life
with moderation. It has little to do with radical
reformers. The men who think it wicked to
smoke a cigar, drink a glass of ale, or see a clean
play at the theatre, are not attractive to the
philosophic temper. Few things are evil in

themselves.　In the heart of man, and not in the forces of nature, are the malign and deadly influences we deplore.　Our Puritan fathers distrusted the world and feared its contaminating influence.　Even good things, if they were not of a distinctly religious nature, were to be avoided. Sorrow and renunciation were ministers of grace, but laughter and light-heartedness were nigh unto perdition.　The philosophical temper views life and the world in a different light.　It rejoices in the beauty of the earth, and enters gladly into the pleasures and occupations of human nature and society.　The words of the sacred writer are ever upon its lips: "A merry heart doeth good like a medicine."　"Cranks" of every kind are its aversion.　For heresy-hunters and fanatics who, had they lived two or three centuries ago, would have toasted their fellow-men who were not of their faith over slow fires, the philosophic temper has no liking.　Its gospel is one of hope, and its mission one of love.

From the earliest times Stoic and Epicurean divided the world between them.　The one found its immortal expression in Rome, and the other is best understood by studying the artistic, elegant, and sensual civilization of ancient Greece.　To both schools the race of man will look in vain for a solution of the vast problem of human life on earth, and for a solution of the still greater problem of a life to come.　The worthier characters are, beyond doubt, found among the Stoics.

The disciples of Zeno, who governed themselves by the laws of reason so far as those laws were known in the early days of Greece, were surely the wiser and better men. Epictetus stands out in bold relief, a sublime and noble character. Lecky says in his "History of European Morals":

"Cicero has left us no grander example than that of Epictetus, the sickly, deformed slave of a master who was notorious for his barbarity; enfranchised late in life, but soon driven into exile by Domitian; who, while sounding the very abyss of human misery and looking forward to death as to simple decomposition, was yet so filled with the sense of the Divine presence that his life was one continued hymn to Providence, and his writings and his example, which appeared to his contemporaries almost the ideal of human goodness, have not lost their consoling power through all the ages and the vicissitudes they have survived."

Marcus Aurelius accounted his knowledge of Epictetus to be one of the greatest blessings he had received from biography and the study of ethics. Lecky repeats the old story, in one of the footnotes to his "History of European Morals," of Epictetus warning his master, who was thrashing him, that he would soon break his leg. When the leg had been broken Epictetus calmly said, "I told you what would be the result." Celsus said to the Christians of his day, "Did your Leader, under suffering, ever say any-

thing so noble as that?" Origen replied for
his fellow-believers, "He did what was still
nobler,— He kept silence."

### MARCUS AURELIUS AND EPICTETUS [1]

Twin stars, serene and pure,
In the fear-haunted gloom
Of the wild pagan night,—
So long, so long ago!
In royal purple one,
Philosopher and saint,
With words divinely wise;
The other but a slave,
Yet monarch still who ruled
The godlike minds of men.
Alone, undimmed, they burned
Above a world of doom
Until the morning-red
Flamed crimson in the east,
And the ascending dawn
Of an immortal Christ
Filled the blue heavens with light.

Pleasure, which the Stoics denied, is nevertheless essential to life at its best.    Pleasure is the
sun without which few virtues can ever ripen
save in some exceptional soul.    Marcus Aurelius
said, "To ask to be paid for virtue is as if the
eye demanded to be recompensed for seeing, or
the feet for walking."    Still there would be little
virtue were there no pleasure.

Hegel finished his "*Phenomenologie des*

[1] Marvin: "Poems and Translations," Boston, 1914.

*Geistes* " in his quiet little study at Jena on the memorable fourteenth of October, 1806, wholly oblivious of the wild battle-storm that raged around him. So completely was his mind occupied with the work he had set himself that not the faintest echo of that desperate conflict interfered with his labor. Every man should be in some measure the master of circumstance and an arbiter of destiny. There can be neither strength nor happiness in a life driven by every wind of fortune, be it good or ill. Self-control is one of the most important elements in the philosophic temper. We may, if we will, regulate our passions, and these have much to do with prosperity and welfare. Anger, when violent, is as truly a poison as are toxic drugs. It brings about certain pathological changes and conditions that may easily cause, not only sickness, but death itself. Of that let the physician discourse; our point of view is not so much that of medicine as of philosophy. Anger injures self-respect, limits usefulness, and degrades the man in his own eyes. It will concern the philosopher as well as the physician to remember that violent displeasure is ruinous to the heart and also to the digestive organs. Wise indeed was the physician who refused to dine with a man who was enraged at the misconduct of one of his servants. " Your condition of mind," said the man of science, " is one that affects your body, for mind and body are so closely united that what hurts one injures as well the other. You know very well that you have an imperfect heart that may be stopped at any moment by an explosion of wrath. I will not dine with you while your mind is in its present disturbed state."

I believe that the cultivation of the temper under review leads to kindness of heart and would make the world a much better place to live in. With all his brusqueness, and even, at times, brutality, Bismarck had much of the "live and let live" philosophy, and it humanized him so that men loved him and willingly followed after him. The story of the last cigar at Königgratz [1] illustrates what has been said.

"The value of a good cigar," said Bismarck, as he proceeded to light an excellent Havana, "is best understood when it is the last you possess, and there is no chance of getting another. At Königgratz I had only one cigar left in my pocket, which I carefully guarded during the whole of the battle as a miser does his treasure. I did not feel justified in using it. I painted in glowing colors in my mind the happy hour when I should enjoy it after the victory. But I miscalculated my chances. And what was the cause of my miscalculation? A poor dragoon. He lay helpless, with both arms crushed, asking for something to refresh him. I felt in my pockets and found only gold, and that would be of no use to him. But, stay, I had still my treasured cigar! I lighted this for him and placed it between his teeth. You should have seen the poor fellow's

[1] The name given by the Prussians to the battle of Sadowa.

grateful smile! I never enjoyed a cigar so much as that one which I did not smoke."

The campaign against tobacco has always found the kindly and friendly associations of the weed too much for the fanatic. It was the calumet, or pipe of peace, that made it possible for the white man to have conference with the red man. The treaty of peace was made and confirmed in a fragrant cloud of smoke, for men never smoke together who are not on terms of amity. Dr. Adam Clarke, the Bible commentator, was a good man, but he was a poor philosopher when he made up his mind that the instincts of all nations were wrong, and that tobacco was the devil's weed. He held that tobacco was a deadly poison, to be shunned by all Christians, and especially those of the Wesleyan variety. Some one asked him why God made such a wicked plant, and the question distressed him greatly. After much holy meditation he decided that tobacco was a medicine, to be taken at times in pills, tinctures, and so on, but never to be smoked or chewed. King James was of the same opinion, as all know who have read his " Counterblast." He argues that smoking is worse than drunkenness. Cromwell ordered his troopers to destroy the crops of tobacco by trampling them under foot. Never was plant more powerfully opposed. But to-day all over the world that genial herb promotes peace and fosters good feeling.

Its fragrant leaves are the symbol of fellowship
and of the philosophic temper.

It should always be remembered that no
philosophy is sound that leaves God out of consideration, or that fails of perceiving his goodness and of confiding in his character. Day and
night we are in the encircling embrace of infinite
Love. That Love called us into being, and upon
its bosom we are cradled. "Beneath us are the
everlasting arms." Thus do the sacred writings
teach us to view the Creator, and all the later disclosures of natural science point in the same direction.

Kant holds that it is the office of philosophy to
answer three questions: 1. What can I know?
2. What ought I to do? 3. What may I hope
for? It seems to us that true philosophy goes
further, and makes to us disclosure of our present possessions. It opens the eye to the vision of
an infinite, eternal, and unchangeable Friend,
and renders forever true the words of the
poet:

> "Out of the shadows of night
> The world rolls into light;
>   It is daylight everywhere."

# IV

## MAUPASSANT AND POE

Maupassant saw life with his senses, and he reflected on it in a purely animal revolt, the recoil of the hurt animal. His observation is not, as it has been hastily assumed to be, cold; it is as superficially emotional as that of the average sensual man, and its cynicism is only another, not less superficial, kind of feeling. He saw life in all its details, and his soul was entangled in the details. He saw it without order, without recompense, without pity; he saw it too clearly to be duped by appearances, and too narrowly to distinguish any light beyond what seemed to him the enclosing bounds of darkness.

*— Arthur Symons.*

Had Poe possessed a small, bright intellect, proportioned to his nature, he would have been a happy and successful man, but unknown. Had he possessed a nature commensurate with his intellect, he would have been one of the greatest of the human race.

*— Hawthorne.*

# MAUPASSANT AND POE

IT may be we should never have heard of Guy
de Maupassant had there been no Edgar Allan
Poe. Both men were masters of the short story;
both were gifted with that clear, penetrating intellectual sight which goes at once with unerring
certainty to the heart of the thing to be portrayed; both were able to compress a world of
meaning into the narrow compass of a few pages;
both were cynical and took dark, pessimistic
views of life; both passed in youth through the
dismal process of endeavoring to adapt a highly
poetic temperament, fine tastes, and unusual
gifts to a commercial pursuit; and both made a
failure as dismal as the process itself. But when
you come to the substance of their work, the material selected, the situations chosen, and the effect produced, you find in the productions of
Maupassant, to remind you of Poe, only here and
there a lowering storm-cloud that soon dissolves
in light and flowers and song. Of Poe's soul of
horror, that "mystic obsession" of terror, that
weird and desolating beauty that unites in one alluring romance and companionless despair, almost nothing is to be found in the brilliant pages
of our French author.

Though both writers were cynical, pessimistic,
and at times despondent, Maupassant's view of
life had in it some of those brighter and more
pleasing features the want of which often ren-

ders the work of Poe distressing to the ordinary
reader.    Maupassant had great delight in nature.
He could lie for hours upon the grass or beneath
the spreading branches of a leafy tree, perfectly
happy in the contemplation of the verdured
earth and so much of the blue sky as could disclose itself through interlacing boughs.    Flowers gave him exquisite pleasure.    The sounds of
nature intoxicated him.    The moaning of the
wind in the tree-tops, the chirp of insects, and
the song of birds,— especially that of the nightingale,— filled him with indescribable satisfaction.
The roar of the ocean rendered him oblivious of
all else.    The sights of nature had upon him
much the same effect that natural sounds had.
Cattle browsing in the fields, the simple life of the
peasant, the landscape, and, above all, the joyous existence of children,— of these he could not
have too much.    His was not the old pagan
pleasure; it was rather the artistic delight of the
modern mind.    His senses were keen and alert.
He had what has been called " a joyous animal-
ism," in which the spiritual element was singu-
larly wanting.    He reveled in form and color
with an artist's joy.    His ears were sensitive to
every sound.    The whisper of love, the cry of
passion, the note of terror, and the shout of
triumph all seized upon him and held him fast.
But the seizure was upon the physical side of his
nature.

Of course he reappears in his books.    Every
man is in a measure the hero of his own story.

His life was not pure; why should we expect to
find immaculate purity in his work? Where
the flame is not without smoke there must be some
smudge of soot. His stories are coarse and some
of them are, if we mince not our words, libidi-
nous. But they are not all of them evil, and perhaps few that are evil are wholly so. He portrayed vice, but it can hardly be said that he rendered it attractive. There was with it too much
of the horror of its fruitage. His descriptive
powers were great, but he could describe only
that of which he had himself knowledge. Passion he could paint, and as well " the raptures and
roses of vice," but of love in its better meaning
he knew nothing. Of marriage he had a poor
opinion. His soul was incapable of that sacred
union. " Boule de Suif," which gave Maupassant his sudden recognition, illustrates what we
are saying. The *motif* of the story is certainly
not elevating. It presents us with a clear, remorseless, and witty picture of selfishness and in-
sincerity. It brings out the sordid side of human nature. It shows up the meanness and rot-
tenness of those who pretend to a virtue they do
not possess. Uncleanness plays a large part,
but surely the reader is not made to love evil.
The reading brings with it an inward disgust, a
loathing, a sense of foulness, but the story is
moral in the same way that Daudet's " Sappho "
is moral. The latter romance may be played
upon the stage in such a way as to make it las-
civious to the very last degree,— it was so played.

But the tale as we have it from Daudet is good and only good. Any young man reading it may see with fearful distinctness how from first to last a bad woman may ruin a pure life, how under her baneful shadow the most noble and manly virtues may themselves become the servitors of vice.

It is a good thing to know that Maupassant, unlike most young authors, restrained himself from premature publication. For seven long years he toiled at the unattractive duties of a clerk of the navy and education departments. Wearisome work it must have been. The old life in Normandy during all that time haunted his imagination. He dreamed of the dear hills, fields, and brooks of earlier days. He grew homesick and despondent, but still he worked on. Only upon a Sunday could he visit the beautiful environs of Paris. Sometimes a holiday gave him a few hours of canoeing on the Seine — an occasional "holiday and six francs!" During all that time he wrote, but no one knew what he wrote. He entered into no communication with any one, until suddenly the young toiler made his début, and astonished Paris gave him cordial recognition,— gave him more, for the immediate demand for his work was so great that neither he nor his publishers could meet it. Fortune and fame came with a sudden rush.

The unclean life of the gay French capital was not good for the delicate and sensitive author.

Why repeat the sad tale?  Suffice it to say that
overwork, licentiousness, drugs, alcohol, entire
neglect of the ordinary laws of health, were more
than his fine temperament could endure.  Over
the blinded mental vision of our gifted writer the
shadows began to fall.  Slowly at first, and later
with great swiftness, melancholy thoughts pursued him.  The mental faculties crumbled, and in
a fit of despair he made an assault upon his own
life.  A watchful friend prevented the suicide,
and foreign travel was tried as a remedial agent,
but with no marked result.  His physician prescribed a period of rest and retirement in a villa
at Cannes, but this also failed to benefit him.  It
was too late.  The gifted author,— gifted as few
have been, praised and admired by an enthusiastic public,— lingered eighteen months in a strait-
jacket, and then died of general paresis.

Poe's life also was one of dissipation.  So far
as the world knows the author of " Ligeia,"
" The Fall of the House of Usher," " The
Raven," and " Annabel Lee " was pure in all his
relations with women.  He married the woman he
loved, and he faced the great sorrow of her death.
Whatever wrongs Maupassant may have committed, he never committed that of wedding a pure
and devoted woman.  Among the women of Paris
who understood him and who chose to live as he
lived, he counted, it is said, " his *bonnes fortunes*
by the score."  Poe's life, as has been said, was
pure.  If he used narcotics we do not know of it,

though true it is the suspicion has been entertained. His one great enemy was alcohol, and of it he died.

Maupassant's sensual enjoyment was restricted by a constant fear of death which, Goncourt thinks, grew out of an intense love of life. Maupassant's theories of both life and death were wholly materialistic. He held that with the last breath one ceased to exist. When a man lost life he lost everything. He found solitude unendurable. Like Aaron Burr, he was unhappy when alone, and preferred almost any company to no company at all. He obtained relief in the presence of other lives, for the presence of such lives seemed to add a measure of stability to his own.

You have the whole of Maupassant's intent and purpose in the story he tells, whatever it may be. The interest centers always in the story, and in the story alone. He introduces no problem and suggests no theories. There are few preachments. He is to be read solely for the story. Since the story is true to life, it conveys its own lesson; but the lesson is always a part of the story, and what may be its contents does not concern the writer.

Here again we come upon a point of resemblance between Poe and Maupassant. Poe makes himself the hero or principal character in many of his tales, and in most of his poems, but you do not feel his personality. So far as the story goes, he is a mere phantom or abstraction mas-

querading in a personal pronoun.   In his tales,
as in those of Maupassant, the interest is in the
tale itself, and not in any thing it suggests.
What moral conclusions may come of the narrative is immaterial to him.

# V

## HUMAN DERELICTS

Addison, in the Spectator, gives an account of a gentleman who determined to live and dress according to the rules of common-sense, and was shut up in an asylum for the insane.

> Chaos of thought and passion all confus'd;
> Still by himself abus'd or disabus'd;
> Created half to rise, and half to fall;
> Great lord of all things, yet a prey to all;
> Sole judge of truth, in endless error hurl'd;
> The glory, jest, and riddle of the world.
> — *Pope.*

# HUMAN DERELICTS

UNUSUAL characters have always greatly interested me. They possess a peculiar fascination that I have never been able to understand. Even the rag-tag and bob-tail army of religious tramps and adventurers is not without a remarkable attractiveness or allurement. Fanatics are nearly always picturesque, and certainly the unique places some of them fill in both secular and ecclesiastical history give an added interest to their personality, and even invest them with a certain charm that may easily blind an observer to not a few of their worst faults.

I have discovered, among other things connected with the world of eccentric men and women, that religious fanatics and impostors are, with few exceptions, entirely devoid of that helpful and tonic sense of humor which lies at the foundation of sound and reasonable thinking and feeling. It is sometimes more than sad, it is even distressing, to see with what sincerity and earnestness these distraught minds toil in the construction of air-castles and brood over insoluble problems; though true it is that they are often found " building better than they know." The man who is wholly destitute of the sense of humor is to be pitied. The power of seeing the incongruous and absurd is a power to be most devoutly coveted. In seasons of despondency and of moral and intellectual unrest, that power has

been to me as a firm and enduring rock in the
midst of a wild and stormy sea. It is, doubtless,
just because I have in some measure this most
helpful sense that I find pleasure in studying and
conversing with the unusual characters which always come to the surface in a transitional period,
and which in this paper I shall briefly discuss.
I use the word " discuss " in a broad and general
sense, giving it a very free meaning. What I
have to say will not be said from any distinctly
scientific or philosophical vantage-ground, nor
will it be said with any thought or hope of mend-
ing matters. If it shall entertain the reader
and, it may be, incidentally instruct him, the end
in view in writing this paper will be attained.

Eccentricity is in many ways closely associated with insanity, and yet the two are not necessarily the same, and care should be taken to
prevent the confounding of the one with the other.
Both are not infrequently the concomitants of
genius. There are many theories with regard
to the nature of genius. Helvetius makes that
special quality to be nothing more than the power
of continued attention. Buffon called it " pro-
tracted patience." Still another theory ad-
vanced by Lombroso represents genius as in itself insanity. He thinks the gifted men and
women of every age and land are to some extent deranged. The folly of such a view must
be apparent. Lombroso was a greatly over-
estimated man, many of whose views and opinions are justly doomed to swift oblivion. No

theory, explanation, or description of genius is adequate; and certainly no endowment that puts its possessor in advance of his age, or that is in itself of a creative nature, can be catalogued among the mental disasters that overthrow reason and wreck those characteristics that distinguish a man as belonging to our human race. Nor can that homely and everyday quality we call common sense be regarded as in any way opposed to genius, though the two mental possessions named are not always, and perhaps not commonly, found in the same person. Everywhere men make the average common sense, or what they think is the average common sense, of their age the measure of intellectual soundness and moral uprightness. No doubt they are often mistaken, but what other standard can be suggested? The rare genius must bear the misunderstanding and consequent persecution with such equanimity as can be commanded. The age in which he lives may do him great injustice, but posterity must be trusted to recognize his worth.

I call attention to the fact already stated that religious fanatics and impostors have little or no sense of humor. We laugh at them, but they never laugh at themselves, though how they at times manage to refrain from doing so is something of a mystery. Not one of them has the faintest conception of the spectacle presented. I suppose the fact that they cannot see themselves accounts in some measure for their

calmness and sobriety at a time when the rest of
the world is convulsed with laughter. The sense
of humor is saving and conservative of reason.
It holds up before the enthusiast a mirror in
which he may see, if so inclined, the ridiculous
exhibition he is himself making. Could zealots
and castle-builders behold themselves, if but for
one brief moment, there would be fewer visions
and revelations, though I am by no means sure
the sum of human happiness would be increased.

Ann Lee, Joseph Smith, the Fox sisters,
Joanna Southcott, and more choice spirits of the
same variety, never dreamed of the real condition
of things. Ann Lee took her twitchings very
seriously. Joseph Smith kept his face straight
while he told the world about his sacred goggles.
The Fox sisters never winced. Joanna Southcott seems to have been perfectly at her ease
when she turned her dropsy to so good an account. She made more than ten thousand followers wait in the street one dark night, eager
to hear that she had given birth to the promised
Messiah. Edward Irving was by no means an
impostor like the eccentric characters already
named. He was a good man, and a man of
education and of fine mind, but he, like all the
rest of the crew, had the sign-manual of the dis-
order,— he had no sense of humor. He never
at any period in his career saw himself. The
Voices were ridiculous, but he listened to them
with devout attention.

Swedenborg was sincere when he wrote his

"Diary," but what a book it is for a scoffing world to read! Could the immortal Swede have caught sight of himself, when, urged by religious fury, he ran around his own room, chased by a thinly clad and lustful angel intent upon debauching him, do you think he would have been quite so sure of some things as he seems to have been? He beheld the angel very distinctly, but himself he could not see. Swedenborg was, beyond doubt, a great man. Emerson describes him as "a colossal soul" requiring "a large focal distance to be seen." The New England essayist does not hesitate to represent him as "one of the mastodons of literature, not to be measured by whole colleges of ordinary students." Yet so great a man as Swedenborg could write:

"A married woman desired to possess me, but I preferred an unmarried one. She was angry and chased me, but I got hold of the one I liked. I was with her, and loved her; perhaps it signifies my thoughts.

"A certain devil fancied himself the very devil who deceived Adam and Eve, according to the vulgar opinion. . . . It was given me to hear Paul saying he wished to be his companion, and that they would go together and make themselves gods . . . but they were rejected wherever they went.

"Paul is amongst the worst of the apostles, as has been made known to me by large experience. The love of self, whereby he was governed before he preached the gospel, continued to rule him afterwards; and from that love he had a passion for scenes of controversy and tumult. He did all things with the end of being greatest in heaven and judging the tribes of Israel."

Swedenborg believed that he saw, conversed with, and associated with beings in the spirit-world. On every side were angels and ghosts. A person walking with Swedenborg along Cheapside in London asked the seer who it was to whom he bowed so very low. "That," replied Swedenborg, "was Moses." In the street he lifted his hat to David, and sometimes to Paul, or to one of the Evangelists. All this is to many only a source of amusement, but the great mystic was serious enough. He saw no incongruity in his marvelous claims.

Mary Baker Eddy makes us smile, but the smile is wholly ours. We are amused, but she is not. Her sublime self-assurance well nigh obscures the colossal absurdity of her claims. She stands out silhouetted against a background of popular incredulity (and, alas! credulity as well) as the discoverer of a new religion which she has called "Christian Science."

Contemplate John Alexander Dowie, "First Apostle and Third Elijah." Grotesque to the last degree, and ridiculous in manner, speech, doctrine, and personal appearance, he yet governed the consciences of hundreds of sincere men and women, and retained to the end of his life their love and devotion.

It is strange that these adventurers never
want for followers. Few prophets have been
so mean and few revelations so preposterous as
utterly to fail of awakening enthusiasm. What
shall be said of the tens of thousands of believers? Were they as wholly devoid of the sense
of humor as were most of their leaders? Certainly there were among them some who had
keen vision, and the ability to see how humorous
was the incongruity of the situation. What
was it, then, that captured such men and women
as these for adventurers like Joanna Southcott?
I cannot think it was any one thing alone.
Peculiar circumstances had much to do with the
success of Joanna Southcott. Her personality
was remarkably attractive to a certain class of
fanatics. She had marvelous self-assurance.
Not a doubt ruffled her serenity, or interfered
in the least degree with her self-complacency.
A doubt might have dissolved the spell, but she
voiced no doubt. She declared herself pregnant, and represented that the fruit of her
womb was to be the Saviour of the world. To
her dropsical abdomen she pointed with a
solemnity that, had it not been calculated to
awaken pity, must surely, it would seem, have
awakened laughter. Yet what appears to us so
absurd was at the worst only serio-comic, and re-
sulted in an even stronger faith. Strange to
say, certain physicians were for a time deceived
into a belief that she was really pregnant. It
may be that some powerful hypnotic suggestion

had to do with the persuasiveness of her astonishing claims.   Our fathers had no definite knowledge of hypnotic influence or control, and it
is far from strange that they never thought
of occult and mysterious phenomena as an explanation of those wonderful forces that defy
the learning of our modern psychologists.

Richard Brothers was another enthusiast who
drew after him a great host of followers.
Brothers saw visions of very great wonder and
astonishment, and received a commission from
Heaven to lead the Jews back to Palestine.   He
styled himself the " Nephew of God," and proceeded to publish new Scriptures which he said
he had obtained from Heaven.   After a time
he found himself in a lunatic asylum, where he
fell in love with a Miss Cott whom he discovered
to be " the recorded daughter of both David and
Solomon," and as well his own destined wife " by
divine ordinance."   While in the asylum he
had apocalyptic visions without number, and conversed freely with the illustrious dead of all lands
and ages.   What the illustrious dead thought
of Mr. Brothers during those astonishing inter-
views is not recorded, but we know what many
intelligent persons of his own day and country
thought of him, and we are all the more surprised to find that there were so many apparently reasonable men and women who followed in his train.   Brothers gained his liberty
in 1806, and lived until 1824.   Up to the last
day of his disturbed life he continued to teach

and preach and to exercise his wonderful power over the minds of men.  And even after he had been laid away in the grave his influence lived on, and those who had known him in the flesh mourned for him when he was gone from them. It is recorded that the clergyman who was with him in his last moments died not long after of a broken heart, and that the physician who attended him committed suicide.  Southey and Coleridge did not like him, but they could not put him out of their minds.  A stanza in the former's " The Devil's Walk " runs thus:

> " As he walk'd into London leisurely,
>    The streets were dirty and dim;
> But there he saw Brothers the Prophet,
>    And Brothers the Prophet saw him."

Jacob Bryan is another choice " specimen " in my psychological cabinet.  Not much is known about him, but it is recorded that William Sharp, the engraver, who was a friend of most of the religious " tramps " of his time, and who was himself a visionary of the first water, found Bryan one morning stretched out on the floor between two printing-presses at his office in Marylebone Street, London, utterly crushed by the weight of the sins of the world which he had been helping our Saviour to bear.  It was while some fine plates were on the press that Bryan had a vision in which he was commanded of God to proceed at once to Avignon with a new disclosure of the Divine Will.  And so it came to pass that Sharp not only lost his best printer, but had to care for Bryan's family until such time as it was the desire of Heaven that the said Bryan should return to England. Bryan came back, but having received another revelation, he gave up the trade of printing and became a dyer. The last we hear of him, he is making a profane pun upon the tender and sad words of the apostle Paul, " I die daily."

A very scurvy fellow was Jacob Bryan, and yet he had followers who loved and trusted him notwithstanding the folly of his claims and the tomfooleries of his life. Was he a conscious and wilful impostor? I think not. That he was rude and vulgar no one can for a moment doubt. He was ignorant, loquacious, and lacking in reverence. But having no sense of humor, he could not see himself, and so it came to pass that he was undisturbed by a sight of the hateful spectacle which he presented to the vision of his fellow men. He thought himself an inspired prophet, and all the time he was only a coarse harlequin. Bryan, like most religious fanatics, was self-centered. He lived, moved, and had his being, not in God, in whose service he thought himself engaged, but in himself. He fed upon his own thoughts, feelings, and desires, and, being the rude man he was, he never knew upon what mean fare he subsisted.

What shall be said of " Father " Noyes? Perhaps the less said of him the better; and yet his name cannot be expunged from the list of

American fanatics. That man was educated for the Gospel ministry at both Yale and Andover Theological Seminaries; he was a Congregational clergyman, an author of some ability, and an educated lawyer. Notwithstanding all his learning, he founded the infamous Oneida Community, which, strange to say, flourished in the enlightened State of New York for forty years. His "Confession," printed in William Hepworth Dixon's "Spiritual Wives," is certainly most interesting material.

John Humphrey Noyes was born at Brattleboro, Vermont, September 3, 1811. He was graduated from Dartmouth College in 1830, and from Andover Theological Seminary in 1834. He read law at Putney, Vermont, and in 1840 founded, four miles from Oneida, Madison County, in the State of New York, the Oneida Community, which in a few years became famous because of much that was good and more that was bad in its doctrine and practice. That for a considerable time the community prospered cannot be denied. In the year 1867 there were two hundred and fifteen persons in its circle, of whom twenty-five were under fourteen years of age. The members, both male and female, held all property and their own persons in common. They ate at a number of tables in one large hall, and used neither tea nor coffee, and seldom touched animal food. The diet was mostly confined to vegetables, fruit, milk, butter, cheese, cakes, puddings and pies. The menu was certainly excellent. Compare it with the French *potages, poissons, entrées, rélèves, rotis, entre-mêts, rélèves des rotis,* and *glacés* that fill our insides with pain, while they distend the doctor's pockets with cash.

Coarse eating makes coarse men, and too much animal food is not good for our intellectual and spiritual natures. I am persuaded that hunting and fishing were once and are still the natural occupations and amusements of savage people; and it may be that the consuming of creatures that have shared with us the same animal life is simply a survival from an earlier and less civilized period. In man the ages long departed still live. In many an eye may be seen at times the wild light of early forest life; in many a handgrasp may be felt the clutch of fierce creatures that became extinct long ago. Physicians describe what they call " arrested development." The quadruped by a process of development becomes an ape; the ape, according to some of these gentlemen, will in time rise to the condition of a savage; and that savage will, after a long period, develop into a civilized man. At any place in this long process the development may be, for a brief period or for a very much longer one, arrested. Sometimes we have an arrest even after human conditions have been reached. Not physical parts alone, but also dispositions, tastes, and inclinations enter into the development. There are men who still retain the ferocity of early tiger-

or wolf-life in forest and jungle.   There are human serpents.   I think we have, all of us, seen and conversed with donkeys.   Oriental religions, some of them, make the great future a round of developments not unlike those of our early racial and pre-racial states.   The transmigration of souls is a doctrine that suggests in many ways the development of which we are writing.   According to its teaching, as set forth by an Eastern poet,

" The illustrious souls of great and virtuous men
In godlike beings shall revive again;
But base and vicious spirits wind their way
In scorpions, vultures, sharks, and beasts of prey.
The fair, the gay, the witty and the brave,
The fool, the coward, courtier, tyrant, slave,
Each one in a congenial form shall find
A proper dwelling for his wandering mind."

At last the good man, made good through many stages of after-death development, arrives at the longed-for Nirvana, as set forth in these ten lines: —

> " Flown is the bird;
> Empty the cage;
> Nor death nor birth
> To the dull earth
> Confines the soul.
> Nirvana calls;
> The tale is told;
> Forevermore the bird
> Floats free
> In the still air."

The Oneida people had a large library and
subscribed for the leading daily and weekly papers.  They published a paper of their own
which they named " The Circular," but it was
not worth reading.  They never employed a
physician, and, being Perfectionists, they had no
need for either lawyer or preacher.  They welcomed neophytes or new believers to the privileges
of their community, but there was always an implied warning:  " No  preacher  need  apply."
The fact is, " Father " Noyes was preacher-in-
chief, and did all the pulpiteering the members of
the community could stand up under.  The community renounced both baptism and the Lord's
Supper.  The Bible was received as the Word of
God, but its teachings were so interpreted as to
make them accord with the peculiar views of
" Father " Noyes.  It was held that Christ's second coming and the establishment of his kingdom
on earth took place within one generation from
the time of his ministry among men.  Their views
were firmly held.

The communism of the Oneida Perfectionists
was founded upon the words of Scripture:
" The multitude of them that believed were of one
heart and of one soul ; neither said any of them
that aught of the things which he possessed was
his own, but they had all things in common."
The Oneida Communists were not compromisers
— they had absolutely all things in common, in-
cluding husbands and wives.  At first Mr. Noyes
and his wife, who has been described as a very

beautiful and accomplished woman (her maiden name was Harriet A. Holton), signed a compact not to live exclusively each for the other. Mr. Noyes was married to all the women who had become believers, and Mrs. Noyes was wife to the entire community. There was, to use their own words, " entire sexual freedom " in the community, subject only to what they called " the doctrine of Male Continence "— a doctrine that I may be excused from discussing. Whoever would study the subject may find interesting material in the " Hand-Book of the Oneida Community," published in 1867 at Wallingford, Connecticut, where was situated another communal family of like faith and similar methods of life.

There were few children; but for so many as the community had, there was an attractive nursery; and when the little ones were old enough, they attended a school which had been established by Mr. Noyes, and wherein they were taught the principles of communism and the peculiar doctrines of the Oneida fellowship. Every mother was regarded as the mother of all the children in the community. Nobody could use tobacco or ardent spirits. The women wore short dresses, and all men and women followed some department of industry. There were among them farmers, gardeners, brick-masons, job-printers, bag-makers, blacksmiths, and an editor. They preserved and sold fruits, vegetables, and jellies. They had silk works where they manufactured sewing silk. There were among them builders who were able to construct large and modern houses for domestic and commercial uses. They did a large business in carpentry. There were also a number of shoemakers and tailors. They had a satchel factory and machine shops. The community became very rich, but the theory and practice of sexual promiscuity finally wrecked the enterprise, and Mr. Noyes had to make good his escape into Canada in order to avoid arrest. He died at Clifton, Ontario, April 13, 1886, aged seventy-five years.

Life in the Community, apart from the sexual feature, had much to recommend it. The vexations of housekeeping were all escaped, for the burden fell upon no one person. The servant question, which is now uppermost in family life, did not disturb the communal household. It is said that winter evenings in the library were delightful. Old and young, men and women, and the few children connected with the household gathered about the large open fire that burned with generous warmth upon the hearth. Books of all kinds and many papers and magazines were to be found upon the library table. In the darker corners of the room the older members conversed, while the children had their games by the fireside or in the large open hall. Stretched out upon the home-made rug in front of a blazing fire, the old cat slumbered away the peaceful hours. The creature was a great pet, and there is a story that it came to its death through overfeeding at the hands of those who were themselves distinguished for their temperance in both eating and drinking.

Life in the Community, leaving out of view the sexual features, was in many ways an improvement upon our ordinary family life. In the surrounding world were cruel competitions, every kind of rivalry, deception, and a merciless social and business warfare. But within the sacred enclosure of the Community none of these evils had power to plague the heart of man. Here no one lived for self alone. What was of advantage to one was of advantage to all. Strife for place and authority, distress of mind with regard to financial and other provisions for sickness and old age, and the bitterness and humiliation of disappointed ambition, were unknown within the charmed circle of the Oneida Community. Sometimes of a Sunday evening the family would gather around " Father " Noyes to hear him read selections from the poets, or recite interesting stories. There were members of the communal circle who could sing, and there were others who could play upon various musical instruments. Nearly all the younger members were in the chorus. Impromptu concerts and entertainments were common.

The life of an organized community is in some ways like that of the cloister; the same feelings and desires draw men to both. The burdens and sorrows of our human state are too heavy for the weak and irresolute. Freedom, whether of mind or body, is held to be a very precious thing; men

will die to secure and preserve it for themselves
and their children. The Protestant Reformation
and the American Revolution were both of them
struggles for freedom; and the suppression of re-
bellion in the Southern States half a century ago
had for its inspiring purpose the emancipation of
more than four million men who had been deprived of liberty for no crime of any kind, and
simply because of race and color. But men will
in many cases part even with freedom if thereby
they may secure peace of mind and quietness of
spirit. Freedom is not the greatest, nor is it the
noblest, thing in the world; truth, honor, and
character are of larger value. Not infrequently
escape from responsibility is well worth the surrender of liberty. There can be no doubt that
the cloisters of the Middle Ages were filled with
men who, in many cases, sought not so much communion with God as the longed-for escape from
personal responsibility and the anxiety of com-
petitive life in a great world of toil and strife.
There were, no doubt, in the Oneida Community
men and women who were there mainly because
of the freedom from anxiety and contention that
communal life secured them.

It has been said by some that the peculiar
sexual features of Mr. Noyes's community must
have drawn to the fold evil and worthless persons. But there is scant evidence that such persons were present. No one could enter without
undergoing careful and thorough investigation.
The social promiscuity that might be sought in

the Oneida Community could be had with no loss
of liberty and no sacrifice of property in the outside world.

One would naturally suppose that communal
life would be likely to attract the lazy and worthless, men who work only when they must, and then
as little as may be.    But we do not find any large
number of indolent or self-indulgent men in the
various societies, whether religious or wholly
secular, that have flourished and now flourish in
this and other lands.    " How do you manage
with lazy people? " inquired Mr. Nordhoff, the
author of a careful work on American communities, of a Shaker elder at Mount Lebanon.    The
elder replied:

" There are no idlers with us.    The shiftless fellows who, as cold weather approaches, take refuge
in Shaker and other communities, professing a desire to become members; who come at the beginning
of winter with empty stomachs and empty trunks,
and go off with both full as soon as the roses begin
to bloom,— even these poor creatures succumb to
the systematic and orderly rules of the place, and
do their share of work without shirking until the
mild spring tempts them to freer life."

There is something in communal life that lays
hold of man.    Of course incorrigible characters
are occasionally encountered, but in well-nigh
every community there are definite and well-un-
derstood methods of getting rid of worthless men
and of eliminating " false brethren."    The men

who preside over these communities are not ordinary men. They are peculiarly well qualified to guide and direct communal life, and to preserve such order and good behavior as are essential. They are themselves, in most cases, firm believers in the doctrines taught or the principles to which the community is committed. They are men of decided character, determined will, and good judgment. They have large knowledge of human nature, and cannot easily be deceived. They have many of the qualities that go to the making of a good general. A considerable number of them are shrewd business men. They have great tact and marvelously developed resourcefulness.

Communal life has a marked tendency to prolong individual life. Healthful and regular habits are cultivated. The members eat at regular and prescribed times, and there is usually plenty of good food, well cooked. The best that they themselves produce upon their farms is set aside for their own table. Little animal food is used, and alcohol and tobacco are avoided. They are relieved entirely from care and worry. If they happen to be sick, they are well nursed, and in old age life is made easy and pleasant. Surely such a life must prolong one's years upon earth.

The monastery in the Middle Ages, and at the present time as well, furnishes the best example we have of the religious community. It was not strange that men in periods of great public

agitation, disaster, and distress, sought shelter
and repose in religious houses. I am surprised
that at the present day larger numbers do not
crowd the inviting cloisters of faith. I should
expect to see both Greek and Roman sacred shel-
ters more than full of apprehensive, troubled,
care-worn souls, seeking rest, hope, guidance, and
encouragement in the fellowship and under the
immediate government of the church that commands their confidence.

Mr. Alger has said, in his "Genius of Solitude": "The majority of men in every age are
superficial in character and brittle of purpose,
and lead undedicated lives, swarming together in
buzzing crowds." These words are surely true,
and yet even the most frivolous and petty covet
at times something better. Grief, doubt, anxiety,
and the consciousness of inward guilt render
"buzzing crowds," noise, the empty chatter of
the world, and the companionship of thoughtless
men and women a burden to the soul and a weariness of the flesh. Solitude is ardently longed
for; tranquillity and repose are desired and
sought. The wholly modern community, whether
religious or secular, does not furnish the peculiar
solitude that thoughtful men earnestly desire;
nor does it provide for a man any real refuge
from himself. It is the monastery, in whatever
country or in whatever faith, that has this blessed
touch of peace found in no other communal home,
unless our Shaker friends may be said to possess
it. The closed door of the monastery shuts out

the world.  In that abode of peace, sacred and inviolable associations and usages bring with them a sweet and restful sense of repose and tranquillity.  The presence of others like-minded with one's self, holding a common faith, and engaged in the same religious exercises, cannot but restore lost equilibrium, reinvigorate spiritual powers, and renew self-control.  It is by no means strange that women especially, with their finer nervous equipment and greater sense of spiritual need, fill the sacred houses of their faith.

" Hark, from yon cloisters, wrapt in gloom pro-
      found,
The solemn organ peals its midnight sound;
With holy reverence round their glimmering shrine
Press the meek nuns, and raise the prayer divine;
While, pure in thought, as sweet responses rise,
Each grief subsides, each wild emotion dies."

No doubt the old-time monastery gave the world many a lazy beggar, but it sheltered the scholar as well, and nourished the saint.  There were cruel persecutors behind its impenetrable walls, and sometimes there were within its inclosure the dishonest sons of drunken revelry and dissipation; but these were not the only men who grew up under its influence.  We have to-day many manuscripts of great value that would have been lost had they not been preserved in the ample libraries of religious houses during the dark period between the fifth and fifteenth centuries. There was often great peace and safety within the monastery while in the world prevailed war, treachery, bitter hatred, and hostility. Long before Cowper lived, many a weary soul entertained his great wish:

" O for a lodge in some vast wilderness,
Some boundless contiguity of shade,
Where rumor of oppression and deceit,
Of unsuccessful or successful war,
Might never reach me more! My ear is pained,
My soul is sick, with every day's report
Of wrong and outrage with which earth is filled."

I have in my psychological cabinet still other specimens of the human derelict. There is Frederick Rapp, with his German religious community. He was not a derelict in any contemptible or evil sense; on the contrary, he was a well-meaning and devout man who strove to please God and serve his fellow men. But he was a dreamer of like dreams with those entertained by the other visionaries of whom we are discoursing. There was also Robert Dale Owen, with his New Harmony; Andrew Jackson Davis, one of the fathers of American Spiritualism; Stephen Pearl Andrews, with his Universology; Symmes and his Arctic Hole; the Walworth Jumpers; and a countless multitude of strange advocates of marvelous schemes of religion and philosophy. Place any one of the enthusiasts named under the literary, philosophical, or scientific microscope, and a whole world of interest is revealed.

I have a friend who is an entomologist, and

possesses a collection of gnats worth, I suppose, many thousands of dollars. The tiny creatures are fastened to little blocks of wood by minute pins, and under each of them is written its own proper name in the precise and distinct hand of the collector. Under each is also placed a description of the characteristics and habits of the gnat named. Some of the gnats are so small that a pin-thrust would destroy the specimen; these my friend has pasted securely to little white cards. I confess that when I saw for the first time that valuable collection, there was awakened within me a great desire to have all my psychological specimens as correctly and as systematically arranged. But that could not be brought about. No one would think of running a pin through Andrew Jackson Davis, nor would it be possible to paste Madame Blavatsky, with her peculiar *embonpoint*, to a slip of cardboard. The founder of Theosophy is no longer with us in the flesh. Her body was incinerated and the Theosophical societies of India, England, and the United States have taken charge of the cinders. All that remains to us of that gigantic humbug is the story of her not-over-fragrant life, the books she published, and the movement she initiated. It is evident that my collection could have only a literary arrangement, and so I have neatly classified the " specimens " in books, and some day, when my executor settles up my estate and disposes of the collection, it may be that all the " specimens " now in my possession will find their way to the Library of Congress at Washington. Why not? Several of my finest " specimens " were members of Congress.

Thomas Lake Harris, who wrote " An Epic of the Starry Heavens," was and is absolutely unique. He was born in England in 1823, and came with his father to the United States. Early in life he entered the ministry of the Universalist church. Later he organized an " Independent Christian Society," to which he ministered until he became a convert to spiritualism. He lectured throughout the United States and England; he established a spiritualistic journal; and organized on a farm in Dutchess County, New York, a community called the " Brotherhood of the New Life." His doctrines were a sort of combination of those of Plato, Swedenborg, and Fourier. The community was prosperous, and at one time had two thousand members.

Harris was like a great spider. He could entangle in his web of pretence and sophistry any kind of a fly. He caught several human flies of large means. He captured and feasted upon Laurence Oliphant, and the smacking of his lips over the dainty morsel attracted the attention of writers on both sides of the Atlantic. Mrs. Oliphant's book gives us only so much of the story of the terrible sufferings of Laurence Oliphant and his wife and mother at the community as is fit to print. The shame and indignity to which those refined women were subjected cannot be published. Later Harris formed a community in

California, but Mrs. Oliphant's book had dealt him his death-blow, and ever after his career was unimportant.

Harris was the author of several books, among which I name only the one by which he is best known, " An Epic of the Starry Heavens." It is a poem which he tells us was received from the spirit-world. The inspiration took place in the presence of witnesses who saw him go into a state of trance; heard him utter at several sittings the lines which constitute the poem; and examined the manuscript after the lines had been taken down by an amanuensis. His witnesses were men and women of no standing whatever in literary circles, but the book itself is quite out of the common order of literary work. The poem consists of 6,500 lines dictated at intervals during parts of about fourteen days, which would make Mr. Harris deliver nearly 500 lines a day. The actual time consumed in its delivery was about thirty hours (Mr. S. B. Brittan, who edited the poem, says that the time was but twenty-six hours and sixteen minutes). During the entrancement Mr. Harris saw and communed with Dante and Petrarch, and upon several occasions he was caught up into celestial spheres, leaving his soulless body on the earth. He gives us in Part 2, page 31, these ecstatic lines:

" A company of spirits, whose white arms
  Are entwined like lilies, float about the deep,
  Their music lulls my spirit into sleep.

Lo! one most beautiful unveils her form,—
My thoughts are drawn to her as dewdrops to the
    morn.

" O rose-lipped seraph, whose celestial charms
    O'ercome my being with a calm divine,—
    Whose heart of love in love inflows through
      mine,—
Whose eyes are twin-born spheres that blend to-
    gether
    As the sweet ocean and the enamored sky;
Feeling thy presence dear, I care not whether
    My being to its primal life returns. To die,
To be diffus'd in love, and made a part
Of the divinest beauty, which thou art,
    Were better, better far.
Where is thy home? in what beguiling star?"

Mention should be made of Elizabeth Doten
(" Lizzie Doten "), whose " Poems from the Inner Life " were, it is claimed, dictated to her by
the spirits of distinguished poets now dwelling
in the celestial world. Among the bards who
availed themselves of her mediumistic powers
were Shakespeare, Burns, and Poe. Elizabeth
Doten was born at Plymouth, Massachusetts,
April 1, 1829, and in mid-life was for a number
of years known as an " inspirational " speaker;
later she became an improviser of verses, of which
she has published several collections. Her book,
" Poems of the Inner Life," has passed through
a number of editions. Brief notices of her and
of her work may be found in Dixon's " Spiritual

Wives," and in Appleton's "Cyclopædia of American Biography." She is also mentioned in Wallace's " Contributions to the Theory of Natural Selection," and in Hodge's " Systematic Theology."

Preposterous as Elizabeth Doten's claims appear, I have never questioned her sincerity. While preparing this paper for the press there was open upon my desk a letter which Miss Doten addressed to me a number of years ago. I read that letter many times in order to catch something of its spirit, and I find in it only the evidence of sincerity and of a sweet and gentle temper. A few lines from the poem, " Words o' Cheer," which she thinks she received from the spirit of Robert Burns, will give some idea of the kind of work to be found in her book:

> "Lo! Calvin, Knox, and Luther, cry
> ' I have the truth '—' and I '—' and I '—
> Puir sinners! if ye gang agley,
>    The de'il will hae ye,
> And then the Lord will stand abeigh,
>    And will na save ye!

> " But hoolie, hoolie!  Na sae fast;
> When Gabriel shall blaw his blast,
> And Heaven and Earth awa' have passed,
>    These lang-syne saints
> Shall find baith de'il and hell at last,
>    Mere pious feints.

" The upright, honest-hearted man,
Who strives to do the best he can,
Need never fear the Church's ban,
    Or hell's damnation;
For God will need na special plan
    For his salvation."

The poet's theology is hardly that of the New
Testament, in which something more than good
behavior and a kindly feeling are called for.
Burns's real life, of which most of his readers
know little, was scarcely in accord with the
Sacred Book named, nor yet with the above lines
which the author of " Poems from the Inner
Life " attributes to his ghost. But it is not necessary to subject a writer's life to microscopic
inspection in order to enjoy his verses. Burns
may not have been all his admirers could have
wished, but nevertheless we delight ourselves in
his genius, and in the simple and natural beauty
of his songs and longer poems. There let the
matter rest.

" No further seek his merits to disclose,
    Or draw his frailties from their dread abode
(There they alike in trembling hope repose),
    The bosom of his Father and his God."

I think the lines quoted from the spirit of
Robert Burns are among the best of the many
more or less good lines one may find in Miss
Doten's remarkable book. Of course a clever
parody or imitation is no uncommon thing.
Walt Whitman has been so well imitated that one

must look into " Leaves of Grass " to assure himself that the lines are not those of Whitman himself. In " Father Prout's Reliques " the art of juggling with the literary work of other men reaches a perfection possible only to scholars. Was Miss Doten an unconscious plagiarist? She may have been; but I cannot see in her verses intentional deception.

A direct claim of inspiration is made in her " Word to the World," which precedes the " Poems from the Inner Life." Miss Doten says very frankly:

" I claim both a general and particular inspiration. They do not, by any means, conflict; and what I do not receive from one, comes from the other. For the very reason that I have natural poetic tendencies, I attract influences of a kindred nature; and when I desire it, or they will to do so, they cast their characteristic inspirations upon me, and I give them utterance according to my ability. . . . Several days before inspirations were given I would receive intimations of them. Oftentimes, and particularly under the influence of Poe, I would awake in the night from a deep slumber, and detached fragments of those poems would be floating through my mind, though in a few moments after, they would vanish like a dream. I have sometimes awakened myself by repeating them aloud. I have also been informed by these influences that all their poems are as complete and finished in spirit-life as they are in this, and the only reason why they cannot be repeated again and again is because of the difficulty of bringing a human organism always into the same state of exaltation,— a state in which mediums readily receive inspiration and render the poems with least interference of their own intellect.

" Among these spiritual poems will be found two purporting to come from Shakespeare. This influence seemed to overwhelm and crush me. I was afraid, and shrank from it. Only those two poems were given, and then the attempt was not repeated. I do not think that the poems in themselves come up to the productions of his master mind. They are only intimations of what might have been if he had had a stronger and more effectual instrument upon which to pour his inspirations. I have no doubt that time will yet furnish one upon whom his mantle will fall; but I can only say that his power was mightier than I could bear. . . .

" The influence of Burns was pleasant, easy, and exhilarating, and left me in a cheerful mood. As a spirit, he seemed to be genial and kindly, with a clear perception and earnest love of simple truth, and at the same time a good-natured contempt for all shams, mere forms, and solemn mockeries. This was the way in which he impressed me, and I felt much more benefited than burdened by his presence."

Of course the inspiration claimed by Miss Doten has been claimed by a great host of enthusiasts, among whom may be named Ann Lee, Joseph Smith, Joanna Southcott, Richard Brothers, and Andrew Jackson Davis. Some of these derived their inspiration from spirits that once lived upon the earth, and some professed to receive it directly from God.

Jacob Boehme, the German mystic, believed himself divinely illuminated, and gifted with an understanding of the secrets of both nature and grace. Some of his writings are so obscure and occult that they are well nigh incomprehensible; yet he numbered among his followers many educated and some distinguished persons. These all sat at the feet of the " philosophical shoemaker of Gorlitz," and adopted his most remarkable opinions. Boehme obtained his knowledge from Heaven by means of visions; and in his books he opens to the reader divine treasures of wisdom which he received from God. In presenting this wisdom he makes use of chemical terms, thus rendering the comprehension of his disclosures still more difficult. Some of his disciples pronounce him incomprehensible to all who are not believers in his system. The Rev. William Law understood him; but then it must be remembered that Law was a disciple, an expounder, and even an editor of Boehme's works.

It is interesting to observe the poetical trend of a large number of enthusiasts. Even those who write in prose not infrequently think in verse. There is a constant inclination toward poetical terms, figures, symbols, and embellishments. Poetry is the natural language of enthusiasm, passion, emotion, and imagination; and for that

reason it is the oldest of all forms of speech.
When our race was sufficiently developed, it naturally sought to give expression to its newly acquired faculties, which were, in truth, those of
children. The language in which the expression
found its embodiment was that of impulse, emotion, passion, and imagination. Reason and
judgment made comparatively little impression
upon the vocabulary of the infant world. The
development of judgment is necessarily associated
with the recession of imagination; and the ripen-
ing of analysis marks the autumn of sentiment
and the winter of poetry. Poetry was the natural language of the infant world, and is still that
of the infant mind. The poet is forever young.
It is his mission to preserve for us all and within
us all youthfulness of mind and heart. The poet
is the immortal child. Emerson tells us the
world's " poetry was all written before time was."
As racial development unfolds, song fails. It is
then " we hear, through all the varied music a
ground-tone of conventional life " that tells us
the age of reason is at hand. Then it is that our
poets are, as Emerson tells us, " men of talents
who sing, and not the children of music." Whatever reopens the early vision pleases the poet
within us, and as well the world-poet who sings
from without, for the vision is always of youth;
hence it is, to borrow again the words of Emerson, that " bards love wine, mead, narcotics,
coffee, tea, opium, the fumes of sandal wood, and

tobacco, or whatever other procurers of animal exhilaration." Yet these only enable us to imitate from afar what was once real.

Insanity is in a certain way a return to childhood. The intellectual faculties most frequently interfered with in insanity are such as distinguish age from youth. The strongholds of reason break and crumble; the fortress of judgment falls; and how often over its ruins blossoms the wild and luxuriant verdure of emotion and imagination. The insane man reverses the process of development; he turns his back upon the future and retraces his steps. Science tells us that the human race started in the mud, and by a process of evolution arrived at animal life and intellectual consciousness. There was a point in time when the little gray nerve-cells first caught the golden sunlight, and in the mint of their own consciousness turned it into the coin of thought; when they knew for the first time the color of the violet and the odor of the rose as distinct sensations. The currents of thought were at first rudimentary and imperfect; but as the brain strengthened, convoluted, and developed, there came with increasing power along the track of the nervous system such trains of living thought as announced the arrival of the human epoch. The vices and virtues, hopes and fears, all point along the road of progress to human destiny, which is but character in its final and fixed experience; these are but milestones along the road over which our race has traveled and over which it must travel so long as our planet remains habitable.

The insane man, as we have seen, turns his back upon the future, and, retracing his steps, descends the stairway of development, and through a process of devolution returns to the childhood of his race. He may go further, for he may sink to the very lowest depths of imbecility. He may even enter through the shadowy portals of idiocy into the realm of brute nature, and have his part with Nebuchadnezzar of old, who became as a beast of the field. Owing to the good offices of civilization, he may not be driven from among men to make his abode with cattle, and to sleep by night unsheltered beneath the stars, his body wet with the dew of heaven, his hair long and tangled like an eagle's plumage, and his nails like a bird's claw; but the human element may be destroyed. He may become to all the intents and purposes of life a mere animal, well portrayed in the blighting words of a poet:

" Hog in filth, fox in stealth, wolf in greediness,
Dog in madness, lion in prey."

The insane are, so far as our race is concerned, children. The same instinct that long ago taught the savage, who is child of the race, to cower before the ordinary phenomena of nature, and that teaches the infant to shrink from an unaccustomed sound, leads the insane to recoil from things in no way dangerous or frightful. Like children, they live in their senses and are

ruled over by imagination.   The child lives in an
ideal world; so does the savage; so does the mad-
man; so also, in a sense, does the poet.   To
these the ideal things, unreal to the practical man
of affairs, are substantial and near-at-hand.
These all live in an enchanted world in which the
critic has no place.   The critic, whether he praise
or blame, is always a disenchanter.

We learn from Herodotus that Phrynicus produced a tragedy on the fall of Miletus; the citizens wept until the play was ended, and then
fined the author for torturing their feelings.
What audience in England or America ever wept
through a play and then censured the dramatist
because of the tragic power and truthfulness of
the work?   I venture to say no such reproof
was ever administered.   We are not children;
our judgment never so relaxes as to deliver us
wholly into the hands of imagination.   We crit-
icize a play while it is enacted before us.   It
was not so with our remote ancestors; they witnessed a play very much as a child listens to a
ghost story.

As knowledge and reason develop, the inven-
tive arts triumph over the imaginative.   The
same thing was true centuries ago in Greece,—
the imaginative school of poetry was followed by
the critical.   After Pindar came Sophocles; after
Sophocles, Euripides; and after Euripides, the
Alexandrine versifiers.   Latin and Greek literatures both illustrate the same great truth, and
place before us the same invariable succession.

Homer, Shakespeare, and Goethe are not exceptions to the general rule. They are described as poets and such they are; but they are, in truth, something more: they are the representatives of our race. Everything pertaining to mankind interested those great writers and found adequate expression in their work.

Those who in this age cultivate poetry as an art, by that very cultivation destroy in some measure its free life and natural beauty. Culture implies criticism. In it are elements that, if not closely watched and guarded against, war upon warmth and youthfulness, which are factors inherent in all true poetry. It is to

> "Olympian bards who sung
>  Divine ideas below,
> Which always find us young,
>  And always keep us so,"

that we owe the sweetness and spontaneity of life. These are the makers of joy through whose eyes we behold worlds that never age. By the natural instinct of a child's heart they believe in what they see and enjoy. No questions are asked. Discussion, born of doubt, has neither place nor recognition in the world they inhabit, for it is a beautiful world, and none the less beautiful because unreal.

Whether we are to include Dr. R. M. Bucke, the author of "Cosmic Consciousness," among the strange characters of whom we are now treating is a question not so easy to answer. Per-

sonally he was a man of attractive qualities.  He
was an upright and sincere man, and a most
loyal friend.  The friendship between Walt
Whitman and Dr. Bucke was one of the beautiful friendships of temperament and literature.
But Bucke was, as well, a man of very peculiar
mental characteristics, and his " Cosmic Consciousness " details some astonishing experiences which he explains in a still more astonishing way.  He tells us that cosmic consciousness is not a mere " expansion of the self-
conscious mind," but the super-addition of a
function as distinct from any possessed by the
average man as self-consciousness is distinct
from any function possessed by one of the higher
animals.  Dr. Bucke had himself a most remarkable experience of this peculiar cosmic consciousness.  That experience he has detailed in his
book, from which the following paragraph is
taken:

" I had spent the evening in a great city with
two friends, reading and discussing poetry and philosophy.  We parted at midnight.  I had a long
drive in a hansom to my lodging.  My mind,
deeply under the influence of the ideas, images, and
emotions called up by the reading and talk, was
calm and peaceful.  I was in a state of quiet, almost passive enjoyment, not actually thinking, but
letting ideas, images, and emotions flow of themselves, as it were, through my mind.  All at once,
without warning of any kind, I found myself
wrapped in a flame-colored cloud.  For an instant

I thought of fire,— an immense conflagration somewhere close by in that great city; the next, I knew
the fire was within myself. Directly afterward
there came upon me a sense of exultation, of immense joyousness, accompanied or immediately followed by an intellectual illumination impossible to
describe. Among other things, I did not merely
come to believe, but I saw, that the universe is not
composed of dead matter, but is, on the contrary,
a living Presence; I became conscious in myself of
eternal life. It was not a conviction that I would
have eternal life, but a consciousness that I possessed eternal life then; I saw that all men are immortal; that the cosmic order is such that without
any peradventure all things work together for the
good of each and all; that the foundation principle
of the world, of all the worlds, is what we call love;
and that the happiness of each and all is in the
long run absolutely certain. The vision lasted a
few seconds and was gone; but the memory of it
and the sense of the reality of what it taught has
remained during the quarter of a century which has
since elapsed. I knew that what the vision showed
was true. I had attained to a point of view from
which I saw that it must be true. That view, that
conviction, I may say that consciousness, has never,
even during periods of the deepest depression, been
lost."

Mr. Trine tells us, in his " In Tune with the
Infinite," that he knew an officer on the police
force who, while off duty and on his way home in
the evening, came under the power of an Infinite
Presence that he could not understand. It was

very much like Dr. Bucke's cosmic consciousness. While under its influence he could hardly keep to the pavement. He was so buoyant and exhilarated by its inflowing tide that he had great difficulty in avoiding the curious gaze of those who were in the street with him. Mr. Trine does not call the officer's experience one of cosmic consciousness, but rather one of harmony with the Infinite. Yet the experiences of the officer and of Dr. Bucke were in fact one and the same thing. Both experiences were of a mystical nature, and have been in some measure paralleled by that of Benjamin Paul Blood, though Mr. Blood's experience was artificial, having been produced by the inhalation of ether, as he explained in a pamphlet which he published, called " The Anæsthetic Revelation and the Gist of Philosophy."

Some of the unusual men and women here discussed were very interesting characters, and a few of them were also useful in their day and generation, but, viewed as a class, they were derelicts. As such they were a burden and, in some instances, a menace to the normal men and women of their age. What shall we do with human derelicts? When they are able to care for themselves and are satisfied to chase their own shadows, leaving others to go their way unmolested, the question is answered. But when the derelict lies directly in the way of sound vessels, impeding progress or rendering shipwreck a near contingency, the question is far from answered. An American alienist recommended some years ago the killing of all weak-minded, incompetent, and vicious persons. We deal in that way with maritime derelicts that endanger our ships of commerce and war. We send out a vessel prepared to find the floating hulks and sink them. Dr. Porter, of Harvard University, said in an address on the subject of public charities, reported in the New York " Sun ":

" It is evident that there is not enough money to go around. And it is equally desirable to spend money on a thing from which we get the most value. . . . It may seem cruel but . . . we must concentrate our relief on the most hopeful side of our population and allow the rest to go the way of nature. . . . The whole question is one of economy. It is a mistaken idea to believe that everything depends on charity for the old and not on prevention for the young. Charity means that those who receive it give up hope. Charity is the gravest psychological factor in the life of the poor. It is an official stigma. Instead of organizations for charity there should be a citizens' union for preventing charity. When a person gets to that point where he is physically unfit to live, the most economical thing for a community is not to give him relief."

Well, that is a comparatively easy way of disposing of the broken-down and broken-hearted men and women who obstruct the way. It is what the Sacred Book calls " Going by on the other side." The other side is always the easy side. Let the derelict hulk be abandoned — no, not that, let it be at once and wholly demolished.

Newer and stauncher vessels have the right-of-
way.   All very good,— but there seem to be certain objections to Dr. Porter's recommendation.
He loses sight of the important fact that we are
civilized, and that as civilized men and women we
are more or less under the control of an enlightened sympathy.   The loveless man is the worst of
all derelicts.   To treat the human derelict as one
would treat the maritime derelict is to treat men
and things in the same way.   No, Dr. Porter,
your system may be, for anything we know to the
contrary, on a level with your sympathy and will-
ingness to help the under dog, but we cannot
abandon nor can we sink the human derelicts.
There lived nearly two thousand years ago One
after whom we name our era and our civilization,
and whom we love,— One who taught the world a
very different doctrine, and who said, " Inasmuch
as ye have done it unto one of the least of these,
my brethren, ye have done it unto me."

   John Fiske states in a footnote to his delightful book on " The Discovery of America,"
that when he was superintending the cataloguing
of Harvard University Library he made a class
for books which he called " Eccentric Literature,"
under which name he grouped a large number of
foolish works which disputed the roundness of the
earth and indulged in other vagaries of the kind.
Among such books he placed " The New Manual
of Biblical Cosmography," a book published so
late as 1877, and " The Truth-Seeker's Oracle
and Scriptural Science Review," and more of the

sort. Strange indeed are some of these books.
They are more or less foolish, but they are not
all of them wholly devoid of interest. Such books
and men will increase in number as our civilization ripens and decays. But we cannot lose sight
of the fact that there have been among the men
and women we call human derelicts some of the
brightest minds our race has ever known. To a
few of these we owe much. Tolstoy was of their
number, and so also was the philanthropist, John
Howard.

Cranks are not always unappreciated. There
are other cranks who approve and encourage men
like unto themselves. There were in Brittany
not so very long ago those who believed, as did
the ancients, that the insane were inspired and
that epileptics were in close fellowship with the
unseen world. Captain King said that he saw in
Brittany persons who looked with great regard
upon idiots, and who actually requested the
prayers of those idiots, believing the prayer of a
fool to be peculiarly acceptable to God. In
India, even now, the insane are held in great
reverence.

Perhaps it is, after all, an open question, what
we are to understand by a derelict. If fools are
wise men, does it not follow that our wise men are
fools? And if such they are, our world must be
a foolish world indeed. And yet not all fools are
wholly devoid of sense. The best of Edward
Rowland Sill's poems is, beyond doubt, "The
Fool's Prayer." The mind of that poor fool was

not in every way distraught, for he understood
all too well his own humiliation.    Sill's fool was
a court fool.    He was more than anything else a
jester,— a man of " cap and bells."    But he
could pray a prayer that hushed the room into
silence, and that so opened the king's eyes that
he saw what he had never seen before,— that he
also was a fool.    Many simpletons have worn
crowns and possessed thrones.    But better so
than that those crowns and thrones should have
fallen to such monsters of cruelty as have sometimes possessed them.    Better were it for Germany that some fool with a child's trinket for
scepter were upon her throne than that a man
like William II, the scourge of his country and
of the world, and the remorseless murderer of
millions of men much better than himself, should
fill, as he does, a station so exalted, and

> " Play such fantastic tricks before high Heaven
> As make the angels weep."

He, too, is, notwithstanding all his wickedness, if
not a fool, at least a derelict, for wickedness is
only a worse kind of folly.

# VI

## MINOR POETS

Those gentler voices float across the centuries to cheer and encourage the human heart. We listen to the peaceful, tender, and reassuring tones, and are refreshed. They are not like the commanding and dominating world-singers that with power and authority stir the pulses of men and lead the nations forth to battle. Very gentle are the minor poets; they fill our hearts with tranquillity and guide our willing feet in the path of peace; yet have they a noble dignity that everywhere and always commands respect.

— *Cirederf Nivram.*

If thou indeed derive thy light from heaven,
Then, in the measure of that heaven-born light,
Shine, poet, in thy place, and be content!
— *Wordsworth.*

# MINOR POETS

TWO dissimilar events occurred about the same time,— Barrie, the author and playwright, was made a baronet, and Austin, who followed Tennyson in the office of poet laureate, died at his beautiful home in Swinford after seventeen years of official glory and mental commonplace. They buried the poet with honor, and his name will be transmitted to posterity. Few will read his verses, and yet, because for a season he occupied the seat of Wordsworth and Tennyson, English literature will celebrate his work and record his glory long after more gifted but less distinguished singers shall have passed from our remembrance. Shadwell, Tate, Rowe, and Pye were, all of them, laureled verse-makers to one majesty or another; and though now no man can be found so dull as willingly to con their cobwebbed pages, their names will still be cherished because for a brief season they sipped inspiration or something more to the point from the traditional butt of Malmsey, and because they belonged officially in the charmed circle that inclosed the author of " In Memoriam."

" A little Latin and mathematics will do very well," said Napoleon; but Frederick the Great was of another mind: bringing down his fist with force upon the table, he exclaimed: " My son shall not learn Latin; and, more than that, I will not suffer anybody even to mention such a thing to me." There you have it,— you can take your choice. Whitehead had much Latin and but little inspiration. The old masters of English song were, all of them, Latinists, partly because the English of long ago was not so completely or so well formed as it is to-day, and partly because at that early time no man was accounted well educated who had " small Latin and less Greek." The old writers were full of both languages, and (sorry I am to say it) that is one reason their lines are so dull and obscure to the "uncrowned sovereigns" and jingledy-jingledy poets of our present time.

Austin was a college man. He was graduated from the University of London. He had in view a barrister's life, and to that end much of his education tended. But, as good old Thomas à Kempis has it, " Man proposes while God disposes," and so it came to pass that Alfred Austin never practiced, but at eighteen published his first poem. From that time on he gave the world many books, some of which are interesting, and none of which are worthy of the laureateship he filled so respectably and with so little inspiration. Some of his best verses are in " English Lyrics." The book came out under the editorial care of William Watson, but after Mr. Watson wrote " The Woman with the Serpent's Tongue " the reading world lost confidence in his judgment. And yet Austin was surely deserving of a portion of the praise bestowed upon him. It by no means follows that because a poem or a picture is not an achievement of the highest order of genius, it is therefore worthless. Few in any age or land stand upon the summit, and it is by no means certain that those who do stand there create for our world the largest satisfaction or the truest pleasure.

When Will Carleton died there came to thousands of plain men and women all over this and other lands a deep sense of personal loss. No one ever thought him the possessor of great genius, but he was a true poet, and everywhere he was recognized as such. Plain farmers, with but little knowledge of books, when they heard of Carleton's death read again " Betsy and I Are Out," and found it had not lost for them its early charm. Thousands of men and women who never read a line of Milton have the " Farm Ballads " near at hand; and, what is more, they hold their hearts wide open to the homely allurement of lines that record so well the annals of the poor. It has been said of the minor poet that he " plays upon the one string of our common humanity "; that was true of Carleton. The everyday troubles and joys of our common human life were the materials out of which he made all those artless and unadorned, yet charming, pictures of rural life. Carleton was himself very like his own verses. He had a large and sympathetic heart. He was instinctively kind and generous. He was outspoken, and had a straightforward and manly way of looking at things. I have passed with

him many a happy hour of frank and unguarded
fellowship, and I am unable to recall one bitter
word or an uncharitable surmise concerning
friend or foe.  He was very entertaining; rarely
was he without a good story; he was quick-
witted; and never was he slow to see the ludicrous
or incongruous side of things.

Carleton, unlike Austin, was a conservative
only in those social and domestic circles and
scenes of which he wrote; in all public and national affairs his sympathy was very largely with
the other side.  Carleton was a democrat and believed in popular government.  He saw nothing
absurd in an administration and common-
wealth guided and directed by the wisdom of
Tom, Dick, and Harry.  Austin's sympathies
were with the aristocracy and landed interests.  To the best of his poor ability he sang
of England's greatness on land and sea.  He
was at the time of his appointment the only possible selection.  Other poets were living, but
none of them were even remotely available.  The
author of "Atalanta in Calydon" could not be
for a single moment thought of in connection with
an office inherently conservative and closely connected with national ideals and traditions.  The
old Puritanism, still strong in England, could
never have adopted the author of "Faustine"
and "Dolores."  Morris, it is true, had written "The Earthly Paradise," but he was a
Socialist.  Kipling's "Recessional" was even
better than good, but alone it was hardly suf-

ficient for the making of a poet laureate; and
then there were the old " Barrack-Room Ballads," not quite in keeping with the dignity of a
place once filled by Wordsworth and Tennyson.
Still further, the author of those " Ballads " had
called Her Majesty Queen Victoria " the
Widow." No disrespect was felt or intended,
but still there was involved an important matter
of taste. The royal person and name are sacred,
and may not be handled without reverence and
something like a sense of awe. Perhaps it would
have been no more distasteful to Her Majesty
had he called her " the Old Woman." She was
at the time both a widow and an old woman, but
what of that? Truth will often make a matter
worse. The thing that Kipling should have remembered was that she was the queen and an
empress. Men wriggle and squirm when *lèse
majesté* appears upon the horizon; they resent
the circumspection required in the presence of
royalty; but without external observances it is
hard to see how there could be maintained anything like strong and abiding authority. A
rowdy government would be no government whatever. It may have been, though I do not know
that it was so, that that slip of the pen, " the
Widow," cost Kipling more than most men have
stopped to consider. Austin, the commonplace
proser whom no one ever thinks of as very much
of a poet, was nevertheless a courtly gentleman
of the old school, who had respect for authority,
and so it came to pass that, authority being the

arbitrator, he was invited to a seat with the gods on Olympian heights. Why should there have been another poet laureate? The court fool with his cap and bells is now no more, and will never again make an appearance among the living; is it not time the court poet as well should find his way to rest and oblivion?

Yet men do not so think, for England has made choice of Dr. Bridges, who is now her poet laureate. He, too, is a courtly gentleman of the old school, full of good Latin and even better Greek, with a sincere love for the England of other days. He will give the world few great poems, but we shall be spared the sluggish dullness of Austin. The minor poet (and both Austin and Bridges must be accounted members of that great brotherhood) is by no means a contemptible figure in literature. His gifts are not of the first order, nor yet of the second, but they are, nevertheless, gifts.

The " Farm Ballads " are not to be named among the brilliant results of supreme inspiration, nor, for that matter, is the " Fable for Critics," though both compositions are real poetry of widely sundered kinds. Still, Carleton and Lowell are not to be placed in the same class, for the latter wrote as well " The Vision of Sir Launfal " and certain other poems that the former could never have written had he given his whole life to the work. Viewed from an artistic standpoint, the poems of Carleton are of no great value, and yet they have cheered and will

continue to cheer and comfort common men and
women. They have a homely beauty all their
own that the dainty maker of elegant and choice
lines might well covet.

Elizabeth Akers Allen would hardly be called
a poet, viewed from an artistic standpoint; and
yet many a year will go by before the world has
forgotten some of those short poems that render
her name dear to thousands of plain men and
women in all parts of our land. " Annie
Laurie " lives on and will continue to live, though
not one in a hundred of those who derive pleasure from the song remember that William Douglas was its author. Who was William Douglas?
Not often will you find his name in a biographical
dictionary, nor, indeed, will you often find it in
any list of poets. Yet the whole world has been
made happier by his brief and obscure life.
Payne is called a poet because we do not know
how else to describe him. He wrote " Home,
Sweet Home," and for that one poem, sometimes
set forth as " immortal doggerel," his dust was
brought with reverence and something of love
across the sea and given a resting place in the
land of his nativity.

No, the minor poet is not to be despised. The
buttercup is not a rose, but it nevertheless adds
beauty to the wayside and a loveliness to the
meadow. One would much rather be an " American Beauty," but it is something to be a buttercup, a daisy, or even a yellow dandelion. The
fields are everybody's garden. God cultivates

them for the great world, and whoever will may gather from them so much of fragrance and beauty as he cares to enjoy.

The trouble with our minor poets is that there are so many of them. Were there fewer daisies, buttercups, and dandelions in our fields and by the road, we should admire and enjoy them more. Florists would then cultivate their little rings of yellow gold, and would sell them in graceful clusters at, it may be, extravagant prices. Were the humbler bards in the meadows of literature not quite so common, we should, no doubt, prize them more. The publishers would then find them more interesting and profitable, and great libraries would give them more distinguished places in accessible alcoves. There are too many of them for their own good. Of course some of the best things are the most common. Light, air, and water are free to all, and without these, so abundant and so essential, there could be no life upon our planet. Still we do not easily value the thing that costs little in toil or money. All common things, and common men, are at a discount. We want the unusual possessions, difficult to obtain, and so it comes to pass that a vast world of beauty goes unrecognized and unenjoyed.

Unlike other libraries, the Grosvenor Library at Buffalo, New York, has accumulated an extensive collection of books of verse, all of which are in the English language. In that collection there were some time ago 3,542 printed volumes and 296 pamphlets; there must now be a much larger number, most of them, of course, being the work of what we call minor poets. There is place enough for one such collection, and there may be in all the land a considerable number who care to consult it; but surely there could not be a call for many collections of the kind, even were poetry more pleasing to the common people than it is at the present time. A large percentage of the books and pamphlets in the collection are not worth the printing, but there is, of course, a residuum that goes far toward making the accumulation of real value.

There are many books upon those shelves written by poets wholly unknown to fame; and yet some of them contain poems of rare beauty. It is a mistake to say that merit alone will always secure for its possessor a hearing. It will often secure for him nothing of the kind, no matter how great may be the merit. The mere pretender can often blow a louder blast upon the trumpet of his self-appreciation than the writer of real worth could sound were he to give undivided attention to self-exploitation for many years. Commonplace men are often unrestrained by a sense of shame, while men of genius, aiming high, are not infrequently humiliated by failures wholly invisible to the eye of dull and vulgar vanity. It is the loud blast that rivets attention and challenges admiration. Blaze and detonation win popular applause. Often it is true that the more commonplace a man is, the more attentively he will be listened to, and the more he will gratify the rude and uncultivated. The savages in Africa demand a " big noise "; savages in New York and other American cities demand noise of the same kind. Not a few of our most successful journals are mostly headlines.

It does not follow that because publishers are glad to print certain books, those books are worth printing; nor does it follow that because a man cannot find a publisher, his book is of no value. The editor is often as vulgar as his subscriber, and the publisher is sometimes too ignorant to know whether a book is of value or is wholly worthless. This world itself is at best a very vulgar world.

There is a general feeling that the work of a minor poet must be at best only fair; but it is a veritable fact that the minor poet may be even a great poet. He may have written but one or two poems, and his inferiority may be a matter of quantity and not of quality. O'Hara's " Bivouac of the Dead," Randall's " Maryland," and Finch's " The Blue and the Gray " are works of genius of no mean order. But the three authors named never did any other work in verse worth remembering, unless we make an exception in O'Hara's case, for his " Daniel Boone " is certainly not bad. Had any one of the three written ten or even eight poems of any length equal to the one poem by which he is known and which we have named, it may be he would have found his place among the more honored sons of genius whose works are praised and treasured by all who take pleasure in good verse.

How many of my readers know anything about Walter R. Benjamin, who has for more than a quarter of a century sold autographs in the city of New York? He does not call himself a poet, nor does any one of the hundreds of his customers ever think of him as in any wise inspired. A few of his verses (some of them good and more of them of no real worth) have found their way into "The Collector," a paper which he publishes, and in which he catalogues the letters and manuscripts he desires to sell. He is a delightful companion, but there is nothing in his presence, or in the many verses he has printed, that leads you to suspect him of being one of the gifted few. You happen to know that his father, Park Benjamin, was once accounted a poet of ability, but father and son are not the same person. Well, the man who wrote "The Drums!" which appeared in the "The Collector," is to the extent of that one piece a true son of inspiration; a minor poet, but a real poet nevertheless. Should he write eight or ten poems of equal excellence (and he is not too old to write them), it may be that we should no longer use the word minor in describing him and his work. The chance, however, it must be admitted, is very much against his writing even one other

poem so good as the one named.  The chance of
any man's writing a superior poem is seldom
great.

It would not be just to Mr. Benjamin, after
all that has been said, nor would it be just to
my readers who have had, it may be, their curiosity excited, should I fail of placing before
them the poem to which attention has been called.
Here it is from a copy he was himself so good as
to send me:

### THE DRUMS!

" The drums!  The drums!  There is music in the
        beating of the drums!
The heart grows gay and lighter as the brass band
        onward comes.
One falls in step and takes a stride,
And with the band walks on in pride,
And banging, crashing at his side,
    The drums, the drums, the busy, busy drums,
    The drums, the drums, the rattling, battling
        drums,
    The drums, the drums, the merry, merry drums,
How they set the blood a-tingling as the brass band
        onward comes!

" I take no joy in drumming,— yet I have a broken
        drum
That is laid away securely in a sacred place at
        home.
My lost boy held it when he died.
Had they but seen it by his side

I know the very drums had cried,
  The weeping and the wailing of the drums,
  The moaning and the groaning of the drums,
  The sobbing and the sighing of the drums,
How they set the blood a-tingling as the craped flag
    onward comes!

"Oh, when I hear their dirges, I can but think with
    pain
That never more his little hand will strike that drum
    again.
Perhaps in that far distant land
He marches in an angel band.
Perhaps they echo to his hand,
  The drums, the drums, the golden, golden drums,
  The drums, the drums, the sweet, celestial drums,
  The drums, the drums, the corps of heavenly
    drums,
How they set the blood a-tingling as the bright band
    onward comes!

"When my sojourn on earth is o'er and my last hour
    is come,
I'll listen in the future world for music of his drum.
My little boy will welcome me;
His laughing face once more I'll see.
How sweet will then their music be!
  The drums, the drums, the great eternal drums!
  The drums, the drums, the grand, supernal
    drums!
  The drums, the drums, Jehovah's mighty drums!
How the soul will sing in glory when that happy
    moment comes."

Not one critic in a hundred distributes commendation and censure with impartiality. The reviewer too often confines his investigations to the Table of Contents, or if by chance he proceeds further, the reader will get little more than two or three of his hastily formed impressions. My publisher usually prints, with whatever book he brings out, a circular somewhat descriptive of the work, and calculated to create for it a favorable impression. A copy of the circular generally goes with each copy of the book. The circular is not intended for the reviewer but for the general reader. I have been greatly interested and amused by observing how faithfully many of the so-called reviewers and penny-a-liners save themselves trouble by copying as their own the material my publisher provided for the reading public in his circular. All the while the unsuspecting multitude of simple-hearted men and women believe they are getting the serious opinion of a competent and faithful reviewer. A bright publisher in the "wild and woolly West," where "everything goes," stated in his somewhat flamboyant circular that the book he was printing was "off-color" and should not be too generously distributed in seminaries for the education of young ladies and in other places of the kind. It so happened that the book was of an irreproachable character. But the writers of the book notices in papers far and near made their usual levy upon the aforesaid circular, and so it came to pass that the sale of the book was a thing to envy.

I cannot think that our professional critics are, most of them, qualified to take the measure of the minor poets. They judge them by exceptional standards. From the critic's point of view there are no minor poets, for no one is a a poet, in any sense of the word, who suffers by comparison with Homer, Shakespeare, Milton, or Dante. They would not themselves like to be measured as critics by any such standard of ideal excellence. The Golden Rule, which is also a rule of common sense and good feeling, does not seem to them to have very much value apart from morals and religion. No man is to be judged by his fellow men, however he may be judged by his Creator, from any criterion of unusual excellence. Why should Carleton be compared with Milton? Why should Riley be measured by Dante? Our critics will deny that they apply such standards, but nevertheless they do apply them with remorseless rigor in very many cases. I will not say that they always know they apply them, nor yet that they would themselves justify such application; but you cannot read a brief paragraph in any serious review of a popular but commonplace poet without feeling the implied if not outspoken depreciation of the writer upon the sole ground that he is not a star of the first magnitude. That the writer thus dealt with is displeased goes without saying, but the critic's

scarcely concealed contempt for those who read
that writer's lines and like them is offensive to a
still larger circle. Added to all this there is a
lack of fair play about it that we instinctively
resent. We do not believe the critic is himself
so superior to the rest of us that he is justified
in patronizing us and in patting upon the back
our household gods. Matthew Arnold could
never write about the middle class in England
without in one way or another insinuating that
its members were well-nigh all of them ignorant
and narrow-minded. I have often wondered how
one man could contain so much old-fashioned
British conceit; and still more have I wondered
how a man of Arnold's knowledge and training
could fail of seeing that his own implications were
those of a narrow Philistine. The larger the
man, the more charitable will be his estimate of
his fellow men. It is just there that our critics
fail. Their lack is that of breadth and catholic-
ity of mind.

It is sometimes represented that Keats died
of a broken heart, and that the fatal fracture
was occasioned by the sledge-hammer strokes of
a critic who, being of a brutal nature, used his
pen somewhat as a thug in India would use a
club. Well, no doubt, the poet, being peculiarly
sensitive, suffered in his mind because of certain
rude and foolish things said of his literary work
by a narrow and foolish reviewer; but the real
cause of Keats's death, if we eliminate all sentiment, was nothing more than plain pulmonary

consumption. The physicians of to-day would
call it "phthisis." It is of little consequence
what most of the critics think of any author or
of any of his books. Keats lived at a time when
those who made a profession of reviewing were
believed in and greatly honored; and it is in no
wise strange that he shared the common superstition of his day, and reverenced the recognized
critic far beyond that always irritable and often
unjust gentleman's actual desert.

Now we know how very human are the literary
fault-finders of the various papers and magazines; and their opinions (if opinions they really
are) carry with them little or no weight. As has
been said, not a few of the men who write short
book notices seldom read a line in the book they
praise or condemn. Some of them do not even
open the book, but, having derived an opinion
from an inspection of the cover, they straightway sell the volume to an ever-ready book-dealer
who knows at least the commercial value of the
material he handles. Some of the so-called reviewers make even more generous use of the various press-notices and descriptive matter issued
by the publisher than we have stated; all of which
amounts to the publisher's reviewing his own
output. And this is by no means the shortcoming of country journals only; some of the
largest city papers save brain and time by using
material that the publishers are only too willing
to provide. When you read in a periodical that
Miss Lily Daffodil's new novel is "the most

brilliant and absorbing piece of fiction," you think you are reading the opinion of a competent reviewer based upon careful examination of the book, but you are really absorbing nothing but the fulsome advertisement of a publisher who has the book to sell, and who got the above advertisement in exchange for a copy of the novel sent to the periodical for review.

When I was a youth preparing for college, Walt Whitman and Swinburne made their appearance in the literary world. Both writers were denounced by the very papers that now laud them to the skies. Whitman was ridiculed, derided, laughed at, and insulted. Not one paper in a thousand could see anything good in " Leaves of Grass." Now the periodicals that laughed at him are the loudest in his praise. Have they changed their minds with regard to his work? Not at all; most of them had no mind upon the matter to change. They derided him when it was fashionable so to do, and when the fashion changed, they changed with it. Well, what did it all amount to? Nothing at all. Whitman knew, or thought he knew, the value of his work; he certainly knew how fickle is the popular mind; and, furthermore, he knew how little importance attaches to an ordinary book-review. Knowing all these things, he took the ill-treatment he received with the quiet contempt and indifference it deserved. He continued his literary output, and waited for the tide to turn. In due time it did turn, and now

the old reviewers cannot be made to remember
that once they reviled the man they praise.
He refused to die of a broken heart, of phthisis,
or of anything else, and lived out the full term
of his years. The critics went their way, and
Whitman went his, and at last it all came to the
same thing. The writer who breaks his heart
over adverse criticism is foolish indeed.

We are sometimes asked in a conspicuous advertisement to purchase a certain book simply
because it is not worth purchasing. The book
is announced as the work of a peasant, a rustic,
a workman, a man of no education, or a little
child. We read that Anne Yearsley, the Bristol
milk-maid, has appeared in print; that the David-
son sisters, both of them untrained children, have
given the world what they and their publishers
are pleased to call poems; that a little girl yet
in her early teens and short frocks has blossomed
into verse; or that a lad in the high school has
published one of his compositions. Mrs. Hemans, when a child, published a book of verses
having little beauty and no worth. I have in
my library " Poems by Felicia Dorothea
Browne " (Mrs. Hemans's maiden name), in the
preface of which an indulgent public learns that
" the following pieces are the genuine productions of a young lady between the ages of eight
and thirteen years." The " pieces," as they are
called, are trivial, commonplace, and jejune,
and could never have seen the light but for the
foolish generosity of the Right Honourable Vis-

countess Kirkwall. The authoress lived to become a distinguished poet, but she never reprinted a line of the book once so bravely exploited. I have in her autograph a letter addressed by her in mid-life to her publisher, rebuking him for seeking to reprint for mercenary ends those "pieces," regardless of her later judgment.

Green apples may interest the pomologist who gives himself to a lifelong study of fruit from seed to ripeness, but one does not care to feed upon green pippins. Some years ago a book of verses was announced as the work of a village cobbler. I will not say that such a man might not produce a reasonably attractive book. Samuel Drew, a maker of shoes, once interested the English world in his " The Immateriality and Immortality of the Soul." Robert Bloomfield, who wrote " The Farmer's Boy," and Kitto, the Biblical scholar, were both of them shoemakers. But not many of the followers of St. Crispin have come to such exalted places in the world of letters, notwithstanding all that Mr. Winks has said about " the achievements of illustrious shoemakers."

Southey was a very moderate poet, if, indeed, it be lawful to call him any kind of a poet; and yet that most generous of men, Sir Walter Scott, thought " Madoc " and " Thalaba " the work of a great genius, and all the while he feared that his own poems were wholly without value. James Ballantyne once asked Scott's little

daughter if she liked " The Lady of the Lake."
She answered with a child's simplicity that she
had not read it because " Papa says there is nothing so bad for young people as reading bad
poetry." But other poets than Scott over-
valued the good, but insufferably dull, Southey.
Think of Lamb's letter to Coleridge, in which
the delightful Elia wrote, " On the whole, I think
Southey will one day rival Milton; I already
deem him equal to Cowper, and superior to all
living poets besides." But dear old Lamb was
not himself very much of a poet. He knew
more about roast pig, of which he wrote superbly, than about " Bob " Southey, as Byron
irreverently called the English laureate.

Scott was a very modest man. The more
thought he gave to his own productions, the
poorer the display they made before his own
eyes. The verses of Joanna Baillie seemed to
him so radiantly beautiful that he threw his own
poems from him in despair. We can excuse
Lamb for his foolish praise of Southey because
Lamb was himself even less of a poet. Many
of Lamb's verses would disgrace a very youth-
ful schoolboy, and even his best poems are good
only when compared with his poorer ones. Why
is it that poets are so inadequately equipped as
critics? Think of Swinburne, who was really
something of a critic, uttering, as he did, un-
qualified nonsense when reviewing the works of
his brother poets. Think of his description of
the poems of Byron as " jolter-headed jargon ";

and listen to Voltaire mocking with contemptuous merriment the immortal work of Dante, and calling "Hamlet" the writing of one who was in large part a savage.

Julia Ward Howe is, notwithstanding the large place she filled in the public mind, a minor poet. She was, as her friend Colonel Higginson has pointed out, many-sided. She was acquainted with the most distinguished men and women of this and other lands; and she was, as well, interested in all the literary and philanthropic movements of her time. Her name was known everywhere, and her poems were translated into many languages. Still Mrs. Howe is, beyond all question, a minor poet. Her one great contribution to literature is "The Battle Hymn of the Republic," a poem as felicitous in its title as it is beautiful in its expression. By that one effort, and by that alone, she will be remembered when all who knew and loved her have passed away. She is a poet of one poem so far as immortality is concerned.

The only reason I can think of for placing James B. Kenyon among the minor poets is one not very creditable to the age in which he lives. I have known Dr. Kenyon these many years, and am well acquainted with his work. His literary output, if I may use so unpoetic a term in describing literature of so high an order, should place his name among those of our foremost writers. I am acquainted with no better sonnets than his in all our English language, leaving out of account, of course, those of Shakespeare and some of the old English authors who must be upon all occasions excepted out of courtesy to public opinion, if for no other reason. Kenyon should not be accounted a minor poet, but such he is, simply because, being a modest and retiring man, he has not sought recognition. Those who know his work are amazed at the slight attention it has received.

Where so many poems are good and more than good, it is difficult to select; but surely a dainty tribute to the memory of Edmund Spenser, printed in "Songs in all Seasons," one of Dr. Kenyon's earlier books, should not fail of appreciation.

## EDMUND SPENSER

" How have the years flown since that golden day
　　When where the Mulla rolls her dimpling flood,
　　Thou heardst the birds sing in the Irish wood,
And Raleigh with thee on the upland lay!
Again through gloomy forests old and gray,
　　O'er many a waste and trackless solitude,
　　Whithersoe'er thy Muse's knightly mood
May lead us in thy tale, we seem to stray.
O master, it was not on oaten reeds
　　Thou madest music for the world's delight,
　　　　Nor yet on Pan's shrill pipe didst thou e'er
　　　　　　flute;
To sing of courtly grace and lordly deeds,
　　Of lovely Una and the Redcross Knight,
　　　　Behold! thou hadst Apollo's silver lute."

I have pleasant remembrances of Niclas Müller, the German poet, who was born in Langenau, Germany, in the year 1809. In early life he was apprenticed to a printer in Stuttgart, and during that apprenticeship he wrote a number of patriotic and revolutionary poems which attracted the attention of the government, and led to his flight from the fatherland. He came to America after a brief stay in Switzerland, and settled in New York, where he carried on a general printing business. In his new home he brought out a number of very striking poems that at once secured him recognition in literary circles. During our Civil War he published a volume of verse which he called " Neuere Gedichte,"— a broad title and hardly distinctive, yet one that singled the poems out as being among his more recent productions. Some of the verses were exceedingly beautiful, and several were later translated into musical English. At the time of the Franco-Prussian War he published his " Frische Blätter auf die Wunden deutscher Krieger." Still later, he gave the world " Lieder und Gedichte," a little book of many charming verses.

Müller was a poet by nature. In his life as well as in his verses the spirit of the bard was everywhere seen and felt. William Cullen Bryant was so pleased with Müller's " Paradise of Tears " that he translated it into graceful English. Why the translation never appears among Bryant's poems I am unable to say; but

because it does not appear, I think I am not out
of the way in reproducing it here.

" Beside the River of Tears, with branches low,
And bitter leaves, the weeping willows grow:
The branches stream like the disheveled hair
Of women in the sadness of despair.

" On rolls the stream with a perpetual sigh;
The rocks moan wildly as it passes by;
Hyssop and wormwood border all the strand,
And not a flower adorns the dreary land.

" Then comes a child whose face is like the sun,
And dips the gloomy waters as they run,
And waters all the region, and behold,
The ground is bright with blossoms manifold.

" Where fall the tears of love the rose appears;
And where the ground is bright with friendship's
        tears,
Forget-me-nots and violets, heavenly blue,
Spring glittering with the cheerful drops like dew.

" The souls of mourners, all whose tears are dried,
Like swans come gently floating down the tide,
Walk up the golden sands by which it flows,
And in that Paradise of Tears repose.

" There every heart rejoins its kindred heart;
There, in a long embrace that none may part,
Fulfilment meets desire; and that fair shore
Beholds its dwellers happy evermore."

Müller was at the time of his death preparing
a complete edition of his poems, and it is to be

regretted that his life was not spared long enough for him to accomplish the work he had in hand. His death took place in the City of New York, in the month of August, 1875. Well do I remember him, and with tender regard, for he was my friend. Even now, after the lapse of many years, I seem at times to hear his once familiar and ever kindly voice. I have only to open " Lieder und Gedichte," with its cherished inscription, to feel again the gentle presence that added something of beauty to earlier years.

The minor poet, if a real poet, performs a service all his own for weary feet and aching heart. It is to him we turn at last with grateful acknowledgment. He may be only a flickering light, but what illumination he has he freely gives, as Amelia Josephine Burr, herself a minor poet, has beautifully said:

> " The firefly, flickering about
> In busy brightness, near and far,
> Lets not his little lamp go out
> Because he cannot be a star.
> He only seeks, the hour he lives,
> Bravely his tiny part to play,
> And all his being freely gives
> To make a summer evening gay."

Yet they do much more than " make a summer evening gay." Often they pour upon the soul a flood of light, and not infrequently they comfort where great poets overawe and even discourage. They gladden the heart and bring it cheer by an intimacy that comes of an equality with the reader. The minor poet seats himself by the fire-side of the reader's heart, where he is ever wel-come. His presence brings peace, and his songs lighten the burden while they assuage the sorrows of life. So thought Longfellow, himself a poet the whole world loved to honor.

" Read from some humbler poet,
    Whose songs gushed from his heart
As showers from the clouds of summer,
    Or tears from the eyelids start;

" Who, through long days of labor
    And nights devoid of ease,
Still heard in his soul the music
    Of wonderful melodies.

" Such songs have power to quiet
    The restless pulse of care,
And come like the benediction
    That follows after prayer."

Alfred Noyes is a new poet. He has written too much for the years of his literary pilgrimage thus far. We have from his pen some good things, more that are poor, and none yet that take commanding place and give promise of en-during. The " Wine-Press " has slaughter and horror enough for more than one poem of very much greater dimensions. Many stanzas are dull, many lines are prose in everything but measure. The epilogue to the " Wine Press," which should give a strong voice of grateful satisfaction chastened by the dark and long-continued sorrow, is a tame ending. The influence of the poem is sane and helpful, and as an appeal may be called worthy; but it falls short of that song-spirit which is essential to poetry. Mr. Noyes's best lines are, nearly all of them, up to the present time (1915), found in that more than interesting poem in which he tells us so much about the old English inn we know in song and story as the " Mermaid Tavern." In that composition we have some of the poet's best lines, full of spirit and real beauty.

There have been said of late in English and American newspapers many foolish things about a rising Indo-Anglican poet named Rabindranath Tagore. That he has written a few good lines cannot be denied; but he has thus far given the world nothing markedly virile or supremely beautiful. His work is distinguished by a dreamy mysticism always popular in the Orient. The following lines will give the reader some idea of the poet's feeling, if not of his literary style:

" Do you know how the moments perform their
    adoration?
Waving its row of lamps, the Universe sings in
    worship day and night;
There are the hidden banner and the secret canopy:
There the sound of the unseen bells is heard.
Kabir says: ' There adoration never ceases; there
    the Lord of the Universe sitteth on his throne.'
The whole world does its work and commits its er-

rors: but few are the lovers who know the Beloved.
The devout seeker is he who mingles in his heart
the double currents of love and detachment,
like the mingling of the streams of Ganges and
Jumna;
In his heart the sacred water flows day and night;
and thus the round of births and deaths is
brought to an end."

Of course there is a great difference between
a poem in the original and that same poem in
translation. The difference must be allowed for
so far as possible, and yet every author knows
that his appearance in a literature other than his
own must prove to him and his readers more or
less of a disaster.

I do not know whether Mr. Clinton Scollard
is to be named with the minor poets or should be
reserved for consideration in a paper upon wider
literature. He has produced some of the most
delicately phrased verses in our language. His
little poem, " In the Library," is a gem. The
poems that are grouped in his recently published
" Sprays of Shamrock " are, many of them, exquisite. He is a poet of great beauty, but he
has not yet taken his seat by the side of Longfellow, Whittier, and Emerson. He is now in
middle life and may in the years to come take
his place with the most distinguished of our
American authors; yet it must be remembered that
the best poetry is generally written in youth or

in early manhood. There are, however, notable exceptions to the rule.

Maurice Thompson has written well; so has George Cabot Lodge. Mr. Lodge has given us few poems, but I have not seen one that was without its own peculiar grace and dignity. Edwin Markham came to literature late in life, and wholly upon the strength of a single poem. " The Man with the Hoe " will perhaps keep his name before the world, and it may be that his poem on " Lincoln " will be remembered. It is hard to place Edmund Clarence Stedman. There are those who class him with minor poets, but there are a still larger number of readers who would call him a major poet. If he was one of the former class he was certainly one of the very best of them. He was the friend of all worthy authors in his own and other lands, and he will be remembered for many a year because of his great kindness to the men of his own profession. Richard Watson Gilder had marked ability, but public opinion is divided,— and it seems to me that it will remain divided,— upon the question of his merit as a poet. The same uncertainty prevails as to the final appraisement of James Whitcomb Riley, John Vance Cheney, and Henry van Dyke. The three men named are still (1915) with us, and much will depend upon work yet to come. Dr. S. Weir Mitchell has written stories that will endure. Their places are already fixed among the classical products of our age and generation. But I think his little book of verse, " The Comfort of the Hills and Other Poems," will add nothing to his enviable reputation. Rossiter Johnson and Stephen Henry Thayer have given the world work of which they need neither of them be ashamed. Mr. Thayer's " Songs of Sleepy Hollow " is a book of quiet and restful beauty that secures in the home a cordial welcome and in the library a place of honor. Arthur W. Colton has given us good work, but the one thing that interests us most in Mr. Colton is the large literary future that evidently lies before him. Will he live up to his possibility? That is a question no one can ever answer for another. Personally I believe we shall have more work from Mr. Colton, much of it as good as and some of it even better than that which he has thus far given to the world. Richard Edwin Day is a genuine poet of whom few have any knowledge. His modesty and humility have interfered, and will, no doubt, continue to interfere, with a public recognition of his genius and worth in the field of letters. He is a fine scholar and linguist, but his great ability is in verse and not in prose. His poem, " The Conquest of Thebes," is a noble piece of classical word-painting, and the same thing may be said of his " The Fall of Dionysus."

Should Sidney Lanier be assigned a place among the major or among the minor poets? His work is now finished, and he is with us no more save in the marvelously beautiful lines through which he still speaks to the generations of men. Where we are to place him must depend upon what we understand by major and minor poets. If we mean by the former only absolutely first-class bards,— men like Homer, Shakespeare, and Dante,— it must be evident that in this paper we are dealing with only third- and fourth-class poets. Milton comes a long distance after Shakespeare, and yet he surely outranks such modern poets as Tennyson, Poe, Longfellow, and Whittier; and these again outrank Matthew Arnold, Thomas Bailey Aldrich, Campbell, and Oliver Wendell Holmes. I am persuaded that we can never classify men of genius in that way. The simple division of all poets into major and minor will bring together men who have nothing in common, and who differ widely in poetic gifts; but it is a possible classification and one not wholly unjust. Lanier is, I think, a minor poet, but one of the very best of them. Had he lived longer and been the happy possessor of better health, it is more than likely that his later, but now forever unsung, songs would give him a clear title to an enviable place among our major poets.

Thoreau's poems are of little worth. It is fortunate for him that there are so few of them. They not only do not help the reputation his delightful prose has bestowed upon him, but they detract something from it. Fitz-Greene Halleck was a poet of the day in which he lived. He lacked creative genius, as did also N. P. Willis. Halleck's satires upon public characters of his period gave him immediate but local fame. He is not known beyond the boundaries of the United States, and there are few if any translations of his poems. They would not be understood by foreigners, and I doubt the ability of a translator to make him intelligible in other languages than his own.

Joseph Rodman Drake's longest poem is "The Culprit Fay." It is not without attractive lines, but as a whole it is scarcely saved from being dull and commonplace. The one poem that made him famous is "The American Flag." It is a spirited composition, full of patriotic enthusiasm. Drake tried medicine before he entered upon his literary career. He hung out his shingle at No. 121 Bowery, in the then little city of New York. He early became acquainted with Fitz-Greene Halleck, and between the two men there grew up the warmest friendship. Later, Drake formed a partnership with Dr. William Langstaff, and the two together opened a drug-shop at No. 34 Park Row, next to the corner of Beekman Street. Drake had his own quarters over the shop, and there, surrounded by his books, he passed some of the happiest hours of his brief life. With Halleck he contributed anonymously to the "Evening Post," then edited by William Coleman. They wrote together the "Croaker Papers," which attracted general attention, and the "Evening Post" became very popular. No one knew who the Croakers were, and for a long time the secret of their identity was carefully guarded. Later, the Papers and both Halleck's poems and those of Drake were published in separate volumes. On the twenty-ninth of May, 1819, Drake's "Ode to the American Flag" was printed in the "Post," and at once the reputation of Joseph Rodman Drake was established. He died in 1820 in his unpretentious little home over the drug-shop. Not long after the burial of Drake in the lonely and neglected cemetery at Hunt's Point, Halleck published his simple and tenderly beautiful monody upon the "Death of Drake." The first stanza of the poem is, it seems to me, an absolutely perfect piece of versification:

> "Green be the turf above thee,
> Friend of my better days;
> None knew thee but to love thee,
> Nor named thee but to praise."

Halleck's best-known poem is, of course, "Marco Bozzaris." His "Burns" and his "Red Jacket" are never without admirers. His longest poem, "Fanny," was what might be called "a hit"; its local allusions render it unintelligible to readers of the present time.

Mrs. Sigourney, whose longest and best-known poem is "Zinzendorff," was one of our early poets. She was a good woman, respected by all who knew her, but she was a writer of almost no ability. Ray Palmer is seldom counted in with the poets, but in his little book of verse are two beautiful hymns that are sung in all our American churches and that have been translated into a number of languages. The more important of the two hymns is called "Faith" and was written when Palmer was a very young man. The opening stanza runs thus:

"My faith looks up to thee,
Thou Lamb of Calvary,
    Saviour divine;
Now hear me while I pray,
Take all my guilt away,
O let me from this day
    Be wholly thine."

Eliza Scudder is another gifted spirit, and a writer of very beautiful hymns. Much of her early life was passed in the old Salem of seventy-five or more years ago, surrounded by devotional books and the quaint associations of early New England. During the best years of her life she was of the Unitarian faith, but her closing days found her in a Trinitarian communion. Sad it is to remember, but it is true, nevertheless, that her change in religious belief brought with it, for her, alienations and distressing separations. Her change in religious affiliation was brought about in a measure, it may be, through a newly formed acquaintance with Phillips Brooks. "The Morning Watch," discussing the change in her religious views and experience, attributed it to an altered intellectual conception of religious truth, and to a "deepening of her apprehension

of the Incarnation." In her life there was much
of privation and long ill-health.

Eliza Scudder inclined to a mystical view of
life, as did many of our New England writers of
a half-century or more ago. It is difficult to
distinguish between the mystical and the spiritual. Sometimes there is no difference. In the
lonely life of Miss Scudder the two elements mingled freely. Beautifully they flow together in
one of her hymns, which she has named "The
Love of God," and which may be found in many
of our best hymnals:

### THE LOVE OF GOD

" Thou Grace Divine, encircling all,
  A soundless, shoreless sea!
Wherein at last our souls must fall,
  O Love of God most free!

" When over dizzy heights we go,
  One soft hand blinds our eyes;
The other leads us safe and slow,
  O Love of God most wise!

" And though we turn us from thy face,
  And wander wide and long,
Thou hold'st us still in thine embrace,
  O Love of God most strong!

" The saddened heart, the restless soul,
  The toil-worn frame and mind,
Alike confess thy sweet control,
  O Love of God most kind!

"But not alone thy care we claim,
    Our wayward steps to win;
We know thee by a dearer name,
    O Love of God within!

"And filled and quickened by thy breath,
    Our souls are strong and free
To rise o'er sin and fear and death,
    O Love of God, to thee!"

Ella Wheeler Wilcox has written some good poems and many others scarcely worth the reading. Several of her poetical compositions have become very popular, and are sure to reappear in every new anthology. Edith Thomas is a better poet. John White Chadwick, Edward Rowland Sill, Robert Underwood Johnson, and Richard Hovey have all written well. Harriet Prescott Spofford is, though a minor poet, a very beautiful one. Many poets have produced too much, but it is Mrs. Spofford's fault that she has written too little. All her poems have a peculiar grace and dignity. John Addington Symonds has given the world more prose than verse, but his verses are always well worth remembering. William E. Henley, the English poet, will live because of one poem only, as will Julia Ward Howe, John Howard Payne, Charles Wolfe, James R. Randall, C. P. Cranch, and many other writers of verse. A single poem may immortalize its author. Miss Dickinson, who lived her quiet life in the little village of Amherst, wrote what may be called formless poems; they were rough and surprisingly individual, yet genuinely inspired. She paid no more attention to the common rules of versification than did Walt Whitman, and yet no one can be blind to the beauty of her many strange verses. These two stanzas will give some idea of her style:

> " If I shouldn't be alive
> When the robins come,
> Give the one in red cravat
> A memorial crumb.
>
> " If I couldn't thank you,
> Being just asleep,
> You will know I'm trying
> With my granite lip! "

The poet, like every other man, must work if he would succeed. Inspiration is indispensable, but there must be artistic training, and, later on, an artistic experience as well.

> " Man is no star, but a quick coal
> Of mortal fire;
> Who blows it not, nor doth control
> A faint desire,
> Lets his own ashes choke his soul."

Jones Very was a clergyman of the Unitarian denomination; a man of fine spirit, delicate yet vigorous imagination, and great culture. He was fortunate in his literary friends, among whom were Emerson and the New England literati. They did much to further his inter-

ests as an author, and it seems to me that they
in some measure exaggerated his worth as a poet.
His poems are not lacking in inspiration, though
they certainly are wanting in variety.

James Gates Percival was a Connecticut editor, a geologist, and poet. His miscellaneous
patriotic and sentimental verses are now rapidly
fading from American literature. He wrote
with ease, and most of his work has been correctly described as " monotonously unreadable."
William Ross Wallace was known to the readers
of half a century ago as " the ' New York
Ledger ' poet." Every issue of the " Ledger "
made public a new poem by Wallace. He was, of
course, something of a " machine poet," and most
of his contributions are already forgotten.
Those who give any thought in these days to the
work of Wallace regard his " Of Thine Own
Country Sing " as the best of his many productions. John Godfrey Saxe was an American
comic versifier. It would be a fatal stretch of
imagination to call him a poet, though there
were, of course, some fine lines among his many
rhymed jokes.

John Hay was a real poet though a minor
one. It will not be necessary here to dwell upon
his great services rendered to our country. This
paper has to do with his worth as a poet only.
He was never proud of his literary work, and
after he became a statesman of world-wide celeb-
rity he was absolutely ashamed of his " Pike
County Ballads," among which appear " Jim

Bludso " and " Little Breeches." With increasing years he became more conservative, and the semi-irreverent tone and Wild-West style of the two poems named displeased him. Mr. Hay in his later days felt toward the " Pike County Ballads " very much as James Russell Lowell felt toward the " Biglow Papers " which in early life he was so " indiscreet " as to publish. Mr. Hay wrote in a letter which appeared in the " Westminster Gazette ":

" I do not think much of my poems. They have had an enormous success, both in this country and in England, but I think it will be ephemeral. I got the story of ' Little Breeches ' from a sermon by Mr. Winans of Hamilton. The character of ' Jim Bludso ' was to a certain extent founded on Oliver Fairchild of Warsaw; of course it was not intended for a likeness. I have forgotten the real name of the boat on which he perished."

Thomas Buchanan Read, George Henry Boker, Thomas William Parsons, Alice Cary, Lucy Larcom, Rose Terry Cooke, Elizabeth Akers Allen, Celia Laighton Thaxter, Helen Hunt Jackson, Paul Hamilton Hayne, James Herbert Morse, and Joaquin Miller have done some good work, but we cannot concede them places with the great poets whose names will live forever. Oblivion awaits them all, as I believe most of them would be wise enough and candid enough to admit. Yet they belong in the same family with the most gifted of the world's great singers.

They have made our lives more beautiful, and we owe them a debt of gratitude which we do well to acknowledge.

Richard Henry Stoddard was of very humble origin, but he took his seat with men and women of large ability. He began life with manual labor, and he ended it with a national, if not an international, reputation. He had an original and fine imagination. He was capable of the tenderest sympathy, and yet at times he could rise to the noblest heights of heroism. His genius won recognition, and yet,— strange to say,— he did not discover it, and his closing days were saddened by a feeling that his work was not fully appreciated.

Francis Scott Key wrote our national hymn as it is called; it is really a " song " and not a hymn. But I cannot think that " The Star-spangled Banner " makes Key a poet, though I have described him as such in my list of " Poets of a Single Poem " in " The Excursions of a Book-lover." If his single patriotic song makes him a poet, it follows that " La Marseillaise " makes Rouget de Lisle a poet. Both songs are great in their way, but they both owe very much to the music, without which the words would count for little.

Mr. Thomas S. Jones, Jr., has written some fine verses; his " Rose Jar " has its own peculiar charm. The style is at once simple and rich. Phillips Brooks, the good bishop, wrote few poems, but those few are well worth reading and

preserving.    Among them are several hymns that
are now justly popular in church circles.    Brooks
could write love songs as well as sermons, as may
be seen by the reading of these tender lines
written by him in 1859:

" We sit together in our soul's high window, Dear-
        est,
    That looks upon the street of human life,
Within, our happy home; without, the world thou
        fearest;
    Within, our peace; without, man's angry strife.

" Look out! see how strange eyes look here upon us,
    How poor they think our dwelling and how
        cheap;
They dream not of our godlike joys and honors,
    The rich, ripe fields of blessing that we reap.

" Nay, close the curtain; it is wrong, my Sweetest,
    That they should see the love they do not know,—
Our love, the purest, Darling, and completest
    God ever trusted to our earth below.

" Sit here, my Love, with all the world behind us,
    Sit hand in hand, nor dare to speak a word;
'Tis wronging God to share what he consigned us
    With every outcast of the human herd.

" So sit we by the soul's sweet fireside, Fairest;
    The days go by as light winds kiss the flowers;
They seek through all earth's sweetest and earth's
        rarest
    A love so sweet, a love so rare as ours."

All these were minor poets if we drop out the song-writers, who perhaps were song-writers only, and not poets in any large sense of the word. Some of them are still with us, and may yet do much good work. As a general rule noble sentiment and fine feeling will not of themselves impart lasting qualities to prose or verse. Many a poem that has had really nothing of value has been saved to posterity by the subtile and haunting beauty of its artistic expression.

> " All passes.   Art alone
>     Enduring stays to us;
> The bust outlasts the throne,—
>     The coin, Tiberius;

> " Even the gods must go;
>     Only the lofty rhyme
> Not countless years o'erthrow,—
>     Not long array of time.

> " Paint, chisel, then, or write;
>     But, that the work surpass,
> With the hard fashion fight,—
>     With the resisting mass." [1]

An old story shows us how the man who concerns himself with trifles advances to his own destruction. Live for to-day, and the morrow will bring oblivion. The work that endures is done by the man who gives little heed to the opinions of others. He is not the slave of his contemporaries. The general opinion of the

[1] Translated by Austin Dobson from Théophile Gautier.

thoughtless world helps no man to aspire to great things, nor will it help him to rise. This is the old story:

"Anim, the son of Al Raschid, when besieged by his brother in Bagdad, refused to quit his game at chess, although his men were driven from the breach and loudly demanded his presence to reanimate them. 'Stop,' said he, 'let me not lose the glorious opportunity of a check-mate!' 'Good sense and good fortune,' said the irritated messenger, 'are inseparable companions,' and left Anim to his evil destiny. He was conducted to an immediate death by order of the Conqueror."

The Anims of this and succeeding ages linger at their games and allow opportunity to go her way. In a strong and true sonnet by John James Ingalls there is set before the reader the sacred solemnity of the one "hour of fate" that comes, and goes, and nevermore returns. Mr. Ingalls seized the hour of which he so nobly sang. He was several times elected to the United States Senate, and before his public services were ended he was accounted the ablest debater in the Senate. We venture to believe that in the years to come he will be better known as the author of the little poem on "Opportunity" than as the distinguished senator and the most renowed debater of his day. Thus runs the poem:

"Master of human destinies am I!
Fame, love, and fortune on my footsteps wait;
Cities and fields I walk; I penetrate

Deserts and seas remote; and passing by
  Hovel and mart and palace, soon or late
  I knock unbidden, once, at every gate!
If feasting, rise; if sleeping, wake before
  I turn away.  It is the hour of fate;
  And they who follow me reach every state
Mortals desire, and conquer every foe
  Save death.  But those who doubt or hesitate,
Condemned to failure, penury, and woe,
  Seek me in vain and ceaselessly implore;
  I answer not, and I return — no more."

In my student days in the City of New York I
knew a poet, at that time a young man, whose literary promise and future were wholly destroyed
by long-continued illness.  His genius was never
recognized except by a very small and select circle
of cultivated men and women.  Burr Griswold
Hosmer, of whom I write, was born at Mead-
ville, Pennsylvania, September 2, 1841.  I am
particular about the place and date of birth because his name will be found, so far as my knowledge extends, in no biographical dictionary.  He
studied five years in New Haven; visited Europe
in 1860; attended lectures at the University of
Berlin; traveled in England, Belgium, France,
Germany, Italy, and Switzerland; and returned
to the United States in the autumn of 1867,
where he gave instruction in the German language and literature.  He wrote much for papers
and magazines, and published in 1868 a little
book of poems.

He was the son of an Episcopal clergyman,

but when I knew him his father had long been
dead, and he was living with his mother in New
York City.  His health during all the time I
was acquainted with him continued feeble.  His
means were not large, but, being a diligent student
and a teacher of more than ordinary ability, he
succeeded in making for his mother and himself
a comfortable living.  He was a man of brave
heart and of scrupulous integrity.  There were
times when sickness clouded his mind, and he was
not always happy.  He was domestic in his temper, fond of children, and simple in his tastes.
Being of democratic opinions and associations,
he made many friends among the poor and obscure; yet in his conversation, which was always
markedly original and often rich in interest,
there was a fine sense of propriety.  He was
a  true  friend,  and  his  friends  loved  him
well.

His little book of one hundred and seventy
pages contains fifty-eight poems arranged in
three periods, each period corresponding to a
period in the poet's literary life.  The poem
called " Utterance " is, I think, among his best,
and I venture to reproduce it in its entirety:

> " How fine is feeling,
> And how rough is speech!
> How, through the gossamer
> Of reverie,
> The rude word bursts,
> And shatters it amain!

"Ah, when shall language rise
Above its stammering?
How long shall every foremost mind
Despise the word,
While from the need
Of intercourse,
Still wooing it?

" The God within,
Striving to speak
With human mouth,
Recoils from discord
He has made.
Perfect musician he;
But base his instrument.

" Yet patience schools
The voice at last
To sweetly hint
Its birth divine.

" O peace-restoring Art,
That givest to the formless, form,
And to the voiceless, voice;
Mouldest deformity
Into a sterner loveliness,
Even as Nature rounds
Her wayward shapes
To symmetry!

" The arts receive
The natural man;
And educate him, step by step,
Unto the master-art,—
The art of Life.

"Afar, behind expression, hides
The thing to be expressed.
Deep underneath all that we do
And all we seem
Lies what we feel;
And what we feel, we are."

Was Phyllis Wheatley, of early fame, a poet?
Why inquire? She thought herself a poet, and
there were in her day those who thought as she
thought. It is said that she was of pure African
blood. She was, as all the world knows, a colored maiden, but I do not know whether she had
or had not in her veins a drop or two of white
blood, and I do not think it likely that any one
ever will know. That a negress had appeared
who could write verses was, a century ago, a nine-
days wonder; and after she was dead the combination of African blood and American letters
conferred upon her a certain kind of immortality.
She indited verses to George Washington and
sent the great man a copy. He, being the gentleman that he was, acknowledged the compliment
and so conferred upon her such fame as a place
in our primitive history affords. The theolo-
gians say, "Once a Christian, always a Christian." The physicians treat sick ex-doctors
without compensation on the same ground,— a
physician remains a physician so long as he lives.
Thus it is, I suppose, with the poets,— once a
poet, always a poet. They called her a poet in
those primitive times. She got into literature
and there she will remain. Think of all the ob-

scure English poets whose lives are preserved for
us by Dr. Johnson! They have fixed places in
literature, and you could no more pry them out
from those places than you could pull a limpet
from a rock with your unassisted hands. Fame
is hard to win, but, once won, it adheres like one's
own skin. Dr. Johnson's poets are most of them
forgotten, but when you are so improvident as to
purchase a complete set of the good doctor's
books, you buy the story of all those uninteresting
lives.

Well, Phyllis Wheatley is preserved like a fly
in amber. Some day there will be a statue to
the colored poet if there is not one now. If
the statue is not of bronze but of marble, the
stone will be as white as the finest marble that
can be found in the Italian hills. Why not?
All who knew her knew her for a good woman.
But being good does not make one a poet. To
those who survive there comes an age of ideali-
zation. That age has come to Phyllis Wheatley.
It is said that she possessed a refined and intellectual face. We are told that there was
something about her presence and in her society
not easily described. A certain college professor
tells the world that he has not yet discovered
just the word by which she is to be distinguished.
My dear professor, is the word " genius " the
one you are seeking? Well, she had no genius;
but why higgle about a little thing like that?
When one is idealizing, why not go the whole
figure? They are now beginning to make at-

tractive pictures of the young woman, but, in truth, the people of her day did not think of her as anything more than a somewhat gifted colored woman. They were surprised to find that a colored woman could have any gifts. I have seen early pictures of Phyllis Wheatley, and they do not make her enchantingly attractive. To tell the truth, she had a pug nose and characteristic lips. But she was an early writer of verses, such as they were. She got into print. And the fame that a not over-critical age in its surprise conferred upon her adhered. Her little book has been reprinted, and the first edition brings a large price.

We have had with us in these later years an African writer who was a true poet. Paul Laurence Dunbar fills a worthy place in American letters, and he will hold the place that belongs to him, not because of time or circumstance, but because of real and enduring ability.

# VII

## THE RECENT DISCOVERY OF A POEM BY SAPPHO

The isles of Greece! the isles of Greece!
Where burning Sappho loved and sung.
— *Byron.*

The world has suffered no greater literary loss than the loss of Sappho's poems. So perfect are the smallest fragments preserved . . . that we muse in a sad rapture of astonishment to think what the complete poems must have been. . . . Of all the poets of the world, of all the illustrious artists of all literatures, Sappho is the one whose every word has a peculiar and unmistakable perfume, a seal of absolute perfection and illimitable peace.
— *J. Addington Symonds.*

# THE RECENT DISCOVERY OF A POEM BY SAPPHO

D R. GRENFELL and Mr. Hunt have distinguished themselves by digging up treasures of ancient art and letters from the dust-heaps of Oxyrhynchus in Egypt. Now (1914) they have discovered parts of a new poem by Sappho. Mr. Osborn, who is known the world over as a learned and skilled critic and classicist, was so affected by the discovery that, forgetting he was an invalid, he leaped from his bed, and demanded that a copy of the Greek lines should be shown him at once. The "find" is a very great one, but the damaged condition of the papyrus makes the heart of every lover of classical literature to ache. Conjectural readings are, of course, necessary, and those of Mr. Edmonds restore the poem fairly well. Here is the text (all we have of it), Mr. Edmonds's readings being bracketed and the poem being given just as it appeared in the "Classical Review": —

Ο]ἰ μὲν ἰππήων στρότον οἰ δὲ πέσδων
οἰ δὲ νάων φαῖσ’ ἐπὶ γᾶν μέλαιναν
ἔ] μμεναι κάλλιστον· ἔγω δὲ κῆν’ ὅτ-
τω τις ἔραται.
πά]γχυ δ’ εὔμαρες σύνετον πόησαι
πά]ντι τ[οῦ]τ’· ἀ γὰρ πόλυ περσκό-
πεισα
κα[λλος ἀνθρώπων Ἐλένα τὸν ἄνδρα
κρίννεν ἄρ]ιστον
ὃς τὸ πᾶν] σέβας Τροία[ς ὄ]λεσσ[ε,

175

κωὐδὲ πα]ῖδος οὐδὲ [φίλ]ων το[κ]ήων
μᾶλλον] ἐμνάσθη, ἀ[λλὰ] παρᾶγαγ'
  αὖταν
πῆλε φίλει[σαν
Ὦρος· εὔκ]αμπτον γὰρ [ἀεὶ τὸ θῆλυ
αἴ κέ]τις κούφως τ[ὸ πάρον ν]οήσῃ·
οὐ]δὲ νῦν, Ἀνακτορί[α, τ]ὺ μέμνα
δὴ] παρεοίσας,
τᾶ]ς κε βολλοίμαν ἔρατόν τε βᾶμα
κ]ἀμάρυγμα λάμπρον ἴδην προσώπω
ἢ τὰ Λύδων ἅρματα κἀν ὅπλοισι
πεσδομ]άχεντας·
εὖ μὲν ἴδ]μεν οὐ δύνατον γένεσθαι
λῶστ' ἐ]ν ἀνθρώποις· πεδέχην δ'
ἄρασθαι
[τῶν πέδειχόν ἐστι βροτοισι λῶον]
[ἢ λελάθεσθαι.]

What an evening with Sappho " the beloved "!
All the long night her lines were ringing in my
ears, and here, after the enthusiasm born of so
great a discovery, is my translation. That it is
true to the original (excluding the conjectural
readings) I know beyond peradventure. I wish
I could be as sure that the deeper spirit of the
Lesbian singer had been caught and held fast by
the rendering.

The fairest thing in all the world some say
  That mighty horsemen are,— a noble host;
And others judge it is a force of foot;
  Still more of arméd ships would make their boast.

But, as for me, I hold the one beloved,
  My soul's desire, is fairest of them all.
To make this plain no task it is, I think:
  Helen her heart obeyed at Love's strong call.

The man who ruined Troy she swiftly chose,—
Nor child, nor parent gave her such delight:
One burning love all other loves consumed,
So fierce the flame, so quenchless, and so bright.

Pliant is woman when her nearer loves
Surrendered are, and then forgotten quite.
Even so, my Anactoria, dear,
When with you dwells your heart's supreme de-
light,

When her sweet voice hath tender power to charm,
Her lightest footfall and her beaming face,—
These I'd rather have than chariots bright,
And arméd troops the Lydian land doth grace.

I know men have not in this world the best,
Yet pray to share what once was shared, for so
'Tis better far than to forget and lose
The flower of love that blooms for us below.

Beyond doubt two stanzas at the very least
are wanting to the papyrus. The last two lines
in the Greek as given by Mr. Edmonds are conjectural, and are bracketed as such. Mr. Osborn says:

"It must have been heartrending to the search-
ers in the Egyptian sands to read, on the last of
fifty-six fragments of papyrus from which barely
a dozen whole stanzas can be restored, the subscription: 'The First Book of the Lyrics of Sappho,
1,332 lines.' Yet if all those lines, golden honey
and blood-red wine commingled and so strangely

strained clear, had been recovered, I suppose the man in the club window would still have preferred the Budget as a theme of conversation, for all that he thinks he has a classical education.

" Fragments of a second roll, containing the ' Second Book of the Lyrics,' have also been found; one of them sings of the return home of Hector with his bride Andromache. Portions of poems by Alcæus have also been recovered, but such tidings do not stir the heart,— for we know as much as we want to know about that fluent poet of fluctuating moods, who is but a pallid and superficial creature in comparison with the mother-in-art, and more than sister of Gongyla and Doricha (the names of these pupils occur provokingly on fragments of unknown context). It is but little, after all, when there might have been so much. Nevertheless, let us be grateful for a boon beyond expectation, and hope that further search may yet restore to us all the Lesbian's lost lyrics. And to that end let some millionaire give a tithe of his millions to equip the quest fully — for if his miserable money were to give us back the heart of Sappho out of the dust of death, he would have earned his immortality, the gates of heaven's glory would not be closed on his silly little soul."

Of Sappho we know so little that we may almost be said to know nothing. She was born on the island of Lesbos, and later removed to Sicily, where she seems to have composed many of her finest poems. We are not absolutely sure about the date of her birth, nor yet about that of her death. From one of her verses we infer that she

was living in the year 568 B. C., and if our in-
ference is correct, she had written some of her
immortal verses before Gautama, the founder
of Buddhism, had been cradled in the loving
arms of his royal mother. It is a long, long
time ago that our Lesbian poet sang in the
world's ear those sweet songs that are with us
still, and that never in all the future of our race
can be forgotten. It was during her lifetime
that the two great prophets, Jeremiah and Daniel, lived. Solon was then at Athens, and Tar-
quinius Priscus reigned over Rome in the dawning history of that great city. Though some
of her work remains, it is in fragmentary form,
and we are not sure we have to-day a single piece
in its entirety. Still, what remains is more precious to the world than twenty-five hundred years
ago it was to the men and women who knew the
author herself, and who even then recognized her
genius as of the first order.

Of Sappho's parents we know even less than
we know of the poet herself. Herodotus gives
her father's name as Scamandronymus. It may
be he had authentic information, for he lived
within a century and a half of the poet's death.
Suidas, the compiler of a famous Greek lexicon
in the eleventh century, records seven other
names that her father is supposed to have borne.
He also tells us she had two brothers who were
known to the men of their generation as Cha-
raxus and Larichus. Professor Charles Anthon
says, in his " Greek Literature ":

" There can be only one opinion as to Sappho's poetic genius. It is almost superfluous to refer to the numerous passages in which the ancient writers have expressed their unbounded admiration of her productions. In true poetic genius she appears to have been fully equal to Alcæus, and far superior to him in grace and sweetness. Of all Greek lyric poets she is the one who, in her own peculiar branch of inspiration, was held to have attained most nearly to perfection."

In her own age she was called the " tenth muse," and there is a tradition that Solon, upon hearing one of her poems recited, was so deeply affected that he wished to memorize it. Strabo speaks of her in even more extravagant terms than were used by either Catullus or Horace, both of whom praised and imitated her verse. She of course wrote many poems of which we have no knowledge. A considerable number of her verses are described as erotic, but the word " amatory " describes them better. Few, if any, are correctly called unchaste. Ovid's heroic epistle, " Sappho to Phaon," translated by Alexander Pope, comes closer to the erotic than most of Sappho's verses. The story of her extravagant love for Phaon, and that of her leap from the Leucadian rock because he disdained her, have but slight historical foundation. Yet the rock is pointed out, partly because of a venerable tradition, and partly because Strabo, in his Geography, says:

"There is a white rock which stretches out from Leucas to the sea and towards Cephallenia, that takes its name from its whiteness. The rock of Leucas has upon it a temple of Apollo, and the leap from it was believed to stop love. From this it is said that Sappho, in pursuit of the haughty Phaon, urged on by maddening desire, threw herself."

To the lonely rock on one of the Ionian islands journey every year pilgrims of sentiment, even as to the tomb of Abélard and Héloïse in Père-la-Chaise journey from year to year those whose hearts are moved by a like feeling.

But did Sappho really come to her death by that fatal leap? Those who know the most there is to be known about the Lesbian poetess believe that she died a natural death. But in these days nearly every fact is questioned. We no longer hold to the tale of Pocahontas and Captain Smith. Washington and the cherry tree are laughed at. Bacon has absconded with the plays of Shakespeare. Now Sappho and her rock are relegated to the realm of fiction. In a few years, no doubt, our children will read in their school-books that Napoleon, Lincoln, and Grant never lived. This is a wise age, and whoever would keep abreast of it must cast aside the useless burdens of history and content himself with believing nothing.

By a large consensus of opinion Sappho's lines, " To the Beloved Fair," sometimes rendered, " To the Beloved Woman," are among the

best of the works of her rare genius that remain
to us.   Plutarch, Strabo, Athenæus, and Longi-
nus all speak of them.   Critics see their influence
in Horace's ode " To Lydia," and in the fourth
book of Virgil's " Æneid."   How beautiful this
rendition from Sappho by Ambrose Phillips:

> " Blest as the immortal gods is he,
> The youth who fondly sits by thee,
> And hears and sees thee all the while
> Softly speak and sweetly smile.

> " 'Twas this deprived my soul of rest,
> And raised such tumults in my breast;
> For while I gazed, in transport tost,
> My breath was gone, my voice was lost.

> " My bosom glowed; the subtle flame
> Ran quick through all my vital frame;
> O'er my dim eyes a darkness hung,
> My ears with hollow murmurs rung.

> " In dewy damps my limbs were chilled;
> My blood with gentle horrors thrilled;
> My feeble pulse forgot to play;
> I fainted, sank, and died away."

Romance not infrequently dies when the beautiful story is traced to its beginning.   Thus the
lovely Laura of whom Petrarch sang was the
wholesome and virtuous wife of a self-respecting
but uninteresting man.   Dante's Beatrice became
a plain, prosaic wife, but her love was not for
the man who immortalized her.   The admirers of

Sappho (and who that knows her verse is not to be counted among her admirers?) are sometimes greatly taken aback when they learn from Suidas that their poet was a married woman, whose husband, Cercolas, was a man of great wealth but not of much learning. He was a man of affairs, possibly a money-king or a pork-packer. There was in those early days no Chicago for him to do business in, and no American market for him to manipulate; but it may be he sold his wife's poems to a literary syndicate or managed a publicity company in her interest. So far as we know, Cercolas (if he existed) lived happily with his wife, and she bore him a daughter who is referred to by Ovid, who calls her Cleis.

It may be that Sappho was an honored mother in a happy family, was a good neighbor, went to the sewing-circle that met in the Temple of Apollo, or somewhere else, to make socks and mittens for the Lesbian soldiers, and was somewhat ashamed of some of her poems, which, however, she preserved because the priest of this or that tutelary deity told her they were good. It may be she was fond of dress, liked small talk, and found great satisfaction in bangles and jewels; in other words, it may be that she was just simply a woman, *plus* the poet, and nothing more.

Here, again, comes in the war of words and battle of books. Who knows that she had a husband? Suidas says so: but who knows that Suidas tells the truth? Ovid refers to a daughter, but then, in those days one could have any number of daughters without being encumbered by a husband. Now, in literary, artistic, and dramatic circles, a woman may have any number of husbands without being burdened by either son or daughter. Who knows that Sappho was any such woman as we have just pictured? I venture to say she was a very different kind of woman. The comic poets gave her a husband, and they gave her husband his name. They tricked her out in all the small weaknesses of the everyday woman, added domesticity and much else, and then invited us to take a look at our heroine. No doubt Sappho became enamored of some one,— if not of Phaon, then of another; but it does not follow that love must have led in her case to suicide. Her verses are not in any way morbid. They do not look in the direction of suicide. She had strong passions, but they were united to a vigorous mind. She had nothing of the sickly spirit that characterized Cleopatra.

Several persons have been named as her husband, but, so far as we know, Cercolas has the best claim. With him she must have lived for a considerable time in the city of Mytilene,— a beautiful place of many gardens, surrounded by the blue waters of the Ægean Sea. She may have fallen in love with other men, and she may have ventured much for their society, but the story of Sappho's leap does not seem to rest upon a very solid foundation. The cliff from which she is

said to have leaped was used in early times, and
even later, as the place for executing criminals.
They were thrown from its lofty height into the
sea that waited for them below. It is said that
birds were fastened to the limbs of those who
were to be thrown over, so that the fall might be
broken, and little boats were sent out to pick up
the criminal floating in the sea, who, if he survived, was pardoned. Perhaps the throwing of
prisoners from the rock had something to do with
the story of Sappho's leap. Many students of
Greek letters think the entire tale a fable derived
from the myth of the love of Aphrodite and
Adonis.

It is generally believed that our poetess was
an exceedingly beautiful woman. Plato, in his
" Phaedrus," calls her so, but his reason is in
no way connected with any knowledge of her face
or figure. He thinks her a handsome woman
because of the loveliness of her verse. Damocha-
ris and many other ancient authors describe her
as a woman of captivating presence, but I much
doubt whether we should find her beautiful were
she living now. Most of us have formed what
impression we have of her from the picture by
Alma-Tadema. He gives us a face full of animal passion, almost brutally sensuous. In it
there are no traces of genius, not a spark of that
fire divine which made her perfect poems possible.

I do not think we can at this late day form
a correct and sufficient opinion of Sappho as a
woman. All kinds of judgments have been

rendered with regard to her. Six comedies are
known to have been written having her name for
the title. Most of them have been lost; of one
by Antiphanes only three words remain to us.
Countless modern plays and poems have dealt
with the supposed story of her life. Gounod
has given her name to an opera. The Queen
of Roumania ("Carmen Sylva") has idealized
the life of Sappho. We have only a few fragments of her work left, but we have enough books
about her to fill a library of considerable size.
It may be that the world will at some time in the
future discover other fragments, and even, it may
be, some entire poems from the genius of Sappho.
Her person and her life are of less concern to
us. We care not so much about

> "The small dark body's Lesbian loveliness
> That held the fire eternal";

but for "the fire eternal" we do care, and for
what its scented flames have given us of worth
and beauty.

Nearly all of Sappho's verses are of love,
though the passion is expressed in many different metrical forms. She is the author of a number of fragments of epigrams, odes, elegies, and
epithalamiums. Her "Hymn to Venus" is beyond question one of her best compositions.
Some of her odes are of exquisite beauty, and some
of the finest of these are addressed to women who
may have been her lovers; for unnatural vices
were not frowned upon in her day as they are in

ours. Suidas has preserved the names of three of
the women with whom the poetess was intimate.
The story of her amours with Anacreon is generally discredited. It cannot be true, for Anacreon was not born in time for any such disrepu-
table relationship with the Lesbian singer. A
comic poet has introduced into one of his plays
the names of three men who appear as lovers of
Sappho. Of course the theory of a second
Sappho may be used to relieve our poetess of much
of the obloquy that has come to attach itself to her
name; but unfortunately for her there is but
little foundation for the theory. There may
have been many women bearing the name of
Sappho in Mytilene, but there is no reason for
thinking that the poetess knew any of them, or
that there were among them any gifted with a
genius for song. No, there never was a second
Sappho, and it is to be feared there never will be.
The exquisite beauty that distinguishes her verse
must make our sweet singer of those far-away
years absolutely unique. Not in Mytilene or
elsewhere was there ever one woman who shared
her genius or who could have written any of the
songs of flawless music that the best scholarship
attributes to her. In such high esteem was she
held because of her work that statues of her were
erected in the most honorable and conspicuous
places. There was one in the Citadel at Athens.
Pliny tells us of a painter named Leo who drew
her portrait. Aristotle says that the Mytilen-
ians honored her, but he does not tell us in

what way.  She seems to have been an exception to a general rule, for she was honored in her lifetime, and did not have to wait for *post-mortem* recognition.

# VIII

# DEATH FROM UNUSUAL CAUSES

Μὴ καταφρόνει θανάτου, ἀλλὰ εὐαρέστει αὐτῷ, ὡς ἐκ
τούτου ἑνὸς ὄντος, ὧν ἡ φύσις ἐθέλει· οἷον γάρ εστι τὸ
νεάσαι καὶ τὸ γηράσαι, καὶ τὸ αὐξῆσαι, καὶ τὸ ἀκμάσαι,
καὶ ὀδόντας, καὶ γένειον, καὶ πολιὰς ἐνεγκεῖν, καὶ σπεῖραι,
καὶ κυοφορῆσαι, καὶ ἀποκυῆσαι, καὶ τὰ ἄλλα τὰ φυσικὰ
ἐνεργήματα ὅσα αἱ τοῦ σοῦ βίου ὧραι φέρουσιν, τοιοῦτο καὶ
τὸ διαλυθῆναι.
— *Marcus Aurelius.*

Imperial Cæsar, dead, and turned to clay,
Might stop a hole to keep the wind away.
— *Shakespeare.*

# DEATH FROM UNUSUAL CAUSES

FEW men die a natural death,— that is to say, a death occasioned by old age alone. A considerable number reach old age, and, of course, die in old age; but their death is rarely due to age itself. Some disease, accident, or deed of violence is in almost every case responsible for man's taking off. Naegeli, the German botanist, tells us that natural death does not occur in the vegetable kingdom. Trees more than a thousand years old come to their end, not by age, but through some catastrophe. Seldom does a tree die from gradual decay of its vitality. The famous dragon tree of the villa Oratava at Teneriffe was estimated to have had an age of between two and three thousand years. Its trunk was hollow, and yet it continued to live in good condition until at last it was overthrown by a storm. No doubt the storm would have left it standing had it been still young, but it was not age that killed the tree. The baobab is reputed to live from five to six thousand years, but its death is usually due to some catastrophe. Professor Loeb tells us that " valid evidence of the existence of natural death is not obtainable " in either man or plant. Still we know that the unfertilized eggs of the sea-hedgehog die a few hours after they have been discharged, and that surely looks something like natural death. Metchnikoff says:

191

"If natural death does exist, it must have appeared on the face of the earth long after the appearance of life. Weismann has suggested that death arose as an adaptation for the advantage of the species,— that is to say, in relation to the surrounding conditions of existence,— and not as an absolute necessity inherent in the nature of the living substance. He thought that, as worn organisms are no longer suited for reproduction or for the struggle for life, natural death is due to natural selection, it being necessary to maintain the species in a vigorous state by weeding out the debased individuals.

"But the introduction of death for that purpose was superfluous, since the debility caused by old age in itself would eliminate the aged in the course of the struggle for existence. Violent death must have appeared almost as soon as living things came into being."

The same writer, in a paper called "Studies in Natural Death," contends that there is an analogy between death and sleep, both being, in his opinion, due to the accumulation of poisons in the blood. If, then, natural death is the result of toxic accumulation in the system, it is an open question whether it is really so very natural after all. He says, "It may be supposed that as in sleep an instinctive need of rest is manifested, in natural death is also manifested man's instinctive aspiration toward death." He believes that "the aged often long for death instinctively, as tired people long for sleep," and concludes that there may be some instances of natural death, but that they are very rare.

Most of us come to the end before we are very old. The man who dies of heart failure or of any other morbid condition of the body dies an unnatural death, for no death is natural but that which comes of old age. All sudden deaths must, in the very nature of the case, be unnatural, for the disintegrations of age are always slow.

Sir Charles Blagden, the distinguished English physician and chemist, died so quietly that not a drop of coffee in the cup which he held in his hand was spilled. At the time of his death he was conversing with some friends, and the friends continued to converse among themselves for several minutes after his death without the faintest suspicion of what had taken place. A clergyman in the far West died seated in the pulpit while the people were singing a hymn which he had announced. After the hymn came the offering, which consumed some time, and so it came to pass that no one knew the pastor was dead until he had been so for something like fifteen minutes.

In a paper on "Ethan Brand," the hero of one of Hawthorne's short stories, which the reader may find in my "The Excursions of a Book-Lover," mention is made of the burial of an immense ingot of steel which contained the bodies of two workmen who were engulfed therein. The two men were caught in a stream of molten steel which, proceeding from a leaky furnace, fell into a pit in which they were at the time working. In one second not a vestige of the two men remained, and scarcely a puff arose to indicate their complete incineration. Another strange and even more distressing death, because not so quickly accomplished, was that of Henry Bailey, the son of a planter in Mississippi, who was killed by being packed in a bale of cotton at the ginnery of a man named John Glaze, near the village of Lemons. Young Bailey came to the gin with several wagon-loads of cotton sent by his father. In some unexplained manner he fell into the press without being noticed. The tragedy was discovered when a shoe heel was seen to be protruding as the bale was removed from the press. The lad was crushed beyond recognition, but his clothing made the identification complete.

We are reminded in this connection of a certain human brick which some time ago furnished interesting material for newspaper paragraphists. The story is not one of any unusual or strange kind of death, but rather of an extraordinary disposition of a dead body. The brick, which now reposes in a cemetery at West Roxbury, Massachusetts, is composed of five parts of cement and one of ashes, the ashes being the mortal remains of a certain Herman Unger, who took his own life at a Boston hotel. Upon the brick are impressed the name of Mr. Unger, the date of his death, and the words, " Leave me in peace." It appears that Unger believed that the human body after death would be revived in the form of a flowering growth of some kind. This belief, which would seem to most of us a very pleasing one, was repulsive to him, and he set about discovering some way of thwarting nature. He had made up his mind that nothing should change him into a flower if he could by any possibility escape such contingency. To accomplish that end, he left a will directing that his body be cremated and that the ashes be mixed with sufficient cement to form solid rock. His request was complied with in every way, and the brick was forthwith made as directed. The inscription, which was of his own composing, was impressed upon the brick just before it became fixed and solid.

To return to the earlier times of which we have already had something to say, it may interest the reader to recall the serio-comic death of Terpander, the harper, who, while singing in Sparta, opened his mouth very wide and thus tempted a thoughtless and waggish person, who had no pleasure in music though he stood by and listened, to throw a fig directly between the harper's teeth. The fig strangled the musician. In very much the same way Drusus Pompeius, the son of Claudius Cæsar, came to his death. He tossed a pear on high, to receive it again into his mouth. It so happened that the pear fell in such a way as to descend into his throat, and he choked to death before help could reach him. There is a curious story in Wanley's " Wonders of the Little World," about a certain priest who

came to his death in much the same way that
Terpander and the son of Claudius Cæsar came
to theirs. The priest, skilled in swimming and
in groping for fish, had, in a deep place under
the banks, caught a perch. The better to hold
the fish, he put it into his mouth and so started
to swim back to his companions. But the perch,
struggling to be free, slipped down the priest's
throat far enough to choke him to death. Pope
Adrian was strangled while drinking spring-
water, by an insect that fell into the glass. It is
almost unbelievable that so slight a thing as an
insect or a fly in a glass of water could choke a
strong man, and yet that kind of an accident
has happened more than once. The physicians
have, in their literature, the reported case of a
youth who grew so fast that he died. The boy
could not assimilate enough food to keep him
alive, and though he ate three generous meals
every day, he nevertheless starved to death.

Death is never a suitable theme for jest and
merriment. The natural feeling of man in the
presence of death is one of solemnity. In many
European countries, and in some parts of South
America, men lift the hat when a funeral pro-
cession passes. We instinctively drop the voice
to a whisper when we enter the house of mourn-
ing. Noise and loud conversation are regarded
as out of place and incongruous anywhere and
at any time in connection with death. Of course
it is possible that our peculiar bearing, attitude,
and tone of voice, as well as the feelings that

accompany such outward expression, are wholly
artificial; for in nature nothing is found that
suggests any of them. Wind and wave, light and
shade, and all forces of the world are the same,
whether men laugh or grieve. Nature reflects
nothing of our inner mood. The noonday sun
warms alike the infant in its cradle and the murderer bent on crime.

Huxley said with great truth, " Cosmic evolution may teach us how the good and the evil
tendencies of man may have come about; but in
itself it is incompetent to furnish any better
reason why what we call good is preferable to
what we call evil than we had before." Vice
and virtue, pain and pleasure, and all moral distinctions go for nothing with the surrounding
universe. The ethical world is an artificial one,
built up within this unconcerned and unfeeling
cosmos. Man lives in two worlds: the ethical
is his, and he has it to himself, for he alone
draws moral distinctions; but the rude, unmoral,
natural world goes its way with little regard for
man's morals, thoughts, or feelings. Sometimes
it even appears as though nature made, not only
sport, but actual derision, of sorrows and distresses. Men are even called to surrender life
sometimes in ways provocative of anything but
seriousness.

Æschylus, one of the three great tragic writers of Greece, was a man who had not only immortalized his name by great dramatic writings,
but had also distinguished himself at Marathon,

Platæa, and Salamis. Yet the method of his taking off was such as to provoke only laughter. Every drop of dignity was taken out of it. His worst enemy could have arranged for him no mortuary performance more ridiculous than the one gotten up for him by the great irresponsible world of nature and circumstance. Æschylus was walking in a field, doubtless cogitating some dramatic problem, when an eagle, mistaking the dramatist's bald head for a stone, let fall upon it a tortoise, hoping thus to break the creature's shell. The eagle lost a good fat tortoise, and the tortoise escaped injury, but the dramatist's skull was split open, and so he came to his distressing but undignified death.

Think of the unconscious wit of Nature in the choking of Anacreon with a grape-stone. He was eighty-five years old and it was time for him to die in one way or another; but who would have thought of choking the one great poet celebrated as the poet of wine and love with a grape-stone? We rarely associate death with laughter, and yet the fantastic world of circumstance has shaken death and laughter together many times. Chalchas, the soothsayer, outlived the day predicted for his death, which struck him as so comical that he burst into a fit of immoderate laughter, from which he died. In the same way expired Marquette. He was convulsed with fatal merriment on seeing a monkey trying to pull on a pair of boots. So also died Philomenes, who was seized with an equally disastrous merriment when he came suddenly upon an ass that was devouring with greed the choice figs that had been prepared for his own dessert. Zeuxis, the painter, who in early days perfected the management of light and shade, and who, having become rich, gave away his pictures because he thought them so valuable that no price was sufficient for their purchase, died of laughter. He painted, it is recorded, a bunch of grapes that were so natural that a bird endeavored to eat them. When he saw the little creature try to dine upon painted fruit he fell to laughing, and his laughter was so immoderate that he straightway died.

What happened to Agathocles, the tyrant of Syracuse, seems well suited to the ill desert of the man. He came from humble life, for he was the son of a potter, and carried to the end of his days the vulgar spirit and manners of his youth. He became a soldier, and after a time rose to the rank and power of a general. At last he became master of the entire island of Sicily. He was a man of good talents, but sanguinary, faithless, and cruel. All the men of his time and country hated him, and at last, as might have been expected, they brought him to a violent death. The story is that his son gave him a poisoned toothpick, which rendered his mouth gangrenous so that he could not speak. While in that miserable and helpless condition he was declared to be dead, and, having been stretched upon a funeral pile, he was burned alive.

Heraclius, the Ephesian, suffered from dropsy. The physicians of his day were not unlike the medical men of our own time: they were perfectly sure of both their diagnosis and their line of treatment. They advised Heraclius to anoint himself with cow-dung, and to sit, while so anointed, in the light and warmth of the sun. His servants left him alone, for of course he was not an agreeable companion while plastered over with filth. Seeing him unattended, some dogs, supposing him to be a wild beast, fell upon him and his death was the result. The mistake of the dogs does not seem so strange, for even in these later days men are frequently shot in the Adirondack Mountains by guides and others who mistake them for deer.

One would hardly think death by a stroke of lightning a desirable kind of death, and yet there have been those who desired to die by an electric current. The American patriot, James Otis, whose fame is inseparably associated with our war for Independence, wished that he might at last perish by the sudden discharge of a thunderbolt, and it is recorded that his wish was granted. He was standing in the open doorway of his house in Andover during a heavy shower, watching the fall of the rain, when a blinding flash from the heavens stretched him lifeless upon the door-sill. The Emperors Anastasius and

Carus died by lightning, as did also Strabo, the father of Pompey the Great.

Death by an electric shock is commonly thought to be painless, and for that reason some governments make use of it in the execution of criminals. Doubtless electrocution is a more merciful kind of punishment than were many of the penal inflictions of earlier days; but it is by no means certain that the electric current occasions no pain. The current must bring with it a terrific concussion, notwithstanding all that has been said about its velocity being so great that the brain is paralyzed before the nerves can communicate any sense of shock. A number of persons who have recovered from shocks of high voltage have testified to the great distress endured. Nicola Tesla, one of the most distinguished of electricians, said:

" Unless three things combine in the taking of life by electricity, the pain of such a death must be something frightful. The three things are a perfect apparatus, a current of sufficient power, and an expert to apply the current. That many criminals who have been ' electrocuted ' might have been resuscitated is generally admitted. Any person who may be resuscitated is, of course, not dead. You cannot revive a dead man. We will suppose the failure was due to an insufficient electric discharge; but it might have been due to a shortcoming in either or both of the other factors. There can be no guarantee that the apparatus is always in an absolutely perfect condition; and how can we be sure that the expert is in every way an expert? And even if a man be an expert, he is still human and liable to make a mistake or blunder of one kind or another. Think for a moment what such a mistake must mean to the criminal who is supposed to be killed by the electric discharge! The fact that the person subjected to the discharge gives no sign of life has little or nothing to do with the matter. In many cases he could be revived; in other words, he was never dead."

Still further, the French scientist, d'Arsonval, has published it as his opinion that a considerable number of electrocuted persons could be restored to life with little effort; and he tells us that in his opinion death by electricity is one of the most distressing kinds of death of which we have knowledge.

An electrician connected with the Hudson River Water Power Company, at Saratoga, New York, received by accident, in the month of February, 1906, the tremendous charge of 30,000 volts, and though he was severely injured, the charge did not kill him. In the case of a murderer executed in an Ohio penitentiary, the electric current had to be passed through the criminal four times; and in the case of another murderer in the same penitentiary, five applications were required. In the latter case eighteen minutes elapsed between the time when the prisoner was placed in the chair and the moment when he was pronounced dead.

It is seldom absolutely certain that the crim-

inal is killed by the electric current. In too
many cases it has been quite evident that resusci-
tation could have been effected without much
difficulty. Beyond question it is in a large number of cases the surgeon's knife that deprives the
prisoner of his life. But for the so-called " autopsy," which is frequently an inexcusable vivisection, the failure of the electric current to make
death sure would be more apparent. I know
of no state that has thus far dared to adopt
electrocution without adding to it the more
deadly " autopsy." It is not surprising that
physicians and surgeons who dissect living animals in their laboratories without any feeling of
kindness or regret, find no moral difficulty in
conducting a so-called " autopsy " very soon
after an electrocution, with full knowledge of all
the facts in the case; but it is surprising that a
civilized state can render an atrocity of the kind
possible.

Arago years ago divided lightning into four
kinds, each distinguished by its own peculiar
form. Most of the fatal strokes come of what
he described as " zigzag lightning," a kind that
appears in sharp and jagged lines of intense
brightness, traversing the heavens with extreme
velocity. The more common name for this kind
of an electric discharge is " forked lightning."
Arago called the second variety " sheet lightning," because of the diffuseness of its glow. The
peril from this form of the electric fluid is not
so great as is that which comes of the " zigzag "

kind. The third sort of lightning described by Arago was named by that philosopher "ball lightning." He was unable to explain its nature. His fourth kind he called "heat lightning," — a very misleading term. Many people think that because this sort of discharge is usually seen at the end of a very hot day, it must in the nature of the case be in some way caused by the heat itself. The fact that it occurs without the immediate presence of a storm, and without thunder, gives color to the popular belief. The illumination described as "heat lightning" is nothing but the reflection of electric discharges in a distant storm.

That the electric current does not so surely occasion death as the students of criminology who advocate the electrocution of murderers profess to believe, is made clear by the most cursory glance at statistics. These show that lightning does not always kill those whom it strikes. Lightning once struck a church containing three hundred people; it slightly injured a hundred, and made thirty ill, but it killed only six. According to a recent authority a bolt of lightning that struck ninety-two persons in Schleswig-Holstein killed ten of them. It paralyzed twenty, stupefied fifty-five, and slightly injured seven persons. In 1905 lightning struck a tent containing two hundred and fifty people; only two were killed, the rest soon recovered. From 1901 to 1910 lightning caused one hundred and twenty-four deaths in England and Wales, a

yearly rate of one in every 3,000,000 inhabitants. Of those who were killed, one hundred
and eight were men and sixteen were women. In
the United States the annual death-rate from
lightning is comparatively high, about ten in
every million. The difference is probably caused
by the fact that thunderstorms are more frequent
here than in England, and that more persons
are engaged in outdoor work.

It has long been an open question how Rousseau came by his death. Dr. Raspail a few years
ago filled the papers and magazines of this and
other countries with such support as he could
give to the theory that Rousseau was murdered.
He examined with great care the death-mask of
Rousseau made by Houdon, and from the study
of it he came to the conclusion that the philosopher's death was occasioned by violence. He
discovered, or thought he discovered, three distinct wounds upon the cast of the skull. One of
these he found at the corner of the right eye; the
second, which was deeper, appeared on the left
cheek not far from the nostril; while the third
was on the forehead, and must have crushed the
skull. Of course any or all of the wounds described, if they were real and not the result of
a lively imagination, might have been occasioned
by an attempt at suicide. Certain it is that had
Rousseau desired to take his own life, no moral
restraint of any kind would have prevented him
from doing so. He said in his " *Nouvelle Héloïse*," " The more I reflect upon it [suicide] the

more I find that the question reduces itself to this fundamental proposition: To seek one's own good, and avoid one's own harm in that which hurts not another."

I do not believe that Rousseau took his own life; I think he was too great a coward even to contemplate the deed. If ever there was a mean and contemptible soul encased in a human body, that soul belonged to the brilliant and vile-minded author of " The Social Contract," " The New Eloisa," and " Confessions." Of course Thérèse Levasseur, his mistress, and later his wife, might have put an end to his existence. She had ample opportunity, and it seems to the writer of this paper that any woman whose life had been in any wise connected with his might feel herself justified in ridding the world of his presence. Had, however, the ridding process taken place at too early a period in his life, we should have been deprived of " Confessions," which work, it must be conceded, is a human document not without value. We are not out of the way in calling it a " human " document, for it was practically the man himself. There may be some measure of exaggeration in the book, for its author was vain of his evil ways, but nevertheless he wanted to be thought as bad as he was, and he was very much as his " Confessions " represents him to have been. That the book is well worth reading no one who has any acquaintance with it will deny. No doubt " coarse feeding makes coarse flesh," and " evil communications

corrupt good manners "; yet one may reap a har-
vest of good from pathology.   Both health and
disease have their word of wisdom, and we are
not surprised to learn that both Emerson and
George Eliot found Rousseau's " Confessions "
the most interesting book they had ever read.
Those who think they have a complete translation in their hands when they read the book in
English are mistaken.   There are parts of the
work that are generally left undisturbed in the
original French.   That the " confessions " are
real confessions and not something gotten up for
the occasion one will see at a glance when once
he has made himself acquainted with the author.
It is, in truth, one of the few real books of the
world.

The woman who is charged with having killed
Rousseau was with him at Ermenonville when he
died, and it is known that he suspected her of
intimacy with one of the grooms of M. de Gi-
rardin, in whose rustic cottage the great French
author passed the closing years of his eccentric
life.

It was at one time thought by a few who gave
much time to the study of Rousseau's life that
the great writer endeavored to kill himself by
swallowing arsenic.   There is little to support
such belief.   Rousseau was sentimental, egotis-
tic, and opinionated.   He had much to say about
himself, and he was doubtless much of a hero in
his own eyes.   But one thing is, I think, certain,
and that is that he was first, last, and always

a self-indulgent coward. It would require very
strong evidence to convince me that Rousseau
plucked up sufficient spirit to destroy his own
life. He may have found life too bitter for his
liking, but there is every reason to believe that
he found death even less attractive.

A few years ago a communication signed " C.
I. B." appeared in one of the New York papers.
Its author, summing up the evidence for and
against Dr. Raspail's theory with regard to the
death of Rousseau, wrote thus:

" It may be interesting to recall that some fourteen years ago, when, at the instance of Senator
Hamel, the tombs of Rousseau and Voltaire underneath the Pantheon were opened to ascertain
definitely whether the remains of those two great
men were really there or not, the present writer witnessed the exhumation, and, together with M. Jules
Clarétie of the French Academy, saw the skulls of
Voltaire and of Rousseau. They were both in a
fairly good state of preservation, particularly the
skull of Rousseau, which was solid and massive. I
held it in my hands and examined it, but I certainly
did not notice any traces of the wounds described by
Dr. Raspail, although there was a small place on
the top of the forehead where the skull had fallen or
disappeared, leaving a sort of cavity."

I have not succeeded in discovering the identity
of " C. I. B.," but his information seems to be
first-hand. I have not the slightest suspicion
that Rousseau contemplated suicide, nor do I
believe that Thérèse Levasseur or any other

woman had aught to do with his death. He
died as most of us will no doubt die,— from natural causes.

It has been supposed that Shelley was
murdered. The supposition has no other foundation than the confession of a dying sea-robber
who has left it on record that he, with other pi-
rates, captured the poet and his boat, and that,
enraged at finding no treasure with Shelley, they
cast the poet into the sea and sunk his boat.
We are too prone to believe death-bed confessions. There is a general belief that " they
breathe truth that breathe their words in pain."
It does not follow that because a man is near
his end he will tell the truth. It may be he does
not know what the truth is, and it not infrequently happens that the approach of death
makes but slight impression upon the conscience
or moral sense. Most of the murderers who die
upon the scaffold or in the electric chair deny
their guilt, and go into eternity with a lie upon
their lips. There is nothing in the approach of
death to make a man either better or worse.
Men usually die as they live. As the tree falls
so it lies. I see no more reason for believing
that Shelley was murdered than I do for thinking that Rousseau came to a violent end.

In the days of Cæsar Borgia poisoned rings
were used for criminal purposes, and even now
such rings are used for both suicide and murder.
Not long ago a man who resided in Brooklyn,
New York, concealed in a very beautiful ring

a poisonous preparation which he employed to rid himself at once of both neuralgia and life. Hannibal, it is recorded, fearing that he would be delivered up to the Romans, swallowed a poison which he had carried with him in the hollow of a ring. It is a long stretch of time from the Brooklyn suicide to the terror-stricken general, but the crime of one age seems to be that of all ages, for human nature remains the same from generation to generation. It is said that Demosthenes died of a poisoned ring. In the same way died the keeper of the Roman treasures, after the robbery by Crassus of the gold which Camillus had placed there. He broke the stone of his ring in his mouth, and allowed the poison to escape. We do not know just what substance was concealed under the stone, but in all probability it was strychnine, which was in common use among the ancients. The jewel over the poison cavity was so closely fitted to the ring that even a modern jeweler might not discover it. Pope Alexander VI had a key which he used for opening a cabinet. The key was poisoned in the handle. A small, sharp pin, when the handle was pressed, punctured the skin sufficiently to allow the poison to enter the body. When the pope wished to rid himself of an obnoxious person, he handed him the key and asked him to unlock the cabinet. The lock was made to turn somewhat stiffly so that there might be pressure sufficient to puncture the skin. Some of the Borgia rings were so constructed that the hand, when passed over a glass of wine, could discharge the poison into the wine without its being observed.

One of the strangest of deaths was that of a clergyman who expired while conducting funeral services. He had made a short prayer and had taken his seat to allow a quartette to sing the hymn, " Nearer, my God, to Thee," and during the singing he closed his eyes and rested his head against the coffin, near which he was seated. No one, however, thought his attitude unusual, until the time came for him to rise and begin the reading of the Scripture. His failure to rise brought at once a physician to his side, and the announcement was made that he had passed away. One can easily see how great a shock such a death at such a time must have been to people who, attending the funeral of their friend and neighbor, witnessed as well the sudden death of their pastor.

There is somewhere an account of an even more shocking death at a funeral. An undertaker who was superintending the lowering of a coffin into an open grave experienced a sudden attack of heart-failure, and, uttering a distressing cry, fell headforemost into the grave. He died instantly.

In the New York " Tribune " of April 25, 1906, there was a very startling story of the shooting of three men who were on a blazing roof in San Francisco, in order to prevent them from being burned alive. They were upon the roof of the Windsor Hotel on Market Street, and it was impossible to get them down. Rather than see them fall with the roof and roast to death, a military officer directed his men to shoot them, which they did in the presence of hundreds of spectators. In the great fire in San Francisco, following the earthquake, there were many tragic and remarkable deaths. Could they all be recorded in a book for general reading, we should have a wonderful exhibit of the heroism of our often misunderstood and pitifully undervalued human nature.

One of the most repulsive and horrible of deaths was recorded in the New York " Sun " of August 31, 1904. Alfred Thurston, a man who, in dime museums, pretended to eat glass, live frogs, and writhing snakes, and who performed various unseemly feats for money, being, as the phrase has it, " out of a job," went into the barroom of a New York hotel, carrying with him in a box a huge diamond-back rattlesnake. He deliberately removed the reptile from the box in which it had been confined and placed its head in his mouth. The snake stung him in the tongue and he died seven hours later in great agony. Thurston's death was far more repulsive than that of Cleopatra, who applied to her breast a living asp. The man's mind may have been unsettled by want of success in obtaining employment, and perhaps he was in some measure the victim of that peculiar vanity and love of attention which so often accompanies the early stages, and sometimes the later stages as well, of insanity. A large number of the picturesque and startling crimes that alarm and shock society are due to the insane self-exaltation and egotism of unbalanced minds. Doubtless many of the evil deeds of the English suffragettes come, not so much from a desire for political equality, as from an imperious and insatiable hunger for notoriety.

Other animals than the snake have been made use of by suicides. A nobleman in Rio de Janeiro, the Viscount Almeida, invited a number of his friends to a sumptuous repast. After the wine had been disposed of and a few witty stories had been told, the viscount led the party to a cage of lions that had been hired from a traveling menagerie. He described the animals and gave his guests some diverting accounts of their habits and dispositions, after which he suddenly opened the door of the cage and threw himself before one of the largest and most ferocious of the animals. The lions pounced upon him and before he could be dragged from the cage life was nearly extinct.

Not all strange deaths are distressing, though from what this paper has thus far presented, the reader may be tempted to believe no death in any wise agreeable that has in it aught of the dramatic element. Men die in all kinds of ways, and the unusual is as likely as any other to be the way one would choose for himself were the manner of his departure wholly a matter of his own choosing. Some time ago in London, at a musical party given by Sir Nathaniel Barnaby, honorary vice-president of the Institution of Naval Architects, a young lady sang with great tenderness and beauty of expression, a song called " Good Night." All who were present were delighted. But as the last words of the song rang out clear and sweet, suddenly the singer dropped dead. It was a strange and startling ending of both the song and life itself, and yet, if we leave out of our thought the youth of the singer, the death was not an unpleasant one.

Some time ago in this country a young lady died while her lover was asking her to become his wife. Doubtless the lover would have been accepted had not Death returned for her an answer he little dreamed of receiving. Was it well she lost the crown of womanhood,— the happiness of married love? Who can say? Not always are we happy in the possession of that which at first we ardently covet. The brightest dream, like the fairest flower, must fade; and sometimes for both dream and flower the summer ends too soon. But of this at least we are sure,— a death like hers, sudden and without mental distress, has been the desire of many hearts.

Dr. Alexander Adam, the distinguished headmaster of the high school in Edinburgh, did not know that the shadows that were falling around him were those of death; he thought the day was drawing to its end and that it was time to dismiss the school. " It grows dark, boys; you may go! " he gently said, and so fell asleep forever.

We naturally think of death caused by falling from a balloon or an airship as one of the most dreadful of which we have knowledge, yet Fritz Kahn, the German psychologist, believes that a death so caused is not exceptionally painful. Heim fell from an airship a great distance and for a number of days he was unconscious. He told the Swiss Alpine Club that when he commenced his fall his first thought was that he would be unable to deliver the address he had promised that club. He wondered who would have to tell his family the news of his death. It also flashed over his mind that if he could remove his spectacles he would save his eyes from damage that might be caused by broken glass. He had no fear and no pain, but had in his ears a soft sound as of far-away music.

A curious kind of death was that which occasionally overtook a Roman soldier. Roman cohorts carried in place of the modern musket a long spear terminating in a sharp and polished metallic point. They sometimes put their spears aside when a thunder-storm came upon them while they were in camp. Of course they knew nothing about the nature of an electric bolt. General opinion held lightning to be Jove's greater spear, which when angry he hurled at his foe. When an electric storm overtook an army engaged in battle, the spears could not be dispensed with, and the result was in some cases death from what was called in those days the "Divine Rage." Pliny, in his "Natural History," describes the glowing stars that settled upon sail-yards and masts of ships. Livy and Cæsar wrote of scintillating balls, the nature of which we now understand. The French and Spaniards of the present time call those electric balls St. Elmo's fires, and sometimes the fires of St. Peter or St. Nicholas. They are not uncommon. Count de Forbin upon one occasion saw as many as thirty such illuminations blazing upon different parts of a ship in which he was traveling. The illuminations were accompanied by loud sounds as of exploding gunpowder. Not long ago a French soldier was shot by an electric bolt that hit the bayonet attached to his musket; and, strange to say, another soldier had all the brass buttons on his coat melted and also the metal attached to his cartridge-box, and yet he was not himself injured. Some years ago an old sailor had his wooden leg struck by lightning. The leg was splintered into small fragments, but the old tar was only stunned.

It would be no difficult thing to turn this paper treating of singular ways of dying into one concerning itself with narrow and unusual escapes from death. But that I do not intend to do, though I may here and there add a narrative of some such escape, by way of variety. There is a story of the kind that seems to me to be peculiarly deserving of a place in this connection. It is of a woman who, in the days when large and substantial crinolines were worn, determined to destroy her own life. She walked out to the middle of High Bridge, and after taking one long look at upper New York City, climbed over the rail and leaped into the air. She had not dropped more than a foot or two when her hoop skirt, or crinoline, expanded into a parachute in which she descended with great deliberation and perfect safety. A large number of spectators witnessed the descent. She came down with her legs exposed to view and dangling in the air, while her head was on a level with her expanded crinoline. She descended in graceful undulations, making what the police justice described as " an indecent exposure of her lower extremities."

There is a curious story of voluntary trance or simulation of death preserved in Mrs. Crowe's " Nightside of Nature." I can do no better than reproduce the story in the author's own words:

" Doctor Cheyne, the Scottish physician, who died in 1742, relates the case of Colonel Townshend, who could, to all appearance, die whenever he pleased: his heart ceased to beat, there was no perceptible respiration, and his whole frame became cold and rigid as death itself; the features being shrunk and colorless, and the eye glazed and ghastly. He would continue in this state for several hours, and then gradually revive; but the revival does not appear

to have been an effort of will, or, rather, we are not
informed whether it was so or not.  The doctor who
attended the colonel states that his patient said he
could ' die or expire when he pleased,' and yet, by
an effort, or *somehow,* he could come to life again.
He performed the experiment in the presence of
three medical men, one of whom kept his hand on
his heart, another held his wrist, and the third placed
a looking-glass before his lips; and they found that
all traces of respiration and pulsation gradually
ceased, insomuch that, after consulting about his condition for some time, they were leaving the room,
persuaded that he was really dead, when signs of
life appeared, and he slowly revived.  He did not
die while repeating the experiment, as has been
sometimes asserted."

Death did not come to Henry Close in any
strange way, for that eccentric man died at home,
in his own bed, and of a natural cause.  But
nevertheless Mr. Close interested himself in the
preservation of his physical frame, and in the
construction of a tomb that was to receive his
body when death had done its work.  During the
last years of his life he spent most of his time
and large sums of money in perfecting his plans.
He wanted, he said, " a scientific burial."  He
had made up his mind to continue his presence
in this world so far as concerned his body, and
he regretted that it was not within his power to
parallel with his own experience that of the Wandering Jew in the matter of long life on earth.
He left money with the corporation of St.
Michael's Cemetery at Birdsboro, Pennsylvania,

with the interest of which his tomb and the lot
connected therewith were to be kept in perfect
order. For years Close lived a recluse, engaged
in experiments the nature of which was not revealed until he died. Then it became known
that all his study had been concentrated on
evolving a method of burial which he believed
would prevent the decomposition of his body.

Notes left by him disclosed his one ambition
to be " to cheat the worms after death." He
was determined that his body should remain in-
tact for ages. Not long ago he superintended
the construction of a mammoth vault in St.
Michael's Cemetery, at Birdsboro. The vault
was built of brick, faced with plates of steel, between which cement was poured. A granite slab
weighing three tons was placed on it.

Before his death he designed and had made an
outer case of phosphor bronze, weighing a ton,
and a coffin of ironwood. He engaged the best
mechanics obtainable for this work, paying them
big wages. He ordered that after his death
the bronze case should be hermetically sealed and
caulked with molten lead. John B. Rutherford,
an attorney, was retained by Close to superin-
tend the burial, and five hundred dollars was be-
queathed to him for this service.

The foregoing may appear to some who read
this paper little more than a morbid or abnormal
desire and a vicious waste of money. The desire was certainly unusual, and no one can deny
that it was eccentric, but it can hardly be called

morbid. Many persons who never discuss the matter dread the slow corruption of the grave. Cremation is in some ways an improvement upon earth-burial, but it also involves the disintegration of the body. Few know that it is no very difficult thing to treat a dead body in such a way that it will become practically indestructible. The body of the great Italian patriot Mazzini has been rendered incorruptible. The body of President Lincoln is so embalmed that in all probability time can have no effect upon it. If two thousand years hence his tomb should be opened, his face will appear precisely as it appeared during his life; not a feature will be altered.

Most interesting and weird is this strange account of the death of a Buddhist priest which appeared some years ago in a New York paper. The author writes as follows:

" It is an exceedingly rare thing for a foreigner to be permitted to witness the death of a Buddhist priest, and it was only after a residence of nearly twelve years in China that the opportunity came to me.

" Old Ting Ho-Sheng, head priest of the ' Temple of the Spirit Light,' I had known by sight for several years, and had a more intimate acquaintance with him the summer he died; but I did not expect to be a witness of his death, or to see him die sitting up. Not only did ' old Ting ' die sitting up, but he was put into his coffin and buried that way.

" Disease and native treatment had already placed

the seal of death upon the old man, so that at my second visit I could only tell the attendants that his hours were few. Returning to the old priest's rooms a little later, I found him sitting on a broad stool facing the outer door, clad in his fine priestly robes of yellow silk. Being long past consciousness, he was supported by the attendants in this position, with his legs crossed, each foot resting upon the opposite thigh, sole directed upward — an exceedingly difficult and, in fact, almost impossible position to assume in life. The hands were placed, palms together, up before his face, the whole attitude being that which represents Buddha in the state of Nirvana — and the old man was very near that state. The great anxiety of those in attendance was that he should not be placed in his coffin until he was really dead; although I could not bring him back to life, they were willing that I should judge when he was dead. Holding a small mirror in front of his face, I waited until there was no more moisture deposited upon it.

" In the meantime preparations were continually going on around me for further ceremonies. A large pail of paper ' cash ' had been placed outside the door, on top of which was a document I was not allowed to see, but which, from what I could learn, was his history as related to his accession to the priesthood and life in it.

" Upon his being pronounced dead, a flaming torch was applied to the ' cash ' by a young priest,— former disciple, and now successor to the lands and buildings of the old man sitting before him. No sooner was the paper well ablaze than the young man prostrated himself before it, bumping his head on the ground the requisite number of times, for every movement in every ceremony of the Chinese is regulated by rites as inflexible as law.

" The next step in the strange death scene was the placing of the body in its upright coffin. The front and top were removed and yellow silk cushions put in the bottom, on which the old man was placed as gently as possible consistent with the awkwardness of his position. Numerous small cushions and wads of thin paper were put in around him, a pillow under each elbow to sustain the arms in their upright position, and then the front was slid into place. More packing was done from the top until his body was immovable and the coffin filled, the yellow silk knot of his hat being the last I ever saw of old Ting Ho-Sheng, who shall sit and wait until time and decay do their work in altering his position."

An eleven-year-old son of Mr. Owen Dorse was the victim of an accident that cost him his life. He, with his brother and a number of other boys, was playing about the pipe used for compressing air in testing the air-brake hose on the cars in the Baltimore and Ohio yards. While he was seated at one end of the pipe some one turned on the air-cock, and the full force of the air, under a pressure of one hundred pounds to the square inch, struck him. He was injured internally, and suffered excruciating agony until he died.

It is interesting to see how fond a man may become of any one of the detached members of his mutilated body. There is a man in Massa-

chusetts who every year journeys all the way to
Gettysburg upon the anniversary of the great
battle which took place there, for the purpose
of decorating the grave of his leg which, in the
cemetery at that place, is marked by a costly
stone. He spends some time at the grave in
recalling the terrible conflict which cost him so
great a price. Before leaving the grave he cov-
ers it with flowers. In a number of graves in different cemeteries of the land there rest single
legs, arms, and other parts of human bodies. A
gentleman who lost an arm in a railroad accident
had the severed member encased in an expensive
coffin, and but for the counsel of his friends would
have given it an elaborate funeral. I am informed that there is in a western graveyard a
stone marking the resting place of a right hand.
Upon the stone it is stated that the hand was
that of a skillful pianist who buried with the lost
member his hope and ambition.

It is reported (I know not with how much
truth) that Brigham Young, President of the
Church of the Latter-Day Saints, and a leader
among the Mormons, requested a few days before
his death that his coffin should be made large
enough for him to turn over in. The request, if
really made, was not so foolish as may at first
appear. Young was a very large man, and he
had always prized above most men freedom of
motion. He could not endure confinement of
any kind. It is not strange that he looked forward to the hopeless confinement of the grave

with horror. Hundreds of men have the same
feeling, though but few give expression to it. It
is impossible for us to unthink our own existence. We always think of ourselves as conscious. When we speak of ourselves, we mean
body as well as soul. Thus it comes to pass that
when we imagine ourselves in the grave, it is
always as consciously there. We are well aware
that we shall not know we are in the grave
when we are there, but, as has been said, we
cannot imagine ourselves ignorant of the fact
that we are there. Thus, distressing as it is,
we always, when we contemplate our burial, contemplate being buried alive. Young, like all the
rest of us, thus contemplated his inhumation, and
the one thing about it that distressed him most
was the close confinement. He was a coarse man
and took a coarse view of things, and so I hardly
think it strange, all things considered, that he
made the request he is reported to have made.

But though Young was a coarse man, he was
not an ignorant one, and it is possible that he
had in mind the repulsive disposal of the remains
of William the Conqueror who, in the year 1087,
was entombed in St. Stephen's Abbey, Caen, Normandy. The corpse of the king was abandoned
by the nobles and by all his followers, and not
even the humblest of his servants showed any regard for either the character or the exalted station of the sovereign. He was despoiled of his
armor, which was very valuable, of his beautiful
apparel, and of whatever he had that was worth

the taking; and his naked body was left upon the floor. No preparations were made for a funeral until a certain country knight conveyed the body to Caen in Normandy. At Caen a band of monks received the corpse, and were about to do it honor when a great fire occurred in the neighborhood, and the monks hastened to extinguish it. The body remained for a considerable time unattended; but when the monks returned, the funeral sermon, which was droned in a careless and perfunctory manner, was ended, and the stone coffin was placed in the earth in the chancel.

As the body was laid in the coffin there stood up one Anselm Fitz-Arthur and forbade the burial, declaring that the dead king had robbed him of his inheritance, and that the very place selected for the monarch's tomb was the floor of his father's house which the monarch had violently taken in order to build a church. "Therefore," said he, "I challenge this ground, and, in the name of God, forbid that the body of this despoiler be covered with the earth of my inheritance." The funeral services were thus brought to a sudden and dramatic conclusion, and one hundred pounds were paid to Fitz-Arthur in order to secure to the monarch the tomb which had been prepared for his body. The corpse had to be pressed down, the coffin not being large enough, and the result was one as unpleasant to describe as it was offensive to experience. Only two or three monks were brave enough to remain at the post of duty. There have been other troubles of the same kind, and it is quite likely that the one already related, or some other, had a measure of influence over the mind of Brigham Young.

The death, in 1891, of Washington Irving Bishop, the famous mind-reader, awakened at the time great interest. Physicians and the laity were desirous of knowing all that could be known about the occult and mysterious powers of Mr. Bishop. He died at the Lambs' Club, where he had given an exhibition of his ability as a mind-reader. Soon after one of his exploits he became comatose, and in an hour he was dead. The physicians were so anxious for an autopsy that they opened the corpse on the very day of death, without obtaining permission from Mrs. Bishop, the mind-reader's aged mother; moreover, they held the autopsy directly in the face of the fact that Mr. Bishop sometimes remained in a condition resembling death for an entire day. The mother very naturally charged the doctors with murdering her son, and the case was taken into court. The physicians swore that Mr. Bishop wished for and expected a post-mortem, notwithstanding the fact that he had left no paper requesting such an examination and had said nothing to his mother about his having such a desire. The physicians were many and were backed by professional influence and strength, while the mother was a poor old woman with comparatively little backing. The result was just what might be expected. It was thought then, and there are

those who still think, that physicians who cut up
living dogs and cats with no twinge of conscience might view the precipitate autopsy in a
light quite different from that in which it would
present itself to the mind of an affectionate and
broken-hearted mother. Still further, portions
of the viscera were removed for private examination and, it is understood, were never returned.

Some time ago the skeleton of a man was
found in the trunk of a very old tree. The tree
was leveled to the earth by a violent storm.
After a time laborers were sent to cut up the
wood and cart it away. Great was their surprise to find embedded in the very heart of the
tree a perfect skeleton. For a long time no one
could imagine how it came there, but later
it was decided that the skeleton was that of a
hunter who must long years ago have climbed the
tree to get away from a bear or some other animal that had pursued him. The tree must have
been hollow, and the unfortunate man doubtless
slipped down the trunk, where he was wedged in
so tightly that he could not even move. There
he must have endured a slow death from hunger
and thirst,— a death rendered additionally distressing by his inability to move or in any way
change his position. The tree no doubt grew
over and around him, thus incasing the skeleton.
The finding of the remains of an old powder-
horn with the bones increased the belief that the
skeleton was that of a hunter. What a long and
horrible death that man must have faced!

## IX

## ROMANCE AND SYMBOLISM OF ANIMAL LIFE

There is implanted by nature in the heart of man a noble and excellent affection of mercy, extending even to the brute animals which by the Divine appointment are subjected to his dominion. This, moreover, we may be assured of, that the more noble the mind, the more enlarged is this affection. Narrow and degenerate minds think that such things do not pertain to them, but the nobler part of mankind is affected by sympathy.

— *Lord Bacon.*

The philosopher avers
That Reason guides our deeds, and Instinct theirs;
Instinct and Reason, how shall we divide?

— *Pope.*

# ROMANCE AND SYMBOLISM OF
# ANIMAL LIFE

I NEVER saw the story of Balaam's ass in
verse. Perhaps the stolid creature with
which the unrighteous prophet had to deal could
not be made to lend itself with any degree of success to either descriptive or dramatic art. Nevertheless the ass has played a somewhat remarkable
part in the great and varying world of letters.
Victor Hugo's curious account of the philosophic
ass that held its own in a labored discussion with
a savant of no mean ability, not only exhibits
the animal to its own advantage, but displays the
man of learning in a more penetrating light than
he would, in all probability, have chosen for
himself. The writer of Genesis compares Issa-
char to an ass, and Homer likens Ajax to that
valuable but much abused creature. The lover
of classical literature will recall the narrative of
" The Metamorphoses, or The Golden Ass," in
which Lucius undergoes a most remarkable
change, divesting him of man's estate and trans-
ferring him to the *genus Asinus*, but with little
damage to his intellectual parts. He was an ass
in his exterior only. His mind remained un-
changed. He fared better or worse, as you view
it, than Nebuchadnezzar of old, who sank in both
mind and body to the condition of a mere animal.
If the sorrows of a man are to be preferred to
the joys of a beast, then Lucius Apuleius (for

that was the writer's full name) is to be congratulated. The possession of a humar mind would have made the humiliation and distress only the greater in any of the instances of transformation recorded in the old mythological tales. It did increase the misery of Lucius so far as the story goes; but as there was, in truth, no real transformation, so there was no distress of any kind. Yet St. Augustine took "The Metamorphoses, or The Golden Ass" for the veritable autobiography of one skilled in magic, who, for his traffic in the evil things of the black art, came himself to be a victim of that same art. In the romance we are considering occurs the tale of "Cupid and Psyche," and from its many pages Boccaccio and Le Sage drew some of their most pleasing narratives.

Other and greater poets than Coleridge have dedicated verses to the sometimes amiable and always determined beast. The ass, like all other living creatures, is sensitive to kindness. Hawthorne relates in his "English Note-book" that "a donkey stubbornly refused to come out of a boat which had brought the beast across the Mersey; at last, after many kicks had been applied, and other persecutions of that kind, a man stepped forward and addressed the animal affectionately, 'Come along, brother'; and the donkey obeyed at once."

The ass about which Coleridge concerned himself seems to have been like the fatted calf in Scripture that an Irish bull tells us had been a great pet in the family for " a long series of years." The poet addresses the animal in terms of the most tender regard. He not only sings, " With gentle hand I give thee bread "; but he adds, " I hail thee brother." Think of that,— Coleridge, a brother to an ass! As though this were not enough, he pushes the matter to a full conclusion, and in a later line speaks of " mild equality." Surely the gifted Englishman was at heart a thoroughgoing democrat, for he included in his circle of fellowship, not men alone, but also beasts. A bard of humbler capacities sings of one who seemed to him to be " brother to the ox," but so far as we remember, no poet but the glorious singer of " The Ancient Mariner " ever dreamed of brotherhood with an ass. It may be urged that Coleridge was a youth when he so exalted the beast we count to be the symbol of a dolt, but he was quite as young when he gave the world other verses of which no poet need be ashamed.

There can be no reason why we should not recognize a human ass, since we have other animals in man's shape, and sometimes with a man's wits as well. Not many years ago a human ostrich was sent to a hospital because it had become necessary to operate upon his digestive apparatus. He had eaten nails, pins, keys, and several pocket-knives. The evening before he entered the hospital he swallowed still other metal articles, which made his condition worse. The surgical operation lasted three hours, at the

end of which time there were removed from the
stomach of our human ostrich six knives of different sizes, one watch-chain, one ring for holding keys, one hall door-key, one desk-key, four
Yale-lock keys, one button-hook, fourteen wire
nails, and two pins. The operation left him in
a critical condition and I was unable to learn
whether he recovered or died. I suppose he was
insane, though I heard no statement to that
effect. If we may have ostriches, reptiles, and
other loathsome creatures in man's disguise, why
may we not have as well the human ass?

An illuminating sentence from Rossetti gives
us the secret of Coleridge's breadth of sympathy
and extent of fellowship, and shows us why even
an ass may claim a tribute from his lyre. Said
the pre-Raphaelite poet, " The leading point
about Coleridge's work is its human love "; he
might have said, and it would have been as true,
that the leading point of Coleridge's work is its
human quality. We all of us recall the lines:

> " He prayeth well who loveth well
>   Both man and bird and beast.
>
> .   .   .   .   .   .   .   .
>
> He prayeth best who loveth best
>   All things, both great and small."

No animal could be so mean and poor as to lose
the sympathy of the poet's heart. Even the
plodding jackass wandered into his verse.

The ass may be viewed in a religious light. "The Feast of the Ass" commemorated the Virgin Mary's flight into Egypt. A girl, elegantly appareled, with an infant in her arms, impersonated the Virgin. She rode upon an ass superbly caparisoned. The beast was taught to kneel and perform other acts of devotion. When it was led into the church and up to the altar, with the girl upon its back, the following remarkable ode was sung by the people:

### ODE TO THE ASS

"From the country of the east
Came this strong and handsome beast,
This able ass beyond compare
Heavy loads and packs to bear.
  Now, seignior Ass, a noble bray;
  That beauteous mouth at large display;
  Abundant food our hay-lofts yield,
  And oats abundant load the field.

"True it is, his pace is slow
Till he feels the quickening blow,
Till he feels the urging goad
On his back so well bestowed.
  Now, seignior Ass, etc.

"He was born on Shechem's hill;
In Reuben's vale he fed his fill;
He drank of Jordan's sacred stream;
And gamboled in Bethlehem.
  Now, seignior Ass, etc.

" See that proud, majestic ear;
Born he is the yoke to wear;
All his fellows he surpasses!
He's the very lord of asses!
   Now, seignior Ass, etc.

" In leaping he excels the fawn,
The deer, the colts upon the lawn;
Less swift the dromedaries ran,
Boasted of in Median.
   Now, seignior Ass, etc.

" Gold from Araby the blessed,
Seba myrrh of myrrh the best,
To the church this ass I bring,
We his sturdy labors sing.
   Now, seignior Ass, etc.

" While he draws the loaded wain,
Or many a pack, he don't complain:
With his jaws, a noble pair,
He doth craunch his homely fare.
   Now, seignior Ass, etc.

" The bearded barley and its stem,
And thistles, yield his fill of them;
He assists to separate,
When 'tis threshed, the chaff from wheat.
   Now, seignior Ass, etc.

" Amen; bray, most honored Ass,
Sated now with grain and grass;
Amen repeat, amen reply,
And disregard antiquity.
   Now, seignior Ass," etc.

When the people lifted their voices and sang,

> " *Orientis partibus,*
> *Adventavit Asinus,*
> *Pulcher et fortissimus,*
> *Sarcinis aptissimus.*
> *He, sire Ane, he!* "

the priest wagged his head three times. At the close of the ceremony the priest, as the rubric of Beauvais ordered, in dismissing the congregation, brayed three times like an ass, and the people responded with three brays. Curious matter with regard to this subject may be found in the " Mémoire pour servir à l'Histoire de la Fête des Fous," by Du Tilliat, Lausanne edition, 1741; Paris reprint, 1751; also, " Recueil des Cérémonies et Coutumes Religieuses de tous les Peuples," volume viii (edition Prudhomme, 1809).

Du Cange gives the Latin from the manuscript ritual of the Church in Rouen, and adds the English of Steinmetz: —

| | |
|---|---|
| " *Orientis partibus* | In the eastern regions |
| *Adventavit Asinus,* | Chanced an ass to be, |
| *Pulcher et fortissimus* | Beautiful and bravest, |
| *Sarcinis aptissimus.* | Fittest loads to bear. |

| CHORUS. | CHORUS. |
|---|---|
| " *Heh! Sire Asnes, car chantez.* | He-hawn, Sir Ass, you sing,— |
| *Belle bouche rechignez* | Fine mouth you grin,— |
| *Vous aurez du foin assez* | Hay enough you'll have, |
| *Et de l'vavoine a plantez.* | Oats enough to plant. |

" *Lenius erat pedibus,*
*Nisi foret baculus,*
*Et eum in clunibus*
*Pungeret aculeus.*

    CHO.— *Heh, Sire, etc.*

" *Hic in collibus Sichem,*
*Jam nutritus sub Reuben,*
*Transiit per Jordanem,*
*Saliit in Bethlehem.*

    CHO.— *Heh, Sire, etc.*

" *Ecce magnis auribus,*
*Subjugalis filius,*
*Asinus egregius,*
*Asinorum dominus.*

    CHO.— *Heh, Sire, etc.*

" *Saltu vincit hinnulos,*
*Damas et capreolos.*
*Super dromedarios*
*Velox Midianeos.*

    CHO.— *Heh, Sire, etc.*

" *Aurum de Arabiâ*
*Thus et myrrham de Sabâ,*
*Tulit in ecclesia*
*Virtus asinaria.*

    CHO.— *Heh, Sire, etc.*

" *Dum trahit vehicula,*
*Multa cum sarcinula,*
*Ilius mandibula*
*Dura terit pabula.*

    CHO.— *Heh, Sire, etc.*

" *Cum aristis hordeum*
*Comedit et carduum,*
*Triticum a palea*
*Segregat in area.*

    CHO.— *Heh, Sire, etc.*

Slow in foot was he
Unless there was a stick,
And a goad to prick him
In his lazy buttocks.

He-hawn, etc.

He was raised in Sichem,
Pastured under Reuben,
Found his way o'er Jordan,
Trotted into Bethlehem.

He-hawn, etc.

Here he is with big ears,
Primitive clod-hopper,—
Ass as big as ever,—
Lord of all the asses.

He-hawn, etc.

Mules he beats at jumping,
Bucks and goats the same;
Swifter than the Midian
Dromedary is he.

He-hawn, etc.

Gold of rich Arabia,
Incense, myrrh of Saba,—
All, the church now offers
To an ass's virtue.

He-hawn, etc.

Whilst he drags his wagon,
Plentifully piled on,—
Then his jaws are grinding
Hard food for digestion.

He-hawn, etc.

Wheat and barley loves he,
Thistles too he savors,
Wheat from chaff well
  knows he,
Browsing in the barnyard.

He-hawn, etc.

*"Amen, dicas, Asine!*
  [Hic genuflectebantur.]
*Jam satur de gramine;*
*Amen, amen itera —*
*Aspernare vetera.*

Now say amen, O Ass!
  [*Here they fall on their knees.*]
Belly full of clover.
Amen! amen! forever!
And away with fodder.

*"Heh-va! Bialxsire Asnes,*
  *car allez, belle bouche*
  *car chantez."*

He-hawn. Beautiful Sir Ass. You can trot. Splendid mouth of yours to sing!

The line, " See that proud, majestic ear," suggests the passage from Tennyson's " Princess " :

" No livelier than the dame
That whispered ' Asses' ears ' among the sedge,
  My sister."

The story is that Midas was called to sit in judgment on a musical tournament between Apollo and Pan. The king decided in favor of Pan, and Apollo, in revenge, changed the Phrygian monarch's ears to those of an ass. The barber discovered the disfigurement and was afraid to reveal the secret, but being unable to hold it longer in his own breast, he dug a hole in the earth, and, pressing his mouth to it, cried, " King Midas has ass's ears " ; after which he filled the hole and was relieved.

If the ass is entitled to a festival in our Christian calendar, why may he not figure in poetry as a moral philosopher, or even as one of the heavenly muses? Why, if the Italian people may bow before him and sing his praise, is it

wrong for the recluse of Guernsey to introduce
him to a modern audience as a competent teacher
in ethics?   And if the ass, in the exercise of
free will, finally ridicules modern education which
has deprived him of his festival, and repudiates
science which has classified and not sanctified
him, who shall find fault with so just an indigna-
tion?   He was a profane wretch who named the
fifth proposition in the first book of Euclid's
" Elements " *Pons Asinorum*.  The dull pupil
may lose his head when called to cross that narrow bridge, but the ass is the surest-footed of all
animals, as every Alpine traveler knows, and as
we shall learn later when a certain Mr. Barry
compares the horse with the mule.   The irra-
tional prejudice against the " sacred beast " cul-
minated in Spanish song when the elegant linguist and musician, Tomas de Yriarte, soiled his
lyre and libeled a brother singer; and, to show
that whatever merit an ass may have must be the
accident of an accident, thus tore the melodious
creature from " the tuneful choir ":

> " The fable which I now present
> Occurred to me by accident.
>
> " A stupid ass one morning went
> Into a field by accident,
> And cropped his food, and was content,
> Until he spied by accident
> A flute some swain on thought intent
> Had left behind by accident;
> When, snuffing it with eager scent,

He breathed in it by accident,
And made the hollow instrument
Emit a sound by accident.
' Hurrah! hurrah!' exclaimed the brute,
' How cleverly I play the flute.'

" A fool, in spite of nature's bent,
May shine for once — by accident." [1]

Shakespeare seems to have shared the Spanish poet's contempt for " the flute-player," for he makes Conrade call Dogberry, who is little better than a fool, an ass; and Dogberry says of himself, though in wrathful irony, " O that he were here to write me down an ass! — but, masters, remember that I am an ass; though it be not written down, yet forget not that I am an ass."

In the East the ass is respected as a useful beast of burden, and many an Oriental song celebrates his virtues; but in the West things are different,— with us he stands for stupidity and stubbornness. The following story of juvenile simplicity illustrates the intense ridicule connected with his name. Two boys of tender years, who went by the names of Tom and Jack, became members of a district school in a certain New England town. On their making their appearance, the teacher called them up before the assembled school and proceeded to make certain interrogatories concerning their names and ages.

[1] A somewhat different translation may be found in Dr. Marvin's " Flowers of Song from Many Lands," page 49.

"Well, my lad," said the teacher to the first, "what is your name?"

"Tom," promptly answered the boy.

"Tom!" said the teacher, "that does not sound well. Remember always to speak the full name. You should have said Thom-as. Now, my son," turning to the other boy, whose face suddenly lighted up with the satisfaction of a newly comprehended idea, "now, then, will you tell me what is your name?"

"*Jack-ass!*" replied the lad, in a tone of confident decision.

The teacher, convulsed with laughter, motioned the lads to take their seats.

The teacher laughed, and we follow his example, because to a western mind there is something indescribably stupid and ridiculous in being an ass. Dogberry in asking to be written down an ass, and Jack in claiming the same privilege, name themselves consummate dolts.

The lot of the ass is full of hardship, and yet it is seldom terminated in such cruelty as every year ends the misfortunes of more than twenty thousand horses at Bordeaux. The dwellers in the valley of the Garonne cultivate leeches for the medical market. Into the artificial swamps where they breed and grow, old and infirm horses are driven. As soon as a horse enters a swamp, thousands of these hungry vampire-worms fasten upon it, covering eyes, ears, lips, nostrils and trunk, dragging the animal under the mud and slime while they gorge upon its blood.

The proverb about giving a dog a bad name, so abundantly illustrated in the history of the ass, is further illustrated in that of the serpent whose calamity dates from the Garden of Eden. Tradition tells us that the devil besought various animals to carry him into the sacred enclosure where dwelt Adam and his beautiful wife. The serpent alone consented. It carried the evil spirit between its teeth as cats carry their kittens, and so it came to pass that the devil was conveyed into Paradise. The serpent was originally the most beautiful of animals, and walked upon legs and feet as do many others; but its service to the devil brought down upon it the wrath of God, and Michael was directed to cut off its legs. It was also condemned to feed on human excrement. "And the Lord God said unto the serpent, Because thou hast done this, thou art cursed above all cattle, and above every beast of the field; upon thy belly shalt thou go, and dust shalt thou eat all the days of thy life." (Genesis iii, 14.)

It is a peculiarity of the Bible that it leaves no animal without at least a " crumb of comfort." Dragons are commanded to praise God, and owls are permitted to honor him. The serpent is promoted to be an emblem of the tribe of Dan, and our exemplar: " Be ye wise as serpents, and harmless as doves." The Saviour himself is likened to a serpent: " As Moses lifted up the serpent in the wilderness, even so must the Son of Man be lifted up."

The serpent figures extensively in classical literature. The Laocoön celebrates the achievements of two serpents that came from the sea and destroyed the priest who would prevent the Trojans from taking the wooden horse into the city. The serpent is twined around the neck of the three-headed Cerberus, the canine guard of Hades. The Gorgons had in the place of hair hissing serpents, and whoever looked on Medusa's locks was immediately turned into stone. Perseus cut off Medusa's head while she was asleep, guiding his sword by her reflection in a mirror, for he could not look at her face without being changed into stone. He placed the head in an enchanted wallet and fled, the Gorgons in hot pursuit. He escaped them by means of his magic helmet, which enabled him to become invisible.

The most celebrated lines in the " Pharsalia " catalogue the African serpents and display their characteristics:

" Here all the serpent deadly brood appears:
First the dull asp its swelling neck uprears;
The huge hemarrhoïs, vampire of the blood;
Chersyders, that pollute both field and flood,
The water-serpent, tyrant of the lake;
The hooded cobra; and the plantain snake;
Here with distended jaws the prester strays;
And seps, whose bite both flesh and bone decays;
The amphisbæna with its double head,
One on the neck, and one of tail instead;
The horned cerastês; and the hammodyte,

Whose sandy hue might balk the keenest sight;
A feverish thirst betrays the dipsa's sting;
The scytăa its slough that casts in spring;
The natrix here the crystal stream pollutes;
Swift thro' the air the venomed javelin shoots;
Here the parēas, moving on its tail,
Marks in the sand its progress by its trail;
The speckled cenchris darts its devious way,
Its skin with spots as Theban marble gay;
The hissing sibila; the basilisk,
With whom no living thing its life would risk,
Where'er it moves none else would dare remain,
Tyrant alike and terror of the plain."
                    — Translated by *E. Cobham Brewer.*


A curious legend records that Zahak, a cruel
tyrant, moved by the devil, murdered his father
and so ascended the throne. Then the devil,
assuming the form of a young man, became the
royal cook and prepared dishes of unusual delicacy and flavor. He claimed as reward for his
culinary services permission to kiss the shoulders of the king. Zahak granted the request,
and at once black snakes grew from the spots
touched by the infernal lips. Every art failed
to destroy the writhing and hissing creatures.
At length the devil donned the form of a physician and recommended as the only way of quiet-
ing the reptiles, that they be fed every day with
human brains. His object was to depopulate the
earth. Every day two men were slain and their
brains made into a pudding for the voracious
creatures. But after a time the king's cooks

discovered that if human brains were mixed with those of a ram, the snakes were equally well pleased; and so of every two men set apart for death, the servants secretly spared one.

The worm typifies the grave (Job xix, 26; xxi, 26; xxiv, 20), and dishonor (Psalms xxii, 6; Job vii, 5; xxv, 6). In Mark we read of the worm that dieth not. The genuineness of the passage is questioned. It is quoted from Isaiah, who uses it to describe the destruction of the wicked in this life and not in the life to come. In a certain church in Europe there is shown to credulous travelers, I am told, a fragment of " the worm that never dieth," preserved in a phial of alcohol. The most hopeless lyric in the English language celebrates the victory of the worm. " The Conqueror Worm " is a song of despair such as only Edgar A. Poe could write. A miracle of genius, it is also a fearful picture of mortality. On a " gala night " the angels assemble in the theatre of the universe to see the play of " Human Life," and puppets made in imitation of God (Genesis i, 27) strew the stage without aim or purpose. The actors are moved by the hand of a hidden but colossal destiny. The play goes on, and madness, sin, and horror are discovered to be the soul of the plot. Suddenly a blood-red worm, writhing in agony, crawls upon the stage and devours the players; after which the curtain, a funeral pall, descends upon the melancholy entertainment.

" But see, amid the mimic rout,
 A crawling shape intrude!
A blood-red thing that writhes from out
 The scenic solitude.
It writhes! — it writhes! With mortal pangs
 The mimes become its food,
And the angels sob at vermin-fangs
 In human gore imbued.

" Out,— out are the lights,— out all!
 And over each quivering form,
The curtain, a funeral pall,
 Comes down with the rush of a storm,
And the angels, all pallid and wan,
 Uprising, unveiling, affirm
That the play is the tragedy, ' Man,'
 And its hero the Conqueror Worm."

Bildad assures Job that " man is a worm, and
the son of man is a worm." A Hindu poem de-
clares that

" All men are worms, and feed upon the dust,—
 The sons of wealth who sip their dainty wine,
And they who fare upon a simple crust."

Pope is of the same opinion.

" The learn'd themselves we book-worms name,
 The blockhead is a slow-worm;
The nymph whose tail is all on flame
 Is aptly termed a glow-worm;
The flatterer an earwig grows;
 Thus worms suit all conditions; —
Misers are muck-worms; silk-worms, beaux;
 And death-watches, physicians."

It was an old superstition that the angel who drove Adam and Eve from the garden conferred upon worms the power of speech. They were thought to have a social compact and laws of their own. The dead were represented in hideous rhymes as hearing the worms discuss their flavor under the coffin-lid. Swinburne has a little poem, "After Death," in which that idea is carried out. The first two lines are a key to the entire piece:

> " The four boards of the coffin lid
> Hear all the dead man did."

The prophet Melampus understood the language of worms and was saved from death by hearing them converse. They said the one to the other, " Surely the roof will fall, for we have eaten the beams from end to end." It was in a dungeon where he was confined. He communicated to the jailers the information he had received, and they removed him to another part of the building. In the night the roof fell, and the king, convinced that Melampus was indeed a holy man and prophet of God, liberated him, and gave him the oxen of Iphiklos.

A very interesting chapter might be written on the language of animals. The *dumb* beast inhabits the realm of fancy only, for most animals are able to speak for themselves in no uncertain tone. Some of them are as skilful in conversation as was the ass that Victor Hugo introduced to Kant, and whose colloquy with the great philosopher furnished material for delightful reading. "Among the animal series, there are none but the mammalia, the birds, and some reptiles endowed with vocal organs,"— so writes a man of science who seems to have examined the animal kingdom with scalpel and microscope only. But animals do communicate with each other, sometimes by sound and often by gesture. Birds call their young and understand each other's chirp, whistle, and song. The cluck of the hen is perfectly intelligible to the chickens. How eloquent and expressive is the tone of the dog,— what meaning he throws into his bark and growl! Bees, flies, and insects have a language all their own. It is not surprising that fancy and romance have given the animals an almost human vocabulary. What a delightful story is that in the "Arabian Night's Entertainment" which records the adventures of the merchant who, like the prophet Melampus, understood the language of the animals! In Æsop's fables the beasts and birds converse with each other and mankind.

Speech has been ascribed to the following animals: Al Barak, the animal that bore Mahommed to the seventh heaven; Balaam's ass; Arion, the horse given by Hercules to Adrastos; Selah's camel, miraculously produced out of a rock, and which used to go from place to place crying, "Ho, every one that wanteth milk, come, I give milk to all "; the black pigeons of Dodona; Katmir, the dog that guarded the Seven Sleep-

ers; Conrade, Fortunia's horse; Tamliha, the
king of serpents; and Xanthos, Achilles's horse.

The spider is another despised animal. Whatever crawls is repulsive to man,— why, it would
be difficult to say. Perhaps Martial's epigram
comes as near an explanation as possible:

*" Non amo te, Sabidi, nee possum dicere quare;
Hic tantum possum dicere, non amo te."*

The spider is no exception to the rule: hated,
it has its romance, history, and compensation.
Agur tells us, " There be four things which are
little upon the earth, but they are exceeding
wise: the ants are a people not strong, yet they
prepare their meat in the summer; the conies are
but a feeble folk, yet they make their houses
in the rocks; the locusts have no king, yet go
they forth all of them by bands; the spider
taketh hold with her hands, and is in kings'
palaces." (Proverbs xxx, 24-28.) The Tal-
mud says that a spider's web, woven over the entrance of the cave of Adullam where David was
concealed, decided Saul not to enter. The king
reasoned that if the spider had not been disturbed the cave must be empty.

A spider wove its web over the entrance to a
cave in which the prophet Mohammed was hiding from his enemies. The web deceived the pur-
suers. They 'thought, as did Saul concerning the
cave of Adullam, that no one could have entered
the cavern without disturbing the spider and dis-
placing the web. Thus thinking, they passed

by, and so the prophet escaped.  An orthodox
Mussulman holds the spider in great reverence,
and many eastern poets have sung its praise.

"From Mecca to Medina fled our Lord;
   The horseman followed fast.
Into a cave to shun their murderous rage,
   Muhammad, weary, passed.

"Quoth Abu Bekr, 'If they see, we die!'
   Quoth Ebu Foheir, 'Away!'
The guide Abdallah said, 'The sand is deep;
   Those footmarks will betray.'

"Then spake our Lord, 'We are not four, but five;
   'He who protects is here.
Come!  Al-Muhaimin now will blind their eyes;
   Enter, and have no fear.'

"The band drew nigh; one of the Koseish cried,
   'Search ye out yonder cleft;
I see the print of sandalled feet which turn
   Thither, upon the left!'

"But when they drew unto the cavern's mouth,
   Lo! at its entering-in
A ring-necked desert dove sate on her eggs;
   The mate cooed soft within.

"And right athwart the shadow of the cave
   A spider's web was spread;
The creature hung upon her net at watch;
   Unbroken was each thread."

The spider, like the serpent, is sensitive to the charms of music. A violinist who practiced many hours a day always in the same room, noticed that a spider had woven a web on the ceiling and that so soon as the violin sounded the creature made its appearance. Slowly the spider would descend by an almost invisible thread until it reached the instrument, where it would remain until the practicing was over. A warm friendship grew up between musician and spider which was highly creditable to both.

Many animals are so useful and affectionate that we are unwilling to believe they perish in death. The poor Indian

" Thinks, admitted to that equal sky,
His faithful dog shall bear him company ";

and our own Agassiz taught that both man and beast enter upon a future life.[2] Leibnitz, by his doctrine of eternal monads, opened the door of heaven to all living creatures, from the animalcula in a stagnant pool to the eagle upon the lofty crag, and from the insect basking in the sunlight to deep-sea fish and scarlet anemone under the waves of the Atlantic. Coleridge held to the same opinion, and defended it with logical skill and poetical power. Tradition admits to the joys of Paradise the dog that guarded the Seven Sleepers.

Seven Ephesian youths, Constantine, Diony-

[2] Contributions to the Natural History of the United States, vol. i, pages 64, 65.

sius, John, Maximin, Malchus, Martinian or
Marcian, and Serapion,[3] flying from persecution, hid in a cave at Mount Celion. They were
pursued, discovered and walled in, but their lives
were preserved by a miraculous slumber of one
hundred and ninety-six years.[4] During all that
time their dog, Katmir,[5] stood without food,
guarding their sacred sleep. The legend is of
great antiquity and found in well-nigh every
written tongue; it occurs in the Syriac, Latin,
and Scandinavian; the best accounts are in the
Koran, xviii, entitled " The ' 'e Revealed at
Mecca "; " The Golden Legends ' of Jacques de
Voragine; the " De Gloria Martyrum," i. 9, of
Gregory of Tours; and " The Oriental Tales "
of Comte de Caylus (1743). The story of the
Dog of the Seven Sleepers is here condensed
from notes in Sale's " Koran ":

" Their dog had followed them as they passed by
him when they fled to the cave, and they drove him
away; whereupon God caused him to speak, and he
said, ' I love those who are dear unto God; go to
sleep, therefore, and I will guard you.' [6] But some

[3] In the "Oriental Tales" the names are: Jemlikha,
Mekchilnia, Mechlima, Merlima, Debermouch, Charnouch,
and the shepherd Keschetiarch.

[4] The Koran says, "Three hundred years and nine years
over "; Gregory of Tours says the sleep was about two
hundred and thirty years.

[5] Some think it was at Rakîm. The name is used as a
talisman to preserve women in childbirth, and to protect
sailors.

[6] In "The Oriental Tales" the dog speaks thus: "You
go to seek God; but am not I also a child of God?"

say it was a dog belonging to a shepherd who followed them, and that the dog followed the shepherd. The Mohammedans have great respect for this dog, and allow him a place in Paradise with some other favorite brutes; and they have a sort of proverb which they use in speaking of a covetous person, that he would not throw a bone to the dog of the Seven Sleepers."

The story of Rip Van Winkle is like that of the Seven Sleepers in that it is a tale of prolonged slumber. Epimenides is undoubtedly the original of Washington Irving's hero, so admirably rendered by our once favorite actor, Jefferson. Epimenides slept fifty-seven years.

Good-natured tradition has opened the " Golden Gate " to other animals,— as the ram which Abraham sacrificed instead of his son (Genesis xii, 13; Koran, xxxvii). Balaam's ass entered Paradise, as did the ass upon which Jesus rode into Jerusalem, and the mare upon which Mohammed ascended to heaven. Goethe has a little poem upon this subject called " The Favored Beasts," a rendition of which may be found in " Flowers of Song from Many Lands." There is also a very delightful article on " The Seven Sleepers' Paradise beside the Loire," by Moncure D. Conway, in " Harper's Magazine " for September, 1880.

The future life of beasts naturally leads to the consideration of animals as symbols.

The fish, sometimes a dolphin, was the earliest Christian emblem. *Ichthus,* the Greek for fish, contains a name and a creed. Take the word apart:

'Ι-ησοῦς ....................... Jesus.

Χ-ριστὸς ....................... Christ.

Θ-εοῦ ......................... God's.

'Υ-ιὸς ......................... Son.

Σ-ωτήρ ...................... Saviour.

'Ιησοῦς Χριστὸς Θεοῦ υἱὸς σωτήρ (*Jesus Christus Dei filius Salvator*), or (taking the initials only) *ichthus*, fish.

During early persecutions the figure of a fish was used to signify Jesus Christ and the Christian faith. It distinguished Christian graves from pagan, and while it was of the deepest spiritual significance to the believer, it meant nothing to the uninitiated. The fish typified the call of the apostles, " I will make you fishers of men," and the miraculous draught of fishes (John xxi). The fish was also an emblem of baptism.

The fish was used in India and the East as a sacred symbol. The first Avatâra of Vishnu was in the form of a fish. His Avatâras are ten, and are generally given thus: 1. The fish. 2. The tortoise. 3. The boar. 4. The man-lion. 5. The dwarf. 6. The Parasu-Rama. 7. The Râmachandra. 8. The Krishna and Balarâma. 9. The Buddha. 10. The Kalki, or Kalkin Avatâra. The first Avatâra was in the form of a golden fish with a single horn, ten thousand miles long.

The fish has always been associated with myths, legends and romance. We read in Herodotus that Polycrates, advised to cast what he most highly prized into the sea, threw therein an engraved gem of great value. Soon after, a fish was brought to his table, and in it was the same gem. A curious legend is told about the Glasgow arms. A queen, having fallen deeply in love with a common soldier, presented him with a ring given her by her husband. The king, having discovered her illicit attachment, took the ring from the soldier while he was asleep and threw it into the sea, and then demanded it of the queen. In the utmost alarm she hastened to St. Kentigern and made full confession. The saint went to the Clyde, and there caught a salmon in whose mouth was the ring, and thus saved the queen's character. A codfish plays the same part in the story of the arms of Dame Rebecca Berry, wife of Sir Thomas Elton, Stratford-le-Bow, and now seen in St. Dunstan's Church, Stepney.

The lamb was a symbol of the Saviour: " *Ecce Agnus Dei* " (John i, 29).

The lion was a symbol of Christ and an emblem of the tribe of Judah. " Judah is a lion's whelp . . . he couched as a lion, and as an old lion ; who shall rouse him up? " (Genesis xlix, 9). St. Jerome makes the king of beasts stand for solitude,— the hermit's sign. The lion was also a symbol of St. Mark, because, according to tradition, the cubs are still-born, and at the end of three days brought to life by the breath of the sire. The Son of God was restored to life on the third day by the breath of God the Father. St. Mark is called, for obvious reasons, " the historian of the resurrection." Dante represents the lion as significant of ambition. When he began his first ascent he was confronted first by a panther (pleasure), and after that by a lion (ambition).

> " A lion came,
> With head erect, and hunger mad."

Una was attended by a lion. The story is that Una, in her search for St. George, became weary and sat by the road to rest, when a furious lion rushed from the thicket. On approaching her the lion was charmed by her beauty, and became as docile as a dog. The creature followed her wherever she went. Spenser relates the story in the " Faerie Queene " (I, iii, 42; 1590). Some say the story is an allegory of the Reformation.

A lion assisted Sir Geoffrey de Latour in his conflict with the Saracens, and was drowned in attempting to follow the ship in which he left the Holy Land. Sir Edwain de Gallis was served by a faithful lion.

Many great kings and gallant knights have had their names associated with the king of beasts. Henry, Duke of Bavaria, was called " The Lion." Richard I was called " Cœur de Lion," because he is said to have destroyed a lion by plucking out its heart; others say he had himself the heart of a lion. Louis VIII of France was called " The Lion " because born under the sign Leo. Gustavus Adolphus was known as " The Lion of the North," and Arioch al Asser was " The Lion of Assyria." The Golden Lion was the emblem of Assyria:

" Where is th' Assyrian lion's golden hide,
  That all the East once grasped in lordly paw?
Where the great Persian bear whose swelling pride
  The lion's self tore out with rav'nous jaw? "
          — *Fletcher,* " The Purple Island," vii.

The lion is now one of the emblems of England, and in company with the unicorn appears on the English coat-of-arms. The Cape of Good Hope was once called Leão do Mar,— Lion of the Sea. The king of the forest usually stands for all that is noble and generous, but the apostle Peter most effectually guards the beast against pride when he bids us, " Be sober, be vigilant; because your adversary, the devil, as a roaring lion walketh about, seeking whom he may devour."

The pelican was a symbol of our Lord's suffering. The pelican wounds her own breast to feed her young with her heart's blood.

The hart stands for spiritual aspiration. " As the hart panteth after the water brooks, so panteth my soul after thee, O God." (Psalm xlii, 1.)

The peacock is Juno's bird, and signified immortality; it now stands for pride.

The dragon and the serpent are the heathen world and sin. The devil is called a dragon and a serpent. Phineas Fletcher, in " The Purple Island," calls the enemy of our race a red dragon. There are all kinds of dragons,— red, white, blue (the blue devil — Hypochondria), black, yellow, etc. Ahrenian was a dragon slain by Mithra ("Persian Mythology"). The dragon Dahak had three heads and was destroyed by Thraetana-Yacna. St. Romain, of Rouen, slew La Gargouille, the dragon of the Seine. Apollo killed the Python. St. Martha destroyed Tarasque. Cadmus killed the dragon that guarded the fountain of Areia and planted its teeth; from them sprang the Sparti. Jason killed the dragon which protected the golden fleece. St. George killed the dragon with which his name is associated, at what is known as the Dragon's Hill (Berkshire) ; but Percy's " Reliques " say in Sylënê, in Libya.

The eagle was the ensign of the Roman legion. Before the Cimbrian war the wolf, horse, and boar shared with the eagle the honor of the national standard; but when Marius declared in favor of " the Roman bird," all other animals disappeared from the colors. Pindar was called " The Theban Eagle." Pierre d'Ailly, the astrologer, was known as " The Eagle of the Doctors of France." Thomas Aquinas is " The Eagle of Divines." The eagle is a symbol of St. John.

The butterfly is the soul. Psyche is represented as " a maiden with butterfly wings."

The ox is a symbol of St. Luke. St. Thomas Aquinas was called by his fellow-students, because of his reserve, " The Ox." The black ox was sacrificed to the infernal gods, and was therefore a sign of ill-fortune; hence the proverb, " The black ox hath trod on his foot."

Animals were punished under the Mosaic and Persian laws. " Surely your blood of your lives will I require; at the hand of every beast will I require it, and at the hand of man; at the hand of every man's brother will I require the life of man." (Genesis ix, 5.) " If an ox gore a man or a woman that they die, then the ox shall be surely stoned and his flesh shall not be eaten, but the owner of the ox shall be quit. But if the ox were wont to push with his horn in time past, and it hath been testified to his owner, and he hath not kept him in, but that he hath killed a man or woman, the ox shall be stoned, and his owner also shall be put to death." (Exodus xxi, 28, 29.)

Later legislation is acquainted with the same custom. A pig was hanged near Laon, June 4, 1094, for killing and eating the babe of a certain cowherd, Jehan Lenfant. A sow and six sucklings were tried for murder, and convicted of having killed Jehan Martin of Savigny. The sow was hanged on the tenth of January, 1457. There being no direct and positive evidence that the sucklings were accessory to or implicated in

the murder, they were released on bail.  On the
second of March, 1552, a pig was sentenced to
death for killing a girl, and the gallows stood on
the spot where the murder occurred.  In 1612
another pig was convicted of destroying a child.
The church has at various times united with the
state in holding animals responsible for crime.
The Bishop of Laon excommunicated caterpillars, using the form of excommunication employed by the Council of Rheims in unchurching
married priests.  Caterpillars were threatened
with ecclesiastical discipline in 1516, and commanded to leave Villenaxe within six days.

It is generally believed that certain animals
occasionally commit suicide.  Goethe tells us, in
" Sorrows of Werther," that naturalists describe " a noble race of horses that instinctively
open a vein with their teeth when heated and
exhausted by a long course in order to breathe
more freely ": *credat Judæus Apella*.  We have
greater faith in Mr. G. Bidie's account of the
suicide of the common black scorpion of Southern India:

" One morning a servant brought to me a very
large specimen of the black scorpion, which, having stayed out too long in its nocturnal rambles, had
apparently got bewildered at daybreak and been
unable to find its way home.  To keep it safe, the
creature was at once put into a glazed entomological
case.  Having a few leisure moments in the course
of the afternoon, I thought I would see how my
prisoner was getting on; and to have a better view

of it the case was placed on a window in the rays of a hot sun. The light and heat seemed to irritate it very much, and this recalled to my mind a story which I had read somewhere, that a scorpion, on being surrounded with fire, had committed suicide. I hesitated about subjecting my pet to such a terrible ordeal, but taking a common botanical lens, I focused the rays of the sun on its back. The moment this was done it began to run hurriedly about the case, hissing and spitting in a very fierce way. This experiment was repeated some four or five times with like results, but on trying it once again, the scorpion turned up its tail and plunged the sting, quick as lightning, into its back. The infliction of the wound was followed by a sudden escape of fluid, and a friend standing by me called out, ' See, it has stung itself; it is dead.' And sure enough, in less than half a minute life was quite extinct."

We are forcibly reminded of Byron's description of the suicide of the scorpion and the power of a guilty conscience:

> " The mind that broods o'er guilty woes
> Is like the scorpion girt with fire:
> In circle narrowing as it glows,
> The flames around their captive close;
> Till inly scorched by thousand throes,
> And inly maddening in her ire,
> One and sole relief she knows,—
> The sting she nourished for her foes,
> Whose venom never yet was vain,
> Gives but one pang, and cures all pain,
> She darts into her desperate brain.
> So do the dark in soul expire,

Or live like scorpion girt by fire;
So writhes the mind remorse hath riven,
Unfit for earth, undoomed for heaven,
Darkness above, despair beneath,
Around it flame, within it death."

Beasts of burden are often beasts of romance. Camel, elephant, ox, and horse are as intimately associated with literature and religion as with the ordinary duties and everyday life of man. What would the history of Arabia be without the camel,— that " ship of the desert," and the fascinating theme of many an oriental song? How useful is the great, clumsy, loose-jointed creature, striding over the sand and bearing on its huge hump an entire household! In olden times the animal was described as patient, but every traveler knows that patience is a virtue it seldom possesses. Dr. Kitto writes:

"Of all the animals which have been domesticated for higher purposes than to serve mankind merely as food, the camel is, past all doubt, the most churlish, irascible, revengeful, and self-willed. We have heard of strong attachments between man and all other domestic animals, but never between a man and his camel. Of all the creatures promoted to be man's companions in travel and in rest, no one so unloving and unloved exists. Its very countenance, which the inexperienced call patient, is the very impersonation of malice and ill-nature,— even when its eyes are not kindled up into active spite, and when its mouth does not quiver with burning rage. Even among themselves quarrels are frequent; and he who has been summoned by their sharp and bitter cries to witness a camel-fight will not easily forget the scene."

Norman Duncan printed some time ago, in "Harper's Magazine," this somewhat comical description of the ugliness and viciousness of even the most promising kind of a camel:

"There had come to us from Hebron a Turkish soldier riding a young camel, whose virtues he boasted, and, indeed, exhibited: the clean limbs, the stride, and the docility of the beast. It seemed a worthy camel; a camel of excellent humor and of distinguished promise; and it was much coveted by the way. At night, as the custom is, the man was used to sleeping close to his beast, the winds being chill; but now, at Rafieh, while the mules were unloading and the cook was coaxing his fire, he tethered the camel, flung his saddle on the sand, and went off to the mud barracks to hobnob with the Egyptian frontier guard. I was presently alarmed by the cook's outcry and a rising excitement in camp; the docile camel was viciously trampling his master's saddle, stupidly believing that he was engaged in his master's murder,— a savage and dreadful attack, a rearing and heavy plunge.

" ' What! ' ejaculated the Turk, when he was informed of this. ' Have I cherished a man-killer? '

" The camel was heartily beaten and reduced to his knees, whereupon his doubled fore leg was tied so that he could rise but with difficulty, and we withdrew to observe his behavior, for his master was not yet convinced. Rise he did, a persistent, silent effort, and cautiously approached the saddle,

which he attacked as savagely as before, but now
with one hoof.

"'I have had a narrow escape,' said the Turk;
'my camel would have killed me to-night. By God
and Mohammed the Prophet of God!' he swore,
'I will put the beast in the bazar at Beersheba.'

"I inquired concerning the future owner's pros-
pect of long life.

"'He is in God's hands,' was the answer."

Notwithstanding all that may be said and is
said against the camel's disposition, oriental
poets delight to dress the creature up in all the
music and romance of song. There must be some
amiable trait in the camel's nature, or we should
not find such praiseful verses written by men
who knew whereof they were writing. Thus an
Eastern poet sings:

"The camel's table in the waste is spread;
  He gladly picks a meal from out the dirt;
One pleasant herb is all he asks for bread,
  And one sour weed suffices for dessert."

A Persian couplet runs in the same direction:

"With strength and patience all his grievous loads
    are borne,
And from the world's rose-bed he only asks a thorn."

The elephant also has received a large share
of man's attention. It has fared even better than
the horse,— man's delight in every age and
country. The elephant has long been an object

of worship in the East, and the kings of Ava and Siam, desiring to exalt themselves, have assumed the title, " King of the White Elephant."　So we read in a native poem:

" The rare white elephant is widely worshipped in Siam,
　As a fit representative of the unseen I Am."

Had I been born a poet, I should never have tired, for instance, so it seems to me, of the elephant symbol.　It is so comprehensive, so intelligent, so versatile.　Elephants do most things that men do, and many that men cannot.　Every one of them is a whole Cleopatra's-needle-full of hieroglyphics and significances.　They knock down the walls of houses with their foreheads and pick up pins with their trunks.　One elephant bumping against another knocks it over, yet elephants have been taught to dance on the tight-rope.　It seems to have most of the virtues, in ordinary times, of an honest man; at others, it develops a depth of cunning malignity that the entire Newgate Calendar cannot match.

" Behold the castle-bearing elephant
That wants nor bulk, nor doth his greatnesse want
An equal strength.　Behold his massie bones
Like barres of iron; like congealèd stones
His knotty sinews are; him have I made
And given him natural weapons for his ayde.
High mountains beare his food, the shady boughs
His cover are, great rivers are his troughes,

Whose deep carouses would to standers-by
Seem as a watering to draw Jordan drie.
What skilful huntsman can with strength outdare
    him?
Or with what engines can a man ensnare him?"

So writes a poet of earlier days; and after him
many poets refer to the " elephant endorsed with
towers," the " castled elephant," the " towered
elephant," and so forth, omitting to remember
how swine once wrought havoc in the " embattled
front of elephants proud-turreted." The story
is a simple one, and better perhaps in the original
old English. Alexander, invading India, was
told that elephants were terrified by pigs, and
finding opposed to him a formidable array of
" olyphauntes berynge castelles of trees on
theyr bakkes and knyghtes in ye castelles for ye
batayle," the great Emathian ordered up a drove
of swine to the front of the Greek army, and the
" jarrynge of ye pygges " upset the " olyphauntes " altogether, for we read that they began " to
fle eche one and keste down ye castelles and slewe
ye knyghtes. By this meane Alysandre had ye
vyctorie."

The elephant is a creature of colossal bulk,
yet it is the most gently docile of man's servants.
Though of vast strength, it is curiously sensitive
to small annoyances. It detests the squeaking
of mice. Mosquitoes infuriate it. Thus Spenser's elephant, assailed by an ant, is one of the
poet's types of the " World's Vanity."

There is a beautiful story of an old elephant engaged in a battle on the plains of India. The creature was a standard-bearer and carried on its huge back the royal ensign, the rallying post of the Poona host. At the beginning of the fight it lost its master. The mahout, or driver, had just given the word to halt, when he received a fatal wound and fell to the ground, where he lay under a heap of the slain. The obedient elephant stood still while the battle closed around it and the standard that it carried. The creature never stirred a foot, refusing to advance or retire as the conflict became hotter and fiercer, until the Mahrattas, seeing the standard still flying steadily in its place, refused to believe they were beaten, and rallied again and again around their colors. All the while, amid the din of battle the patient animal stood, straining its ears to catch the sound of a voice it would never hear again. At length the tide of conquest left the field deserted. The Mahrattas swept on in pursuit of the flying foe, but the elephant, like a rock, stood there with the dead and dying around him and the ensign proudly waving in its place. For three days and nights the animal remained where its master had given the command to halt. Neither bribe nor threat could move it. At last they sent to a village one hundred miles away, and brought the mahout's little son. The animal seemed then to remember how the driver had sometimes given his authority to the little child, and immediately, with all the shattered trappings clinging as it went, paced quietly and slowly away.

The ox, though highly esteemed, has not been so fortunate as either camel or elephant. Under the Mosaic law the animal might be punished with death. The creature was peculiarly unfortunate in the matter of sacrifice. Solomon slew twenty-two thousand oxen at one time as a sacrifice, and on another occasion seven hundred oxen shared the fate of seven thousand sheep on the smoking altars of Israel.

The horse (not the New York omnibus horse, but the real eastern animal, the " stallion shod with fire ") has had a good time in this changing and fickle world. Kings, nobles, poets, and painters have vied with each other in celebrating the virtues of the horse, and many of the most beautiful poems are in honor of " the desert darling."

> " Mahlek Ben Essedin sings,
> Horses are birds without wings."

Many volumes of absorbing interest might be written about the horse — its speed, sagacity, usefulness, and beauty. Bucephalus, Alexander's horse, was painted by Apelles with such consummate skill that a living horse neighed at the portrait, so the credulous romancers of long ago tell us, believing it to be alive. The real horse cost the Emperor a sum equal in these days to about $17,500, and was so beloved by its royal master that he named a city in its honor; and when it died at the age of thirty, Alexander, it is said, wept bitterly and refused to be comforted.

The horses of the sun were Brontê (thunder), Amethēa (no loiterer), Aethon (fiery red), Pyrasis (fire), Lampos (shining like a lamp), and Philogea (effulgence). The steeds of Aurora were Phaeton (shining one,) and Aleraxas (the Greek numeral for 365 — the number of days in the year). Pegasus was the winged horse of the muses whereon the venturesome Bellerophon essayed to ride to heaven; he was thrown from its back, and the horse, reaching the sky without its rider, was there changed into the constellation that bears its name. It was through a wooden image of the animal Troy fell. The Brass Horse, owned by Cambuscan, King of Tartary, figures extensively in sacred and secular romance. On Merlin's wooden horse Don Quixote rode when he performed so many wonderful exploits. In the " Arabian Nights " we have an enchanted horse. Darius was indebted for his kingdom to a horse. Al Borak (lightning) was a creature, part horse, eagle, man, and precious stone. It had a human face and voice, a horse's head, eagle's wings, and eyes of jacinths. It was commissioned by Gabriel to carry Mahommed to heaven.

It was a horse that made Darius Hystaspes king of Persia. There was a dispute as to who should be the king of that country. The most powerful men of the kingdom determined to assemble on horseback, and it was agreed that the person whose horse neighed first should become the sovereign. The groom of Darius Hystaspes heard of the arrangement, and at once he took a mare to the spot and allowed his master's horse to see the animal. The next day at sunrise all assembled, and of course the horse, remembering the mare, began to neigh vigorously. Not only did the creature neigh, but it indulged in various interesting antics which so surprised the horsemen that at once its owner was declared to be the king.

In a delightful little book by Rev. W. R. Alger, called " The Poetry of the Orient," there is an exceedingly felicitous stanza describing the delicate step of the horse :

> " Hâymour, the peerless chestnut steed
> Of Hussein, Sheik of El Madeen,
> Was said to be so light of foot
> That on a woman's bosom he
> Could dance, nor leave a bruise behind."

This peculiarity has been the fruitful theme of many a poem and of many a story in prose of absorbing interest, both in our own and in other languages. A soldier in the front rank of a German cavalry regiment was thrown while the troops were manœuvring; all the horses passed over him, but not one of them, it is said, trod upon him.

Antar, describing the mare of Shedad, the famous Jirwet, writes :

" Shedad's mare was called Jirwet, whose like was unknown. Kings negotiated with him for her, but he would not part from her, and would accept no offer or bribe for her; and thus he used to talk of her in his verses: —' Seek not to purchase my horse, for Jirwet is not to be bought or borrowed. I am a strong castle on her back; and in her bound are glory and greatness. I would not part from her were strings of camels to come to me, with their drivers following them. She flies with the wind without wings, and tears up the waste and the desert. I will keep her for the day of calamities, and she will rescue me when the battle-dust rises.' "

In the same vein writes Shakespeare: —" I will not change my horse with any that treads on four pasterns. When I bestride him I soar, I am a hawk; he trots the air; the earth sings when he touches it."

The value of a good horse has not decreased even in these days of automobiles, air-ships, and self-propelling vehicles of every kind. Alexander paid $17,500 for Bucephalus, but that was not a large amount for a king to give; modern racing horses cost more, as may be seen by glancing at the following list of prices: Kentucky, $40,000; Norfolk, $15,000; Lexington, $15,000; Blackwood, $30,000; Jay Gould, $30,000; Dexter, $33,000; Lady Thorne, $30,000; Goldsmith Maid, $20,000; Kingfisher, $15,000; Gleneig, $10,000; Smuggler, $15,000; Startle, $20,000; Jim Irving, $30,000; Prospero, $20,000; Rosalind, $20,000; Lulu, $20,000; Clara G., $25,000;

Happy Medium, $20,000; Pocahontas, $35,900; Auburn Horse, $13,000; Edward Everett, $20,-000; Judge Fullerton, $20,000; Mambrino Bertie, $10,000; Socrates, $20,000; George P. Daniels, $8,000; George Palmer, $51,000; Mambrino Pilot, $12,000; J. G. Brown, $12,000; Flora Temple (too old to run, sold for a brood mare) $8,000. The owner of Tom Bowling refused an offer of $25,000; $30,000 was offered for Basset; $50,000 was offered for Woodford Mambrino, and $20,000 for Thorndale.

In England horse-racing, even more popular than in America, was early encouraged and patronized by the British rulers: Charles I, Cromwell, Charles II, William III, and Queen Anne were exceedingly fond of the sport. The racecourse was the delight of ancient Greeks and Romans; thus we find Archias, the friend of Cicero, setting forth in classic verse the sorrows of an old race-horse:

" Me, at Alfæus wreath'd, and twice the theme
Of heralds, by Castalia's sacred stream,—
Me, Isthmus' and Æmæa's trumpet-tongue
Hailed fleets as wingèd storms!— I then was young.
Alas! wreaths loathe me now: and eld hath found
An outcast trundling mill-stones round and round."

The celebrated Flying Childers was bred in 1715 by the Duke of Devonshire. He surpassed every other horse of the period, running three and a half miles in six minutes and forty seconds, and never losing a race. From him were produced four hundred and ninety-seven winners, and he realized stakes to the amount of £200,-000. Eclipse succeeded Flying Childers. West Australian ran two and a half miles in four minutes and twenty-seven seconds, the fastest time then on record, at the race for the Ascot cup in 1854. "The Perfect Horse," so felicitously described by Parson Murray, is pictured on the pages of hundreds of authors, ancient and modern. The horse is the popular animal of the world. So far back as 1496, only four years after the discovery of our continent, we find in "Wynkyn de Worde" the fifteen qualifications of a competent horse:

"A good horse sholde have three propyrtees of a man, three of a woman, three of a foxe, three of a haare and three of an asse. Of a *man*, bolde, prewde and hardye. Of a *woman*, fayre-breasted, faire of heere, and easy to move. Of a *foxe*, a fair tayle, short eers, with a good tratte. Of a *haare*, a grate eye, a dry head, and well rennynge. Of an *asse*, hygge chynn, a flat legge, and a good hoof."

The average age of the horse is from twenty-five to thirty years; but the animal has been known to reach sixty and even seventy years. Flying Childers lived to the age of twenty-six, and Eclipse was twenty-five years old at the time of his death. The heart of the latter horse weighed fourteen pounds. Christie White, in his "History of the Turf," thinks the uncommon

spirit and courage of the creature are explained
by the size of its heart.

Elephants have been known to live more than
four hundred and fifty years. A writer in one
of the English magazines calls attention to the
Indian Ajax. The story runs that "when
Alexander the Great had conquered Porus, King
of India, he took a great elephant which had
fought valiantly for the king, and naming it
Ajax, dedicated it to the sun, and let it go with
this inscription: 'Alexander, the son of Jupiter, dedicated Ajax to the Sun.' The elephant was found with the inscription three hundred and fifty years later."

Whales have been supposed to live from three
hundred to four hundred years, but Cuvier is
sure they sometimes live to be over a thousand
years old. The average age of the ordinary
tortoise is one hundred years; one died in England aged one hundred and twenty-eight years,
another at two hundred and twenty years of
age. But if it be true that "he lives longest
who serves most," one good horse will outlive
an entire menagerie.

Without doubt the horse is the most useful
animal in the world. And yet the horse has not
been without its troubles and distresses. Careless
shoeing, the bearing-rein, the blinders, a cold bit
on a frosty morning, overloading, and abuse are
some of the bitter ingredients in the life of many
a horse.

" I sometimes think," writes Sir Arthur Helps,
" that it was a misfortune for the world that the
horse was ever subjugated.  The horse is the
animal that has been the worst treated by man,
and its subjugation has not been altogether a
gain to mankind.  The oppressions it has aided
in were, from the earliest ages, excessive.  To it
we owe much of the rapine of ' the Dark Ages.'
And I have a great notion that it has been the
main instrument of the bloodiest warfare.  I
wish men had their own cannon to drag up-hill.
Men would rebel at that, I think.  And a com-
mander obliged to be on foot throughout the
campaign would very soon get tired of war."

All that Sir Arthur Helps has said was true
at the time he said it, but now comparatively
little heavy work in dragging instruments of war
to the scene of action is performed by horses.
The Germans have taught the world to use rail-
roads and automobiles constructed for the purpose of moving guns and the heavier munitions
of destruction.

All grades of horses have, however, been made
to experience man's inhumanity; the cart-horses
of England are kicked and beaten; cab-horses
are overworked; in France, worn-out horses are
driven into the leech-swamps; wounded army
horses are left on the battle fields to die of thirst
and agony; and race-horses are often urged to
death.  After a steeple-chase in Liverpool, not
long ago, five horses had to be killed because per-
manently injured.  Three had their backs broken,

and two had their legs snapped. In the market-place of Atri a large bell was hung that could be heard in all the country around for many miles, and whenever a man was wronged he might demand justice by ringing; but as Abruzzo and its little villages were peaceful and law-abiding, the rope was not often used. At last a vine covered it, and no one remembered where it was. A story tells us that an old and ill-treated horse, turned out to die, grazing by the roadside, discovered the vine and began to eat the leaves and tendrils; and as he tugged at them, the bell began to sound. The poor beast had appealed for justice, and at once a proclamation of the king brought relief. It might be a good thing if bells were hung on every highway for the benefit, not only of injured horses, but of the larger animals of various kinds.

" One afternoon, as in that sultry clime
It is the custom in the summer-time,
With bolted doors and window-shutters closed,
The inhabitants of Atri slept or dozed,
When suddenly upon their senses fell
The loud alarm of the accusing bell!
The Syndic started from his deep repose,
Turned on his couch, and listened, and then rose
And donned his robes, and with reluctant pace
Went panting forth into the market-place,
Where the great bell upon its cross-beam swung,
Reiterating with persistent tongue,
In half-articulate jargon, the old song:
' Some one hath done a wrong, hath done a wrong!'

But ere he reached the belfry's light arcade,
He saw, or thought he saw, beneath its shade,
No shape of human form of woman born,
But a poor steed dejected and forlorn,
Who, with uplifted head and eager eye,
Was tugging at the vines of briony.
' Domeneddio! ' cried the Syndic straight,
' This is the Knight of Atri's steed of state!
He calls for justice, being sore distressed,
And pleads his cause as loudly as the best.' "

*— Longfellow.*

Writes the humane Ruskin: " There is in every animal's eye a dim image and gleam of humanity, a flash of strange light through which their life looks out and up to our great mystery of command over them, and claiming the fellowship of the creature, if not of the soul." We are partakers with the animals of a common nature, and that common nature should teach us kindness and mercy.

In the " Fortnightly Review " for August, 1881, may be found an exceedingly interesting article on " English and Eastern Horses " by Sir Francis H. Doyle, from which a single paragraph is selected:

" The Duke of Devonshire was in the habit of buying annually some of Mr. Childers's ' young things '; on one occasion a dispute arose between them as to whether the sum due from the duke to the squire was to be calculated in guineas or pounds. ' Throw in,' exclaimed the duke, ' that ugly little white-faced devil looking over the gate yonder, and

guineas it shall be.' No sooner said than done:
Childers went with the lot to Chatsworth, and was
there used as a hack. Returning one day with letters across the moor, he passed the exercising
ground of the duke's accepted racers. The boys
jeered at him as he went by, crying out, ' Come
now, let us see what that wonderful high-bred nag
of yours can do.' This invitation was straightway
accepted, and the curiosity of Childers's critics satisfied at once. It is needless to add that the horse
was immediately put into training, and the Chatsworth post-pony found himself at once transformed
into the pride and terror of Newmarket. His comparatively small size was considered at first, I suppose, to unfit him for racing. The same thing happened with Gimcrack afterwards,— some such accident disclosed his superiority, and the wondering
groom rushed to tell his master that the ' little crip-
ple colt could beat them all.' Between Childers
and Eclipse little more than forty-five years inter-
vened, and during all this time, whenever superior
power was shown or imagined, the regular formula
was, ' This is the best horse since Childers.' That
was said of Lath, foaled in 1732; of the Duke of
Devonshire's Atlas, foaled in 1752; and doubtless
of many others in the excitement of some unexpected
victory. But after the advent of Eclipse this formula dropped. For the first time men recognized
a race-horse equal, or if not absolutely equal to the
typical Flyer, yet good enough, in Cambridge
phraseology, to be bracketed with him."

A reporter of the " New Orleans Times-Demo-
crat " says:

"During a chat with the foreman of the street-car stables, James E. Barry, the subject turned to a discussion of the characteristics of horses and mules. He has been a close student of both, and the result of his experience is that the mule is entitled to the higher rank in sagacity.

"Mr. Barry went on to say that the superiority of the mule is shown in his absolute refusal to put his foot in a hole in a bridge or crossing. Horses seem to endeavor to find a hole, if there is any lying around, and break their legs. This a mule will not do, nor can he be forced to advance if he thinks there is danger. 'The horse,' said Mr. Barry, 'has more courage; the mule more sense.'

"It has been an amusing study at one of the stables to watch a sly, mischievous little mule that is rather too fond of liberty. It seems that the mules are fastened to their stalls by a chain, on the end of which is a cross-piece of iron, which is slipped lengthwise through a hole in the stall, and when extended crosswise over the hole, prevents the chain being withdrawn. This mule, when standing in his manger, with his teeth and tongue manages to slip the cross-piece attached to the chain out of the hole, and then cautiously backs out the full length of the chain, and surveys the field. If there be a stable-man in sight, he reënters the stall and waits demurely till the coast is clear, when he comes out quickly and makes a dash for liberty and the street. Sometimes it requires all hands to catch him and bring him back.

"In the yard of one of the down-town stables there is a post to which four mules are generally tied after being curried. There was recently one mule there that was fond of slipping his chain-tag

through the ring in the post, and then, to allow
his mates to share in his liberty, he loosened the
others. This he did so often he had to be closely
watched."

Among other interesting items in natural history is the following excerpt from a paper that
has for a long time represented the horse-market
and the racing fraternity:

"My attention was called recently to the peculiar actions of an orphan colt, which perhaps are
worth recording. When the colt was two weeks old,
its mother died. Previous to her death, she was
covered with a blanket. When it was apparent she
could not live, the blanket was thrown over the fence
and the mare removed, but the colt left in the enclosure. The colt, at first very much exercised, ran
up and down the yard neighing; but when it came
near the blanket on the fence, it stopped, smelled
of it, and seemed pacified. It evidently considered
the blanket its mother, and has continued to do so.
If the blanket is removed from the fence, the colt
becomes restless, runs about neighing, but is recon-
ciled again by the sight of the blanket. If any one
throws the blanket over his back, the colt will follow the bearer all about. It will watch the blanket,
and will not wander far away from it; and when it
wishes to rest, will go and lie down by it."

Snake-charmers seldom handle reptiles that do
not belong to them. From this one naturally
draws the conclusion that in most cases the fangs
have been removed. Yet it cannot be that the
fangs are always taken out, for occasionally an

experienced charmer is killed by one of his own
snakes. Well-nigh every kind of serpent is more
or less fascinated by monotonous tunes, by gentle and continuous strokes along its back, and by
warmth. Cobras and nearly every kind of reptile will respond to certain notes which the na-
tives of southern and eastern countries sound
with a reed-pipe. They will, as soon as they
hear the low and unvarying vibrations, creep
from their hiding-places and approach the
charmer. So long as they catch those sounds,
they will follow and obey the man who makes
them. The reptile can from the first be made to
dance, but I must doubt whether the so-called
dancing is anything more than an expression of
uneasiness or alarm. Cobras are capable of
domestication. In the East some of the most
vicious reptiles are trained to perform the same
part that dogs perform for us. They can be so
educated that their owners may trust them as
protectors. They can be trained to follow their
master by day and to guard his home and family by night. I am well aware that what I am
saying will appear to many of my readers a wild
fabrication, but it is sustained by excellent
authority. If any one is moved by this paper
to follow the matter further, I take pleasure in
calling his attention to Dr. George J. Romanes's
excellent book on " Animal Intelligence."

The charmers of reptiles not only use the reed-
pipe, the music of which seems almost to hypno-
tize the creatures, but at times they accompany

the pipe with a humming sound made with the lips, and, on occasions, they sing to the snake in low, monotonous tones a song addressed to his snakeship. The sentiment of the song is well set forth in the following lines by Sir Edwin Arnold:

## SONG OF THE SNAKE-CHARMER

" Come forth, O Snake!  Come forth, O glittering
      Snake!
O shining, silent, deadly Nâg! appear;
Dance to the music that we make,
  This serpent-song so sweet and clear,
  Blown on the beaded gourd so clear,
    So soft and clear.

" O dread Lord Snake! come forth and spread thy
      hood,
And drink the milk and suck the eggs; and show
Thy tongue; and own the tune is good:
  Hear, Maharaj! how hard we blow!
  Ah, Maharaj! for thee we blow;
    See how we blow!

" Great Uncle Snake! creep forth and dance to-
      day!
This music is the music snakes love best.
Taste the warm, white, new milk; and play,
  Standing erect, with fangs at rest;
  Dancing on end, sharp fangs at rest,
    Fierce fangs at rest.

" Ah, wise Lord Nâg! thou comest! — fear thou
      not!
We make salaam to thee, the Serpent-king!

Draw forth thy folds, knot after knot;
  Dance, Master! while we softly sing;
  Dance, Serpent! while we play and sing,
    We play and sing.


" Dance, dreadful King! whose kisses strike men
      dead;
Dance this side, mighty Snake; the milk is here!
    [*They seize the cobra by the neck.*]
Ah, *shabash!* pin his angry head!
  Thou fool! this nautch shall cost thee dear;
  Wrench forth his fangs! this piping clear,
    It costs thee dear!' "


**Dr.** Arthur Stradling, surgeon on board the British man-of-war Elba, undertook to test the bite of a rattlesnake on his own person when treated with antidotes. The doctor shut himself up in his cabin after midnight with ligatures, ammonia, nitric acid, brandy, and the serpent, *crotalus horridus.*

The snake was a small one, with but two rattles, but lively and not at all inclined to lend himself to the cause of science. When the doctor introduced his gloved hand into the box, proposing to be bitten on the fleshless part of the wrist, the snake sprang out at the other arm and inflicted two punctures, leaving the fang in one.

**Dr.** Stradling shut the snake up, pulled out the fang with forceps, and sat down to write out his sensations, and to apply his remedies. He had no sensations and applied no remedies.

About four hours later he suddenly perceived a lump rising on his arm, and turned to the table to get the nitric acid, when he became dizzy and fell on his cot insensible. There he was found an hour or two later, paralyzed in the lower extremities, his breath scarcely perceptible, and his eyes fixed and glassy. Frightful convulsions followed, and it was only after the most vigorous treatment with brandy, sulphuric acid, and ammonia for two days that he rallied. " He was as weak," says his attendant physician, " as a baby, and a mere lay figure for the exhibition of beef-tea, arrow-root, and misplaced sympathy." No good could possibly result from so foolhardy an experiment.

Dr. S. Weir Mitchell, the eminent American specialist in nerve-diseases, made the poison of the rattlesnake and its remedy the subject of years of study and experiment. His monograph on the subject was published by the Smithsonian Institution.

The result of his researches was that no known specific against the bite of this serpent is so certain as whiskey, swallowed until the patient becomes drunk. The hunters and trappers of the lower Alleghanies reached this conclusion long ago without any scientific research. We have heard among them of innumerable instances of bites, none of which proved fatal when whiskey was taken in time and in sufficient quantity, though in cases where the snake was old and its fangs full of venom, the health of the victim was

injured for life. Against the bite of the cop-
perhead (*Trigonocephalus contortrix*), however,
it is said to prove totally ineffectual.

It is certain that the serpents handled by
snake-charmers are in many cases deprived of
their fangs and poison-bags. But there are
cases in which they remain in full possession of
the deadly defense given them by nature. A
gentleman who visited India went with a charmer
to a hole in which a large snake was supposed to
be hiding. The charmer stretched himself close
to the hole, with his lips directly above it. Then
he began to whisper in a low monotonous tone,
" *Burra sap; sabit babut burra* " (Big snake,
your honor, very big). Soon the creature
pushed its tail into view, and the charmer, after
sundry incantations, seized the snake at once, and
brought it forth. It proved to be a deadly
cobra-de-capello, about five feet long. The
thickest part of the creature was eight inches
round. The hood was about five inches in cir-
cumference. While the snake was hissing, it
could be handled with comparative safety.
After a time it was freed, when it at once began
to wriggle toward the charmer with hood expanded and ready to strike. Again the snake
was seized. A tune was softly played to the
creature. This evidently astonished and greatly
pleased its snakeship, and it soon became perfectly tractable and was allowed to go free.
No sooner was it set at liberty than it began
to follow the music, keeping time to every note,

wriggling and jumping in every direction. It
swayed from side to side in perfect accord with
the music. This it did until at last it became
exhausted and subsided.

Again the charmer seized the cobra by the
neck and pressed its mouth open, disclosing the
fangs and poison-bags. This serpent was later
deprived of its fangs, and was trained for a
traveling menagerie.

It may be interesting to know something about
the prices of wild beasts and birds. The prices
change with times and circumstances, but the
following figures will give a fair idea of the average cost of such creatures as usually enter into
the showman's market. A well-trained elephant
will bring from $30,000 to $40,000, though in
Ceylon the beast just captured costs only about
$1,000. A fine lioness costs $6,500, while male
lions bring only from $1,000 to $3,000. Tigers
cost all the way from $800 up to $4,000. The
difficulty of catching tigers keeps the price up;
and then they fret and die in captivity while
the king of beasts, the lion, endures and even
enjoys slavery. A good trick-bear will bring
$1,500, but an ordinary show bear costs much
less. Leopards are valued at from $1,000 to
$2,000. The giraffe is a delicate and sensitive
creature, and no one ever lived longer than two
years in captivity. " It is difficult to teach them
to put their heads down to eat and drink."
They are worth from $5,000 to $10,000.
Camels are cheap; from $500 to $2,000. The

hippopotamus used to cost $50,000, but he is now much cheaper. Monkeys cost $25, but a live gorilla is worth $10,000. A large ostrich will bring from $1,000 to $2,000. The ostrich is short-lived and vicious, and soon worries himself to death. Alaska seals are worth from $1,000 to $3,000. Snakes will sometimes bring over $1,000. It is estimated that there are in the United States more than $4,000,000 worth of wild animals and birds.

The Right Reverend Charles Gore is the Bishop of Oxford, Chancellor of the Order of the Garter, grandson through his father of the third Earl of Arran, and through his mother of the Earl of Bessborough, and, if we mistake not, the possessor of still other honors, to which must be added what is of even greater importance, an extensive and profound scholarship. One would suppose a man so marvelously enriched with golden honors in which his divine Master when upon earth had no part, would strive to imitate that Master in things that cost so little as kindness to animals always costs the person who cherishes it in his merciful heart. But honors, emoluments, money, and " greetings in the market-place " do not seem to soften the episcopal heart, or, indeed, any other kind of a heart. This same Bishop of the Order of the Countess of Salisbury's Garter (she that was the frail inamorata of Edward III) has rushed into print to tell us that it is wicked to pray for animals, and especially for cavalry horses. Some kind-

hearted men and women, disturbed by the fearful sufferings endured by horses and dogs in
the war now (1915) raging in Europe, have offered prayers to God on their behalf.  Against
all such prayers the Bishop of Oxford has issued
a pastoral letter.  He tells us that animals have
no souls and are, therefore, not to be prayed for.
How does he know that animals have no souls?
Wiser men than he have thought the higher animals endowed with an immortal nature.  But
even if it be granted that all animals perish in
death, why may we not ask that God's mercy be
granted them in this life?  There can be no reason why we may not pray for them.

Bishop Gore may not be aware of it, but there
are a number of animals interred in Christian
churches.  Frederick the Great erected in Prus-
sian Poland a magnificent church as a memorial
to his favorite charger, killed beneath him at the
battle of Künersdorf.  It is commonly believed
that the horse is buried beneath the floor of that
building.  The favorite dog of William the Silent twice saved its master from assassination,
and at last died of grief a few days after the
death of William, who was a kind master.  The
animal is at rest among the illustrious dead in the
Nieuw Kirk at Delft.  A pet monkey that once
belonged to the Countess of Lincoln rests in St.
George's Chapel at Windsor.  The little animal
is carved upon the tomb of its devoted friend.

No, there can be no reason why we may not
pray for animals if the prayer is suited to the

occasion. Of course it will be generally conceded that the prayer must always concern itself with such things and circumstances as enter into the lower and narrower life of the beast in field or forest. If the prayer is not devout in the sense in which those prayers are which we offer for our fellow men, it may still be devout in another way, if only it be a true and sincere address to the throne of heavenly grace. It carries with it a spirit of kindly regard, recognizing the fact that both we and the animals beneath us are created and preserved by the same God. The sacred Scriptures tell us that not a sparrow falls to the earth without His notice. If, then, He is interested in all His creatures, it must be our duty also to interest ourselves in them. We have a claim upon the animals, but it is not less true that they have their own peculiar claim upon us; otherwise there could be no such thing as cruelty. If there were such a thing as cruelty, there could be, nevertheless, nothing wrong in it. But from the Scriptures we learn that " a righteous man regardeth the life of his beast." It follows that the man that regards not the life of his beast is not righteous. Cruelty, then, is sinful, and, being sinful, calls for repentance. Repentance and the thought of divine forgiveness bring us into the region of prayer. Of course, if all sin is to be confessed in prayer, it follows that I may surely pray for a kind heart in dealing with God's creatures. Why, then, may I not pray for the

welfare of those creatures? Dr. Mackarness has
written a prayer for the comfort and well-being
of animals, and certain humane societies in England have had the prayer printed upon cards for
general distribution. I wrote some time ago the
following prayer, which has had a reasonable cir-
culation and which has, I hope, accomplished a
measure of good in the direction of kindness to
the animal world:

"Have mercy, O God, on all animals that have
to work for our comfort and welfare. Give unto
us and unto all men a gentle and compassionate
spirit, that we may deal rightly by Thy creatures
of whatever kind. Have peculiar mercy, we pray
Thee, upon such animals as have brutal and cruel
owners, drivers, and masters. May we not increase the burden of such of Thy creatures as must
give up their lives that we may have food. And
may we practice mercy and show a compassionate
spirit in the destruction of such animals as must
be destroyed by man for his own safety and welfare. In all our relation to living creatures may
we be just, gentle, and pitiful; gratefully remembering the goodness of God to us in bestowing upon
us human reason and sovereignty over all living
creatures. This and every good thing we ask in
the name of that Saviour who, when upon earth,
said of the birds, ' Not one of these is forgotten before God.' Amen."

The tragedy of animal life is a thing we cannot, with all our study, understand. Most wild
beasts come to their death through violence.

Very few undomesticated animals reach old age.
They destroy each other not only that they may
procure food, but to gratify a native ferocity
that impels them to attack each other. More
animals than the cat take pleasure in tormenting
their prey. Ocean and forest are vast theatres
of violence. We in some measure share with
the animals their dreadful impulse in the direction of violence. Men who are called kind and
humane take delight in fishing and hunting.
They view with no discomfort the mortal agony
of a deer or a fox that has been shot not so much
for food as for pleasure. What we call a menagerie is, in truth, to the animals confined therein,
nothing but a prison. Beasts of high spirit
have been known to attempt self-destruction in
order to escape the hopeless monotony of such
confinement. Think of the horror of vivisection.
Truly the lives of wild creatures are something
to call forth compassion. And by compassion
I mean more than a sentimental pity; I mean
a desire and an effort to ameliorate or improve
in some way their condition. If we may go thus
far, we may, I think, go further, and seek such
wisdom from above as is needed for our campaign of kindness.

We may teach our children to be kind to animals, and we may, and should, add to that kindness the sanction of religion. A woman who
saw that her child was unwilling to feed a bird,
asked the little one to find in the New Testament
Matthew vi: 26; and when chapter and verse had

been found, she had the child read aloud the words, " Behold the fowls of the air; for they sow not, neither do they reap, nor gather into barns; yet your heavenly Father feedeth them." When the child had read those words, it was more than willing to feed the creatures God himself was ready to feed. In a Psalm may be found these words: " He sendeth the springs into the valleys, which run among the hills. They give drink to every beast of the field; the wild asses quench their thirst. By them shall the fowls of the heaven have their habitation, which sing among the branches." So we discover that religion has very much to do with the relation we sustain to the animals beneath us; and if religion has much to do with the matter, then surely prayer as well has to do with it. I think, then, the question is answered, " May we pray for animals? "

There is an absolutely unique story told of a pet dog that is worth recording because it illustrates the extravagance and wastefulness of those who have money. All around us are homeless and hungry men and women who beg in vain for assistance, while dogs, cats, birds, monkeys, and other creatures are housed and fed in unstinted luxury. Stories like the one I am about to tell have much to do with the unrest and bitterness of spirit that drive desperate men to deeds of violence. The man who, in vulgar bravado, lighted his cigar with a twenty-dollar bill was no worse than are some of our fashionable women who squander small fortunes upon animals that are made sickly and disgusting by the humiliating attentions they receive.

Not many years ago an actress had a diamond of considerable value mounted upon one of her front teeth. Whenever she laughed, the stone, which was a very beautiful one, flashed like a scintillating spark. Now her example has been followed by the owner of a dog. Rex is the name of a full-blooded Gordon setter that attracted much attention two or three years ago at the dog show. The animal has six front teeth of solid gold, and in the tooth most visible when the dog opens his mouth is imbedded a small diamond. The owner of the dog is a dentist. The animal is very intelligent and seems to understand his master perfectly. The dog, so the story runs, was told to jump into the operating chair. Rex did as he was directed. A towel was tied in the creature's mouth to prevent the closure of his jaws, and then the operation commenced. The dog howled occasionally, but he seemed to understand that the master was working for his good. The value of the gold in his mouth is about one hundred and fifty dollars, to say nothing of the diamond imbedded therein.

Chateaubriand has preserved from oblivion the name and exploits of the once famous cat, Micetto. This animal was the constant companion of the Pontiff Leo XII, and always sat at the table with his Holiness. Pilgrims from all parts of the Catholic world brought with them to Rome delicate morsels for the capricious palate of the sacred cat, and were not in the least disturbed when they saw the creature engage in familiar play with the holy ass that the most favored devotees were allowed only to kiss, and that with the greatest humility. It is said that upon one occasion Micetto actually chased the holy ass into the street, to the great scandal of the church. Leo XII was so fond of the animal that he put a golden collar, engraved with the arms of the Papal See, around its neck. The creature is described as " gray, stupid, and tiger-like, with bands of black." It survived Leo XII and was taken by Chateaubriand to France, where it was treated with the greatest reverence. Aristocratic ladies stroked its fur with their delicate hands, and suffered themselves to be scratched by its sharp claws. One lady of royal blood went so far as to boast that she was the recipient of a remarkable favor. Micetto had imprinted, with snow-white teeth, eight deep wounds upon her beautiful hand.

Pius IX was very fond of a cat that he called Morello. He often slept with the creature at the foot of his bed, and at dinner it was at liberty to run all over the table-cloth, and even to pick and steal from the plate of the Holy Father. Petrarch had a cat upon which he bestowed every kind of attention, and when it died he mourned for it as for a very dear friend. He had its remains carefully embalmed after the fashion of the ancient Egyptians. Andria Doria, known as the " Father and Defender of Venice," had his cat's portrait painted, and after the animal's death he preserved its skeleton. It is said he would not render a decision on any question of public importance without first spending an hour in the delightful society of his favorite cat. Cardinal Wolsey never gave audience to a foreign ambassador without enthroning by his side a cat that was his constant companion. Richelieu's attachment to cats is a matter of history. Mohammed has left it on record that he was never happy away from his cat. When the animal was asleep upon his sleeve and he wished to rise, he would cut off the sleeve rather than disturb its slumbers. Rousseau delighted in cats.

Dr. Johnson had a cat he called Hodge, and he was careful never to say anything in its presence that might offend the creature. Sir Isaac Newton was so fond of cats that he made holes in his barn door for their accommodation. He measured the cats and cut the holes to fit them. Southey had Greta Hall, where he settled in 1804, so full of cats that he was accustomed to call it " Cats' Eden." He wrote a " Memoir of the Cats of Greta Hall," and wished to be remembered as the Plutarch of cats. Montaigne used to obtain relaxation by playing with his cats. Colbert reared six or eight cats in his private study, and taught them various tricks. One large Angora slept in his waste-paper basket. Tasso wrote a sonnet to his faithful cat, in which he entreated the creature to assist him through the night with the lustre of its moonlike eyes, having no candles by which he could see to write verses. Béranger made a poem to his tabby. Fontenelle used to deliver orations in the presence of his favorite cat. Gray has given the world an ode " On the Death of a Favorite Cat Drowned in a Vase of Gold Fishes,"— all of which reminds us of the Latin adage, " *Catus amat pisces, sed non vult tingere plautos* "—the cat loves fish but does not wish to wet her paws. Lady Macbeth makes allusion to the line:

" Letting I dare not wait upon I would,
Like the poor cat i' the adage."

From Pope we have the famous distich:

" But thousands die, without a this or that,
Die, and endow a college or a cat."

But the poet little thought that a good and wealthy woman in Dedham would leave most of her property for the support of household pets, and certainly he could not have dreamed that Dr. Lindsay, in his excellent work on " Mind in the Lower Animals," would recommend that every large city have a nursery for cats and other domestic animals.

We often hear of the Kilkenny cats. The story is that two cats at Kilkenny fought with such ferocity that each swallowed the other, leaving behind nothing but the tails of both combatants. There is a different version of the story which tells us that a regiment once stationed at Kilkenny found amusement in tying cats together by their tails, and watching their frantic attacks upon each other in the effort to get free. The colonel determined to stop the cruel sport, and one day, in the midst of the fun, an alarm was given that he was approaching, whereupon a soldier cut through their tails with a sword, thus liberating the animals.

We frequently employ the expression, " cat's-paw," to signify a dupe. It is derived from the fable of the monkey who wanted to get from the fire some roasted chestnuts, and used the paws of the cat to pull them out from the hot ashes. Commodore Rodgers, in a brilliant and famous patriotic address, said, " I had no intention of becoming a cat's-paw to draw European chestnuts out of the fire." There is in one of the art galleries of New York a very good picture of the monkey and the cat. The phrase, " Let the cat out of the bag," is coextensive with the English language. The old-time English farmer would substitute a cat for a sucking pig, and bring the animal to market. Strangers who were not acquainted with the trick would buy " a pig in a poke " without examination. But if they opened the bag to see what kind of a pig had come to market, they were sure to " let the cat out of the bag."

Those who are interested in the life of Napoleon will call to mind the celebrated " Cat Hoax " of 1815. Just before the Emperor started for St. Helena a practical joker printed and distributed a large number of handbills setting forth that the island upon which Napoleon was to remain was overrun with rats, and that a considerable sum would be paid for full-grown tom-cats and also for female cats, and even for kittens if they were lively and could feed themselves. The day set for the presentation of the animals saw hundreds of felines offered as companions and fellow travelers for the distinguished prisoner. The wharf was crowded with men and old women and even little children carrying cats of all kinds and sizes. So anxious were the people to dispose of the creatures that a riot broke out and most of the cats escaped, and instead of infesting the island to the dismay of the rats, they infested the neighboring houses to the dismay of their occupants. Something like five hundred cats were killed.

" A lady friend of mine," said a writer in " Nature," " was at one time matron of a hospital for poor children, which institution was maintained by subscription. One of the inmates was a blind girl, who was not there as a permanent patient, but temporarily, till a home could be found for her. She had learned to feed herself, and at meal time a tray containing food was placed on her knees as she sat in a comfortable chair. Upon a certain day, while she was eating, the pet cat of the establishment placed itself before the girl, and looked long and earnestly at her,— so earnestly that the matron, fearing the animal meditated mischief to the girl, took her from the room. Again the next day at the same hour the cat entered the apartment, but this time walked quietly to the girl's side, reared itself on its hind legs, and noiselessly, stealthily reached out its paw to the plate, selected and seized a morsel that pleased its catship, and then silently as it came, departed to enjoy the stolen meal. The girl never noticed her loss, and when told of it by her companions, laughed heartily. It is evident that the cat, from observation, had entirely satisfied itself that the girl could not see, and by a process of reasoning it had decided it could steal a good dinner by the practical use of a little valuable knowledge."

Hamerton, in his delightful book about animals, says that he knew a French politician whose cats made it impossible to dine with him. They were permitted to run all over the table, taking from any plate whatever happened to please them. On the same page our author observes that " cats frequently appear upon the table in another shape." He once lodged near the Arc de Triomphe, and from his window could see a purveyor of dead cats supply a cheap restaurant in a back street with French rabbits. Cats were regarded by the Parisians during the great siege as a delicacy. The French politician's fondness for cats was surpassed, however, by the attachment for them manifested by a certain Mrs. Griggs of Edinburgh. That lady had in her house eighty-six living cats and twenty-eight dead ones in glass cases. She consumed much of her time in fondling and feeding the animals. It is said that a lawyer in San Francisco had a collection of more than a thousand cats, which he valued at a great price. The most famous cat shows were held in England at the Crystal Palace, on the thirteenth of July and the second of December, 1871, and on the twenty-sixth and twenty-ninth of October, 1872. New York and Boston have had large exhibitions of feline beauty. At the latter city the cats known as Hamlet, Charles Dickens, Lowell, Rolla, and Sebastian Bach attracted great attention by their size, beauty, and agility.

Beattie tells us, in his " Minstrel," that it is hard to climb the " steep where Fame's proud temple shines afar." The cats named had, all of them, the usual feline apparatus for climbing whatever steep seemed to them attractive; but certain distinguished artists saved their catships all trouble of the kind by painting them on orders from their owners. Think of the efforts of some good authors to obtain even a passing recognition. Think of their futile climbing. Then consider for a moment the unearned immortality of those unresponsive, fluffy, silky Angoras. Verily Dogberry might have exclaimed, " Write me down a cat!" Yet Shakespeare made him much prefer to be written down an ass. Well, Dogberry was, in truth, a fool. He also is a fool who prefers the immortality of a dolt to the dignified oblivion of unrecognized worth.

Shelley, who delighted in all strange and supernatural stories, has left us this wild narrative, which he received from a certain inventor of weird and remarkable tales.

" A gentleman, on a visit to a friend who lived on the skirts of an extensive forest on the east of Germany, lost his way. He wandered for some hours among the trees, when he saw a light at a distance. On approaching it, he was surprised to observe that it proceeded from the interior of a ruined monastery. Before he knocked he thought it prudent to look through a window. He saw a multitude of cats assembled around a small grave, four of whom were letting down a coffin with a crown upon it. The gentleman, startled at this unusual sight, and imagining that he had arrived among the retreats of fiends or witches, mounted his horse and rode away with the utmost precipitation. He arrived at his friend's house at a late hour. On his arrival the friend questioned him as to the cause of the traces of trouble visible on his face. He began with some difficulty to recount his adventure, knowing that it was scarcely possible his friend should believe one word of it. No sooner had he mentioned the coffin with a crown upon it than his friend's cat, who seemed to have been lying asleep before the fire, leaped up, saying, ' Then I am the king of the cats! ' and scrambled up the chimney and was seen no more." [7]

There is a story of a certain man who dreamed he was a cat, and so vivid was the impression

[7] *Hamerton's* " Chapters on Animals," page 53.

made upon his mind by the dream that ever after he could not endure the sight of the animal, though before the unfortunate dream he was exceedingly fond of cats. Rev. J. C. Wood, in his "Man and Beast," publishes a letter from a lady in which is recorded a strange adventure. At the time of the occurrence, the lady and her mother were living in an old country château in France. This is her letter:

"It was during the winter of 18— that one evening I happened to be sitting by the side of a cheerful fire in my bedroom, busily engaged in caressing a favorite cat,— the illustrious Lady Catharine, now, alas! no more. She lay in my lap in a pensive attitude and a winking state of drowsiness. Although my room might have been without candles, it was perfectly illuminated by the light of the fire. There were two doors,— one behind me, leading into an apartment which had been locked for the winter, and another, on the opposite side of the room, which communicated with the passage. Mamma had not left me many minutes, and the high-backed, old-fashioned arm-chair which she had occupied remained vacant at the opposite corner of the fireplace. Puss, who lay with her head on my arm, became more and more sleepy, and I pondered on the propriety of preparing for bed.

"Of a sudden I became aware that something had affected my pet's equanimity. The purring ceased, and she exhibited rapidly increasing symptoms of uneasiness. I bent down and endeavored to coax her into quietness, but she instantly struggled to her feet in my lap, and spitting vehemently, with arched back and tail swollen, she assumed an attitude of mingled terror and defiance.

" The change in her position obliged me to raise my head; and on looking up, to my inexpressible horror, I then perceived that a little, hideous, wrinkled old hag occupied mamma's chair. Her hands were resting on her knees, and her body was stooping forward so as to bring her face in close proximity to mine. Her eyes, piercingly fierce and shining with an overpowering luster, were steadfastly fixed on me. It was as if a fiend were glaring at me through them. Her dress and general appearance indicated that she belonged to the French bourgeoisie; but those eyes, so wonderfully large, and in their expression so intensely wicked, entirely absorbed my senses and precluded any attention to detail. I should have screamed, but my breath was gone while that terrible gaze so horribly fascinated me: I could neither withdraw my eyes nor rise from my seat.

" I had meanwhile been trying to keep a tight hold on the cat, but she seemed resolutely determined not to remain in such ugly neighborhood, and after some most desperate efforts at length succeeded in escaping from my grasp. Leaping over tables, chairs, and all that came in her way, she repeatedly threw herself with frightful violence against the top panel of the door which communicated with the disused room. Then, returning in the same frantic manner, she furiously dashed against the door on the opposite side.

" My terror was divided, and I looked by turns, now at the old woman, whose great staring eyes were constantly fixed on me, and now at the cat, who was becoming every instant more frantic. At last the dreadful idea that the animal had gone mad had the effect of restoring my breath, and I screamed loudly.

" Mamma ran in immediately, and the cat, on the door opening, literally sprang over her head, and for upward of half an hour ran up and down stairs as if pursued. I turned to point to the object of my terror: it was gone. Under such circumstances the lapse of time is difficult to appreciate, but I should think that the apparition lasted about four or five minutes.

" Some time afterward I learned that a former proprietor of the house, a woman, had hanged herself in that very room."

In the olden times it was a common sport to suspend a cat from a branch of a tree as a mark to be shot at. Sometimes the animal so suspended was enclosed in a leather sack. We have a reference to the cruel sport in " Much Ado about Nothing ": " Hang me in a bottle, like a cat." It was also a custom to place the cat in a soot-bag and hang it on a line; the players were to beat out the bottom of the bag, hence the saying, " Not room to swing a cat." Thirty or more years ago the expression, " He grins like a Cheshire cat " was common; it came from the habit of moulding cheese in Cheshire into the form of a cat.

It is a mistake to suppose that the modern " cat-call " has anything to do with the domestic pet of which we are now writing. The ancients separated the drama into four parts: the protasis (introduction), epitasis (continuation), catastasis (climax), and catastrophe (conclusion). The "cat-call" is the call for the dramatic cat or catastrophe, or, as we sometimes have it, the *dénouement*.

The "harmless, necessary cat" of which we read in "The Merchant of Venice," was a very costly creature in the Middle Ages, and was protected by law in Wales about 948. The cat is mentioned in the "Epistle of Jeremias": "Upon their bodies and their heads light bats, swallows, and birds, and in like manner also the cats spring upon them." It is believed that the animal alluded to by Aristotle was the wildcat. Every scholar is acquainted with the famous passage in Herodotus (book 2, chapter 66) which treats of the cats of Egypt. Interesting material in this connection may be found in Wilkinson's "Ancient Egypt," volume 1, page 246; Jablonski, "Panth. Ægypte," volume 2, page 66; and in the history of Diodorus Siculus, book 1, chapter 83. Especially interesting are the accounts of the burial and worship of wolves, crocodiles, bears, and dogs in tombs and sacred caves.

Household pets have been made from nearly every kind of animal known to man. Frederick the Great was a dog-fancier. Goethe was fond of a snake, which he kept in a chimney corner. Tiberius, the Roman Emperor, had the same taste, and made a bosom companion of a serpent.

Augustus delighted in his parrot, and mourned with inconsolable grief when his quail died. Honorius declared himself willing to give up the city of Rome and to sacrifice the lives of all its citizens could he but restore to life his hen, Roma. Louis XI, when ill at Plessis-le-Tours, could find pleasure in nothing but dancing pigs. Henry III of France used to carry a litter of spaniels in a basket suspended around his neck. Charles I of England had the same taste. Richter was fond of all animals. Razzi, the painter, filled his house with squirrels, monkeys, Angora cats, dwarf asses, he-goats, tortoises, and Elba ponies. Pelisson, confined in the Bastille, tamed a spider. The Marquise de Montespan amused herself with mice, which she allowed to run all over her elegant apartments at Versailles. Cardinal Mazarin made a friend of an ape. The poet Alfieri delighted in horses. Cowper's great delight was to feed his tame hares. Fournier was devoted to a squirrel.

Charles Kingsley delighted in cats; and upon his lawn dwelt a family of toads which lived from year to year in the same hole in the green bank, which the scythe was never allowed to approach. A pair of sand-wasps, one of which had been saved from a watery death in a hand-basin by the tender-hearted rector, lived in a crack of his dressing-room window, and every spring he looked eagerly for their advent. A fly-catcher that built every year under his bedroom window was a joy to him, and he delighted in a favorite slow-worm in the church-yard, which his parish-ioners were specially enjoined not to kill.

" Who will bell the cat? " is a curious old pro-verb, famous in parable and in history. The mice held a consultation how to secure them-selves from the cat, and they resolved to hang a bell about the cat's neck to give warning when she approached; but after they had resolved on doing it they were as far off from safety as ever, for who would hang the bell? Both parable and proverb have immortalized themselves in history. When the Scottish nobles met at Stirling in a body, they proposed to take Spence, the obnoxious favorite of James III, and hang him to rid them-selves of him. " Ay," said Lord Grey, " that's very well said,— but who'll bell the cat? " " That will I! " said the black Earl Angus; and he undertook the task and accomplished it, and was called " Archibald Bell-the-cat " until his dying day. " You can have no more of a cat than her skin," is an old saying, but surely Lord Grey got more than many skins when once he had the bell about that dreaded neck.

It is reported of a certain Mr. O'Rorke that he invented a living rat-trap. The question with him was not " Who will bell the cat? " but " Who will outwit the rat? " The rats overran Mr. O'Rorke's house and in many ways troubled him greatly. So, after studying their habits and haunts, he trapped several of the obnoxious crea-tures. Selecting the largest and strongest of these, O'Rorke gave it a coating of glue, after which he dropped it into a bag of feathers. Then the animal was turned loose. It scurried away as fast as it could to its old resorts and friends. The other rats, on seeing the feathered rodent, fled in terror from their holes, and for a long time avoided the house wherein they had seen so strange a creature. Were we inclined to be facetious, we might call O'Rorke's performance " The Metamorphosis, or The Silver Rat."

William Dunlap, an early American artist (1766–1839), to whose activity and enterprise we owe the New York Academy of Fine Arts, has given the world a picture of Chloe, the " Florence Nightingale of the Cats." When the yellow fever was ravaging New York in 1822, a large portion of the city, known as the infected district, was deserted and barricaded. The inhabitants fled, but the cats remained in their homes, and would have starved had not old colored Chloe remained to feed them.

Gottfried Mind, who was born at Berne in 1768, devoted most of his time to the painting of cats and bears. So lifelike were his water-color representations of puss that posterity calls him the " Raphael of Cats." Mind passed many of his happiest hours at the bears' den in Berne, where from time immemorial two live bears have been kept. No sooner did he make his appearance than the creatures hastened to him with a friendly growl, and were invariably rewarded with a piece of bread or an apple from the pocket of their benefactor.

The cat was worshipped in Egypt as a god. This deity had a human body and a cat's head. Diodorus tells us that to kill an Egyptian cat, even by accident, was to forfeit one's own life. An ancient tradition has it that Diana assumed the form of a cat, and thus excited to rage the great giants. The creature was a symbol of liberty because of its dislike for all constraint. The Romans represented their Goddess of Liberty as holding in one hand a cup and in the other a broken sceptre, and with a cat at her feet.

But the cat, worshipped in Egypt and petted all over the world, is not without its tale of woe. And in some cases we may exclaim with Carey in " The Dragon of Wantley ":

" What a monstrous tail our cat has got! "

No animal has been more intimately associated with every kind of superstition. The creature was once thought to provoke storms at sea, and was regarded as unlucky by seamen. It was said of the animal, " She carries a gale in her tail." When the cat licked its fur the wrong way, it was a very bad sign. No sailor in the olden time would dare to provoke a cat, and yet the opinion prevailed that the best way to secure a favorable wind was to drown the creature.

Fielding, in his voyage to Lisbon (1775), says: " The kitten at last recovered, to the great joy of the good captain, but to the great disappointment of some of the sailors, who asserted that the drowning of a cat was the very surest way of raising a favorable wind." The Germans have a proverb that any one having a cat for an enemy will be followed at his funeral by rats and rain. There is a Hungarian proverb that a cat will not die in water, hence sailors call flaws on the surface of water, "cats'-paws"; the animal's paws disturb the surface. A greater agitation is called a " cat-skin." So we have, " It rains cats and dogs." In some parts of England the northwest wind is called " cat's-nose." There is an old saying that " Good liquor will make a cat speak." Cats, because they see at night and are of nocturnal habits, are connected with the moon, and are viewed as witches' familiars. Galinthia was changed by the Fates into a cat. Hecate assumed the shape of a cat. The animal was used by witches for raising a gale, and it was believed that the creature could smell a wind in the same way that pigs could see it. Southey tells us in his " Travels in Spain " that old women promised him a fine day because the cats' skin looked bright. The animal is remarkably tenacious of life; hence the saying, " A cat has nine lives." Shakespeare, who knew everything, writes, in " Romeo and Juliet ":

*Tyb.*—What wouldst thou have with me?
*Mer.*— Good king of cats, nothing but one of your nine lives.

The tiger has always been a symbol of ferocity and cruelty, yet Tasso tells us, in his " Jerusalem Delivered," that Cornelia was suckled by a tigress. Story, in his poem, " Cleopatra," makes the Egyptian queen recall the happy time when, a smooth and velvety tigress, she wandered over the desert and through the jungle with her Antony, in the enjoyment of a " fierce and tyrannous freedom." A Buddhist parable represents " Lord Buddha " as giving himself, out of pity, to be food for a famished tigress unable to nourish her cubs:

" The famished tigress howled in vain;
No prey to stay the hunger-pain
Was seen on all the burning plain.

" The savage mother, worn and faint,
Heard, wild with woe, her cub's weak plaint,
Then leaped for joy.   She saw a saint.

" For Buddha, pitying her despair,
Is hastening to the tiger's lair
In answer to her awful prayer!

" ' Take me and feed your young,' he said.
Great Buddha's blood was fiercely shed,
Great Buddha's heart the tigress fed."

William Blake has this fine poem about the tiger:

" Tiger, Tiger, burning bright
In the forests of the night,
What immortal hand or eye
Could frame thy fearful symmetry!

" In what distant deeps or skies
Burnt the fire of thine eyes?
On what wings dare he aspire?
What the hand dare seize the fire?

" And what shoulder and what art
Could twist the sinews of thy heart?
And when thy heart began to beat,
What dread hand forged thy dread feet?

" What the hammer?   What the chain?
In what furnace was thy brain?
What the anvil?   What dread grasp
Dare its deadly terrors clasp?

" When the stars threw down their spears,
And watered heaven with their tears,
Did He smile his work to see?
Did He who made the lamb make thee?

" Tiger, Tiger, burning bright
In the forests of the night,
What immortal hand or eye
Dare frame thy fearful symmetry? "

The Reverend Thomas Hill has recorded his
experience with a friendly old toad that used to
sit under the door of a beehive forty years ago,
and also with a little toad in its second summer.  The experience is so pleasantly related
and so interesting that we venture to quote without abridgment:

" This note is intended as a contribution toward
the psychology of the American toad, simply pre-

senting some evidences of intelligence and of capacity for learning to which I have been witness. In the summer of 1843 an old toad used to sit under the door of a beehive every fine evening, and dexterously pick up those bees who, overladen or tired, missed the doorstep and fell to the ground. He lost, by some accident, one eye, and it was observed by several members of the family, as well as myself, that he had with it lost his ability to pick up a bee at the first trial,— his tongue struck the ground on one side of the bee; but after several weeks' practice with one eye, he regained his old certainty of aim. I have never seen our toad use his hands to crowd his food into his mouth, as the European toads do, although he uses them freely to wipe out of his mouth any inedible or disagreeable substance. When our toad gets into his mouth part of an insect too large for his tongue to thrust down his throat (and I have known of their attempting a wounded humming-bird), he resorts to the nearest stone or clod, and presses the protruding part of his mouthful against it, and thus crowds it down his throat. This can be observed at any time by placing a locust's hind-legs together, and throwing it before a small toad. On one occasion I gave a ' yellow-striped ' locust to a little toad in its second summer, when he was in the middle of a very wide gravel-walk. In a moment he had the locust's head down his throat, its hinder parts protruding. He looked around for a stone or clod; but finding none at hand in either direction, he bowed his head and crept along, pushing the locust against the ground. But the angle with the ground was too small, and my walk too well rolled. To increase the angle he straightened his hind legs up, but in vain. At length he threw up his hind-quarters and actually stood on his head, or rather on the locust sticking out of his mouth, and after repeating this once or twice, succeeded in ' getting himself outside of his dinner.'

"But these instances of ingenious adaptation to the circumstances were exceeded by a four-year-old toad at Antioch College. I was tossing him earthworms while digging, and presently threw him so large a specimen that he was obliged to attack one end only. That end was instantly transferred to his stomach, the other end writhing free in air and coiled about the toad's head. He waited until its writhings gave him a chance, swallowed half an inch, then, taking a nip with his jaws, waited for a chance to draw in another half inch. But there were so many half inches to dispose of that at last his jaws grew tired, lost their firmness of grip, and the worm crawled out five-eighths of an inch between each half-inch swallowing. The toad, perceiving this, brought his hind foot to aid his jaws, grasping his abdomen with his foot; and by a little effort getting hold of the worm in his stomach from the outside, he thus by his foot held fast to what he gained by each swallow, and presently succeeded in getting the worm entirely down.

"A garter-snake was observed this summer in North Conway, pushing a toad down his throat by running it against clods and stones just as the toad crowds down a locust.

"The amount which a toad can eat is surprising. On Tuesday morning I threw a squash-bug to a young toad. He snapped it up, but immediately rejected it, wiped his mouth with great energy, and then hopped away with extraordinary rapidity. I was so much amused that I gathered some more of the squash-bugs and carried them to a favorite old toad at the northeast corner of the house. He ate them all without making any wry faces. I gathered all that I could find in my vines, and he ate them all, to the number of twenty-three. I then brought him some larvæ of *pygæra ministra,* three-quarters grown, and succeeded in enticing him to put ninety-four of them on top of his squash-bugs. Finding that his virtue was not proof against the caterpillars when I put them on the end of a straw and tickled his nose with them, he at length turned and crept under the piazza, where he remained till Friday afternoon, digesting his feast."

The efforts of the Quebec Department of Lands and Forests to stock the Laurentide National Park in the Lake St. John region with wapiti have proved an amusing failure, according to statements in the Quebec Parliament by the Minister of Lands and Forests, who reported that eight wapiti were brought last year by the Quebec government from Labrador for the purpose of stocking the park.

But the journey was a long one by ship and rail, and hundreds of curious and kindly disposed persons looked at the beautiful animals, who took most kindly to the new and wonderfully alluring foods that their new human acquaintances forced upon them.

When at last the wapiti were turned loose in

the park away up north of the city of Quebec, they refused to run away and resume their old Labrador ways.

They just hung round the station agent's house and visited all the farmers' and hunters' houses and shacks. One pair fought a duel to the death over some farmyard delicacy, and the others cling to the outskirts of civilization and are tamer than the cows and sheep,— so tame that the hunters do not consider it good form to hunt them, but " shoo " them away when they try to steal the camp supplies.

Writing of the souls of brutes, Krahmer expresses his firm conviction in the following words: " The intelligence of an animal manifests itself in the same manner as that of a man. No essential difference, but only one in degree, can be proved to exist between instinct and reason." Burmeister adds: " Centuries before the thoughtful writers who have written upon this subject lived, a hero refused to ascend to heaven without his dog; he spurned the car of Indra, exclaiming, ' Companion of my life, heaven would not be heaven without thee! ' "

The doctrine of the transmigration of souls early taught the Oriental mind to contemplate in a religious spirit the mystery of animal life. It was the belief of ancient Egyptians that the human soul, upon dissolution of the body, entered into some one of the lower animal forms, and, having passed in rotation through various terrestrial, aquatic, and aerial beings, again entered the body of a man (Herodotus, book 2, chapter 123). The Hindu believed that the slayer of a Brahman was reborn, according to the degree of his guilt, as a dog, a boar, an ass, a camel, a bull, a goat, a sheep, a stag, a bird, a chandala, or a pukkasa. The Brahman who drinks spirituous liquor must migrate into the body of a worm, an insect, a grasshopper, a fly that feeds on ordure, or some mischievous animal. One who has suffered birth twice and then plunders a Brahman of his gold, will pass a thousand times into the bodies of spiders, snakes, or murderous demons. The man who violates the bed of his gurn will a hundred times migrate into grasses, shrubs, and creeping plants. They who injure men become flesh-eaters. They who embrace women of the lowest castes become ghosts.[8] Contemplating the fearful consequences of an evil life in the countless and loathsome migrations that follow it, a poet thus warns his readers:

> " Shun thou the evil thing,
> Since life is on the wing;
> Thousands of births attend
> E'er thou shalt know the end.

> " Yonder a worm doth lie,
> A song-bird seeks the sky;
> Betwixt them birth on birth
> With anguish fill the earth.

[8] See " The River of Oblivion," being the last paper in this book.

"Love thou the wise and good;
Let evil be withstood;
So shall Nirvana thee
Make henceforth wholly free."

Another Eastern poet voices the same thought:

"Through many different births
I have run, vainly seeking
The architect of the desire-resembling house.
Painful are repeated births.
O house-builder! I have seen thee.
Again a house thou canst not build for me.
I have broken thy rafters and ridge-pole;
I have arrived at the extinction of evil desire;
My mind is gone to Nirvana."

An old legend tells us that Solomon knew the languages of all the animals, and could talk with beasts and birds. A rabbinical story is told of the wise king. As he rode one day out of Jerusalem with a great retinue, an ant-hill lay directly in his way. Solomon heard its little people talking. "Here comes the great king," said they; "but he is not so great as men think. His flatterers call him wise and just and merciful, but he is about to ride over our hill, and he will crush us without giving heed to our sufferings."

Solomon told the Queen of Sheba, who rode with him, what the ants had said of him and also of her. The queen remarked, "The ants are insolent creatures. They would have a better fate than they deserve did we but tread them and their hill under our feet."

But Solomon said, " It is the part of wisdom to learn of the lowest and weakest of all God's creatures." Then the king commanded his train to turn aside and spare the ant-hill. All the courtiers marveled greatly, and the Queen of Sheba bowed her hand and made obeisance to Solomon, and said, " Now know I the secret of thy wisdom. Thou listenest as patiently to the reproaches of the humblest as to the greatest of men and animals."

The doves of Venice are a very beautiful feature in the life of the far-famed city of the sea. They haunt the statues, the eaves of the great buildings, and the marble columns that line the piazza of St. Mark's. Whoever has the courage to go into the central square of Venice having with him a package that suggests corn, will find himself in a moment or two covered from head to foot by the doves of St. Mark's. The creatures were once protected by the city government, but long ago the protection ceased, and now the birds are protected and cared for by private benevolence.

Kwannon is a goddess of mercy, and no man may worship her unless first some favor has been shown her consecrated white ponies. Her ponies are the most beautiful in all the world, and to deny their beauty is a grievous sacrilege. They have their stable close to her temple, and both stable and temple are so like, the one to the other, that passers-by not infrequently take the stable for the temple and the temple for the stable. It is an act of worship to feed the sacred animals. For some distance before their stable is reached vendors of beans and peas may be seen. From them passers-by purchase the kind of food the holy white ponies like best. When men approach the animals they drop upon their knees, and the beans and peas are presented with great reverence and many genuflections. The worshippers write, or buy already written, prayers, and after chewing the paper upon which the prayers are written, they make the pulp into a little ball which they throw at the goddess. If the prayer-pulp sticks, the supplication will be answered as the petitioner wishes; if it falls off, then it must be offered over again. Every time a prayer is thrown, a bit of coin is placed in a box at the foot of the goddess. To kill one of the holy white ponies would be an act of the greatest wickedness. The creatures are supported in luxury while many of their worshippers die in poverty and neglect.

The sacred elephants in India are also maintained in luxury. When we hear of a desolating famine in that country, we may be sure that those huge beasts do not suffer in the least from want of food. Men and women may perish by the thousand, but the holy elephants have all they want and very much more than they can consume. Thus it is that superstition lifts brutes above the deluded people who worship them. There are holy pigeons, cats, horses, and even pigs. These all live as the Roman Emperor's horse lived long centuries ago. It is a pitiful thing to see little children crying for bread while a stupid hog revels in more food than it can by any possibility devour. Pagan religions are cruel. Only when our Saviour comes to reign in human hearts and lives will this world see an end of hard-hearted superstition.

The old Roman world was cruel to animals. The men of those early days took pleasure in the wanton destruction of living creatures. Four hundred bears were killed in the Roman amphitheater in a single day during the reign of Caligula. Three hundred animals came to their death at one time under Claudius. Four hundred tigers fought with bulls and elephants under Nero. When the Colosseum was dedicated, five thousand animals of various kinds were destroyed. Trajan carried cruel amusements to the greatest degree of atrocity. He had lions, elephants, hippopotami, bulls, tigers, rhinoceri, giraffes, stags, and even serpents and crocodiles, slaughtered by thousands, with every conceivable refinement of cruelty.

Vivisection is the modern brutality that in some measure takes the place of the shameful amusements of ancient Rome. Bear-gardens were the delight of medieval Europe. Later came the bull-ring. Even now we have the cock-fight and a few other low and disgraceful entertainments.

If you would read an interesting book about the animals that infest the fields and forests of America, you can, I think, find no better work than one called " Wild Neighbors," written by my friend, Mr. Ernest Ingersoll.   I have known wild neighbors of my own species that I did not greatly care for,— that I, in fact, positively disliked.   Wild animals are better company than wild men.   Mr. Ingersoll writes very entertainingly of the former.   He really helps you to see some redeeming qualities in the skunk, and he even inclines you to excuse in a measure its peculiar way of defending itself.   He seems to recommend the creature as a domestic pet.   I am, however, somewhat lacking in faith,— and it may be in courage as well.   I am by no means sure that I should not greatly prefer the puma or even the shark as a pet.   From my earliest days I have viewed the proprietor of the scent-bags with aversion.   Yet if any book could change my point of view in the matter of the skunk, I think that book would prove to be Mr. Ingersoll's " Wild Neighbors."   I will not say that Ernest Seton Thompson's " Wild Animals I Have Known " is more interesting than Mr. Ingersoll's book.   Perhaps Mr. Thompson's book would please ordinary persons better, but certain it is that Mr. Ingersoll's is more instructive, and its style and method of presentation are very agreeable.

Thoreau's books are full of nature, and nature seen through his eyes has added charm.

John Burroughs is both a popular and an instructive writer.  His books are delightful reading and his facts are generally reliable, but he treats his theme from a literary point of view, often diverting the reader's attention from the facts to the way in which they are handled.  If a scrap-book of natural history giving special thought to exceptional and out-of-the-way occurrences is wanted, Buckland's books will prove an invaluable treasure.  His works are now out of print and, being rare, command a large price. We must make ourselves acquainted with the scientific works of original investigators if we would be ourselves scientific men, but of such works I have not thought it worth while to treat in a popular paper like this.

# X

## THE RIVER OF OBLIVION

Let no one say, " I will not drink of this water."
>                                    — *Cervantes.*

Duller should'st thou be than the fat weed
That rots itself in ease on Lethe wharf.
>                                    — *Shakespeare.*

Out, out, brief candle!
>                                    — *Shakespeare.*

# THE RIVER OF OBLIVION

I.   ACHERON, the River of Woe.
II.  PYRIPHLEGETHON, the River of Fire.
III. COCYTUS, the River of Wailing.
IV.  STYX, the river in Hades over which the
     dead are ferried by the boatman, Charon.
V.   LETHE, the River of Oblivion.

THE above are the five great rivers of the underworld. The last may be, by certain persons, under certain circumstances, and at certain
times, desired, but the other four are to be
dreaded and avoided.

Acheron was a geographical river which the
Greeks believed to be at the end of the earth.
Early imagination pushed it farther away as the
end of the earth receded, and thus was its ever-
widening stream at last transferred to the lower
world itself. The river was one of great length,
because the sorrows of mankind have no end.
Its depth was great, because the sea of human
anguish into which it flows has no bottom. Its
impetuous current broke through all barriers, because there is nothing that may successfully re-
sist the distresses which assail the human heart.
It leaped over vast walls of stone in cascades of
silent foam, and was blown about the earth in a
spray of tears.

Pyriphlegethon was a stream of fire. Its light
illuminated the gloom of the lonely world through

which it was wont to flow. The shadows that
proceeded from the overpowering and piercing
brightness moved as if living. They seemed
about to speak, but in another moment the darkness would fall over them and cause them to disappear. Light and gloom pursued each other
in a never-ending round of meaningless movements,— a dance of shadows.

Cocytus lapped its shores with monotonous
and wearisome vibrations, sending out a wailing
cry of distress, above which rose the lamentations
of the dead.

Styx was the river over which the dead were
ferried by Charon on their way to the land of
woe. It was the principal stream of the nether
world. From that world it flowed forth into
nothingness. It was connected with the Cocytus, and so it came to pass that the dead often
heard the lamentations of that river long before
they came to its shores. Cocytus was, in fact,
a branch of the Styx. Æneas and the Sibyl,
in their journey through Hades, came to the
River Styx; but when they approached the boat
Charon objected to conveying them. He said
that Æneas was not dead, and that therefore he
had no right to cross the river. He said further
that Æneas, being still alive, might offer the dead
violence, especially as he was armed. He insisted that the boat was not adapted to living
men, but only to the light freight of bodiless
spirits. It was strong enough to carry ghosts,
but not strong enough to sustain human bodies.

The Sibyl with great tact assured the ancient ferryman that Æneas would do no harm, that he would not sink Charon's fragile craft, or assault the unarmed ghosts. Finally the golden bough was exhibited to the old ferryman, and at sight of it all objections were withdrawn. Charon at once conveyed the living hero across the Styx to the land of the dead.

Far more to be dreaded, I think, was the dog Cerberus with his three heads, all of which barked at the same time. No dog was more ferocious than Cerberus, and but for the narcotic cake the Sibyl threw the creature, I doubt not that Æneas would have straightway become a ghost.

The region through which the Styx poured was desolate beyond description. Upon its shores all life became extinct. Mountains rose above the tide in fearful grandeur. The torrent tumbled over a fearful precipice more than two hundred feet in height, and, rushing through a gorge, became so dark that it was called Mauronero, or Black Water. Of all the rivers of the underworld there was none greater, unless perhaps it might be Lethe. By it the gods took their most solemn oaths. It was the wish of Cleomenes that he might lead the Arcadian chiefs to this river when, five hundred years before Christ, he sought to make with them a league.

Æneas entered the infernal regions just beyond the mysterious Lake Avernus, where even now one may see the cave of the Sibyl. The ground shook and emitted sulphurous flames and pent-up vapors; but one knows now that all the wild phenomena were due to the proximity of Vesuvius and Etna.

Of all the rivers of the infernal world, Lethe was the greatest. To that river Æneas came. Before him stretched a spacious valley, and on the shores of the stream a shady grove brought sweet refreshment. Along the banks grew countless flowers, and wandered a great multitude of butterflies. They floated in the enchanted air upon iridescent wings of light and gauze. Æneas inquired what all the gay creatures were, and why they resorted day and night to the shores of Lethe.

" These," Anchises answered, " are souls yet to receive bodies. Meanwhile on the banks of Lethe they flutter and wait. They drink from the river of oblivion and lose remembrance of their former lives."

" But," continued Æneas, " can it be that any one would willingly leave this paradise of beauty, refreshment, and delicious forgetfulness? "

Anchises replied, " The Creator made the soul of man from the four elements,— fire, air, earth, and water. In some earth predominates, and these are of the rude, uncultivated, tempestuous, and churlish kind. They must wait a long time for bodies. Other souls receive bodies of a commonplace sort. These love money, pleasure, and such things as interest the men and women of everyday life. A few who are yet to be ad-

mitted to Elysium will have wholly new bodies.
These are sons and daughters of light; beautiful
themselves, they are the creators and lovers of
beauty; among them are the poets, musicians,
and philosophers.   Out of the four elements all
souls are constructed."

" And the high gods took in hand
Fire, and the falling of tears,
And a measure of sliding sand
From under the feet of the years;
And froth and drift of the sea,
And dust of the laboring earth,
And bodies of things to be
In the houses of death and of birth,
And wrought with weeping and laughter,
And fashioned with loathing and love,
With life before and after,
And death beneath and above,
For a day and night and a morrow,
That his strength might endure for a span,
With travail and heavy sorrow,
The holy spirit of man.

" From the winds of the north and south
They gathered as unto strife;
They breathed upon his mouth;
They filled his body with life;
Eyesight and speech they wrought
For the veils of the soul therein;
A time for labor and thought,
A time to serve and to sin.
They gave him light in his ways,
And love, and space for delight,

And beauty and length of days,
And night, and sleep in the night.

" His speech is a burning fire;
With his lips he travaileth;
In his heart is a blind desire;
In his eyes foreknowledge of death;
He weaves and is clothed with derision;
Sows, and shall not reap;
His life is a watch or a vision
Between a sleep and a sleep."

Thus have men believed with regard to the making of the human being himself. If from the seed of the inferior gods the four elements become fertilized, the man must become a rude and vulgar creature. If the fertilization be from the loins of the high gods, then shall man's breath be as that of the flowers, and his speech shall be as the " noise of a hidden brook," tender with love and strong with all noble and gracious qualities.

It came to pass that the Sibyl, observing the shadows, said to Æneas, " It is now time that we leave the banks of the stream, and return to the world of living men."

Lethe was the great " River of Oblivion." In early days and among those who believed that it had an existence as actual as that of any stream in the world we now inhabit, its waters were thought to make men forget themselves. The Lethe that flows to-day around the life of man is not self-forgetfulness, but the great deep into

which we sink when all we have said, sung, or
done disappears,— it may be forever,— from the
remembrance of mankind. In this respect the
overwhelming and all-devouring oblivion of the
fathomless ocean may more closely resemble
man's approaching fate than do the shallows of
any river on earth or in Hades.

Below the tides of the Atlantic, upon vast
floors of sand and coral, lie treasures of every
kind. There rot side by side little fishing smacks
and the great Titanic. There are scattered the
munitions of war and beautiful books of rare
learning. There are spread out gems and jewels
that shine not for want of light. There corrupt the bones of men. A common fate was in
store for all. A much deeper ocean than that of
the Atlantic rolls above them,— the ocean of
rayless, hopeless oblivion. We may be willing
to forget ourselves. In every man's life there
are surely some things it would be good to forget. Forgetfulness of that kind is sometimes the
precursor or forerunner of better things. But
to be forgotten by others, and so to have all the
genius and toil of a lifetime wiped out as one
erases with a wet sponge a mark from a slate,—
that is a very different matter, and yet that is
the sort of Lethe against which we instinctively
contend. We contend sometimes in very foolish ways, and at other times in ways that are
only occasionally successful. We know now
that the water of river and sea has little to do
with the impending fate we dread.

For increasing numbers of men the Lethean tides are stimulants and narcotics. It is not strange that so many men use alcohol; on the contrary, I am surprised that still larger numbers do not resort to it. No one who has any knowledge of life will deny that the troubles, distresses, and tragedies of the world are many and grievous. All these we would be glad to forget when we may not escape them, and alcohol is to thousands upon thousands of our race an open door into a heaven of rest, blessedness, and glory. No doubt the use of alcohol has increased the misery of the world; but it is, nevertheless, an immediate though temporary escape that most men desire, and in stimulants they find what they want. Alcohol used in moderation is not a curse to all who invoke its aid. There are many exceptions to what may be a general rule, and each man, as his turn comes, flatters himself that he is among the exceptions. The increasing number of suicides we attribute to the use of alcohol, but it should be charged to the abuse of that drug, if drug it may be called. It is also true that alcohol has not infrequently prevented self-destruction. It is a fact that in most cases the misdemeanors of those who use stimulants are indiscriminately charged to intemperance; and yet the crime of an intemperate man may have really nothing to do with his intemperance; and also it is true that many temperate men are criminals. There are crimes that a drinking man could not commit. Most political misdemeanors

are the work of clear-headed, sober men.  Deeds
of violence are largely due to the abuse of alcohol, and quite as often to the rage of lust or the
fury of anger.

Opium may also be described as the Lethe of
our modern world.  Its inward sense of untrou-
bled peace the Chinese call " a flame which burns
far from the wind."  " No fancy," says a writer,
" is so bold, no pencil so accomplished, as to be
able to depict the visions which rise out of the
chaos of an opium-eater's brain and which display themselves to his closed eyes.  Alcohol
draws men together.  Its votaries must have
companions to laugh with, to drink with, to talk
with.  The victim of opium goes his way alone,
for the reason that no other human being can
accompany him.  No other eye can see what he
sees, no other heart can know what he enjoys and
suffers."  Again the same author writes:

" The moral effect of opium is the erection of a
veil between its victim and the world.  At first this
veil is of such diaphanous texture as to be scarcely
perceptible.  A man dimly feels that his relations
with the world have undergone a change for the
better, as he thinks, since now he has a refuge from
every ill of life.  Only when he attempts to rend
this slight tissue of illusions does he discover that
it is composed of finest steel.  His inner life may
be a heaven or it may be a hell; the fact remains
that he cannot escape from it.[1]  The veil between

[1] Not quite true at present.  The Combs Chemical Company, Chicago, Illinois, now prepares regular hyos-sco-

him and the world thickens.  He looks out on life
as one sees a light through an alabaster vase."

The old Lethe meant our forgetfulness of ourselves, but the Lethe of to-day means our drop
from the remembrance of others.  The tragedy
of it all is this, that in the latter river our hopes,
desires, and ambitions are drowned.  We see
them perish, and our every effort to save them
comes to pitiable failure.  There can be no
doubt that the impelling motive behind a very
large part of modern literature is the desire of
authors to live in and through their books when
they themselves are no longer upon earth.
Whether an author will in the other world care
in the least that his books continue to sell and
his fame to hold out against the destructive
energy of time is another question.  He does
care now, and that is to him the immediate and
important matter.  A little book of poems was
published in this country about fifty years ago
by a man who was then a youth, but who has
since that time given the world a number of
books.  In the volume referred to was a poem
called " Ambition's Prayer."  It was not much
of a poem, if, indeed, it was worthy of being
called a poem in any sense of the word, but it
gave expression to the hunger for remembrance

phine tablets to be used in the gradual reduction of the
amount of the drug taken, and in the final elimination
of the habit.  The treatment is attended with little or no
pain and is successful in a large number of cases.

with utmost frankness.    Very few verses have the
naked audacity of that composition of fifty years
ago.    The poet sings:

> " O God, that I might be
> When I have ceased to be!
> O God, that I might live
> When I have ceased to live! "

This deep longing for the impossible is a most
pathetic thing, and yet it may be that in that
very longing we might see, if we only would, a
forecast of personal immortality.    But one way
or the other it would be a good thing if only we
could substitute for " Ambition's Prayer," which
seems to us so very poor, the familiar lines beginning with " O may I join the choir invisible ";
and yet I doubt not that George Eliot found satisfaction in anticipation of the regard she well
knew would be her reward.    I once asked a man
where he was born, and was surprised at his
answer.    He said, " I was born in an iron cage,
against the bars of which I have well-nigh beaten
out my life."    I could hear after each sad word
the low moan of the River of Oblivion.

An artist once said to me, " I know my pictures are good, and yet I am compelled to stand
aside and see them neglected or sacrificed while
inferior paintings are appreciated and their makers rewarded.    I have, however, this advantage:
I am not dependent upon my art for a living.
Yet I have ambition, and I naturally desire recognition.    As a man of genius I would be known

and remembered. I wish to live in and for art."

I answered my friend in somewhat the following fashion: " I do not doubt your genius, nor do I deny that men of inferior ability win where you fail. You cannot prevent that. And after all, can you not allow them the brief satisfaction of harmlessly deceiving themselves and others? In the end, for them and for well-nigh all of us, the waters of Lethe will be cold and deep. If the ' art-loving public ' prefer tea-chest chromos to your paintings, nothing that you can say or do will change matters. You have the satisfaction, if it be any satisfaction, of knowing that your pictures are of value while those that win the recognition of the crowd can never hold a place of permanent importance. The producers of poor work may, and doubtless will, establish organizations for self-recognition; they will vote themselves medals. But what will it all come to? Why should any one grudge the butterflies that float their little hour above the shores of Lethe the brief triumph they so enjoy? You are financially independent of your art. Why should you not be morally independent of the poor success of inferior workmen? If you want a medal, employ a good artificer to make you one. You can vote yourself any amount of bric-a-brac, and in the end it will matter nothing to you or to any one else whether you had an assortment of ' articles of vertu ' or died without such an assortment. I should say that the right thing for you to do is to go on producing the very

best work you are able to produce.  Live in your
work, and take delight in it.  Help some other
good painter who shares your want of appreciation but not your financial means.  Save him
from humiliation."

A very amusing thing happened in one of our
American cities some years ago.  An eccentric
clergyman, having looked to colleges a long time
for recognition, helped himself to the degree of
doctor in divinity.  He was asked from what institution of learning he had received the degree.
He said, " No college gave it to me.  I gave it to
myself."  Some one said to him, " Do you not
think that a dishonest act? "  " No," said he,
" I told no lie about it.  I stole no degree from
any man, nor did I steal it from a college.  In
my opinion I deserve the degree.  I have added
D.D. to my name, and confiscated two slivers of
the English alphabet, but there are letters enough
left for all the rest of the world."  A president of
one of the colleges said to him, " But you cannot
confer a degree upon yourself."  " That," said
he, " is nonsense, for I have already conferred it
upon myself."

To my mind the sad thing about that sort of
pleasantry (for it was nothing but jesting, view
it as we may) is the fact that a man of ability,
for he was one, was disturbed by lack of appreciation.  It seems to me that a minister of the
gospel should be above troubling himself with
such matters.  Henry Ward Beecher declined
a doctor's degree.  " Well," some one remarks,

" Beecher was a man of supreme ability." I think
every man of worth to his race should be greater
than any degree that may be conferred. Why
should a clergyman who honors himself covet a
degree, and why should he or any one else take
the trouble to decline it? Let the man of genius
do his work in the joy and confidence of that
work. Let the minister of the gospel look higher
for his reward.

Academus was the original owner of a garden
or grove in the suburbs of Athens. The garden
afterwards came into the possession of the public through a bequest of Cimon, and later still it
was known as the favorite resort of the lovers
of philosophy. Even in those early days the
seat of learning was identified with commercial
interests. The garden was a piece of real estate,
and had an owner, very much as the laboratories
and libraries of Oxford and Harvard have owners
to-day. The bequest of Cimon and the gifts
of Carnegie and others were and are points of
contact between dollars and letters. The Academy in Athens and that in Paris come to the same
thing. In both there were men who received
what they did not deserve, and those as well who
deserved more than they obtained. There were
those in the time of Cimon who practically honored
themselves, forgetting the sacred admonition,
" Let another praise thee and not thyself." Perhaps I should not say that they forgot the admonition, for, living at so early a period, they

may have had no opportunity of knowing anything about it. They wished to be regarded as
philosophers, as men now desire to be known as
poets, historians, novelists, and scholars. Their
desire, in those bygone times, was to escape the
River of Oblivion; but only a few succeeded.

To-day the same desire prevails, and the same
result must follow. On the grave of Keats in
the old Protestant Cemetery at Rome is the inscription: " This grave contains all that was
mortal of a young English poet, who, on his
death-bed, in the bitterness of his heart at the
malicious power of his enemies, desired these
words to be engraved on his tombstone: ' Here
lies one whose name was writ in water.' " His
name was not writ in water, but he thought it
was. Most of us write our names in sand and
wave, but why should there be such bitterness
of heart because our fate is as that of most of our
companions? Life is spoiled by our foolish vanity. A fictitious value is given to an iridescent
bubble. We are belittled by our self-thought,
self-seeking, and self-pity. Dr. Holmes wrote: —

> " Many an eye has danced to see
>     That banner in the sky."

One sometimes wonders how many professors
there may be in Harvard, Columbia, Princeton,
and other seats of learning who would not dance
to see their portraits in the New York " Herald "
or " Times." There will never be any regular

line of steam packets on the River Lethe, for no one will ever pay a farthing for a trip to Oblivion.

But to return to the consideration of our modern Lethe,— alcohol and opium. From most ancient times men have used stimulants and narcotics. They will continue to use them in the face of whatever restrictions may surround them and whatever legal enactments may be adopted. A glance at the world's consumption of intoxicants will, I think, give force to our statement:

Coffee berries are taken, in the form of an infusion, by two millions of the world's inhabitants.

Paraguay tea is taken by ten millions.

Coca by as many.

Chicory, either pure or mixed with coffee, by forty millions.

Cacao, either as chocolate or in some other form, by fifty millions.

Hashish is eaten and smoked by three hundred millions.

Opium by four hundred millions.

Chinese tea is taken by five hundred millions.

Finally, all the known nations of the world are addicted to the use of tobacco.

The matter stands thus: Every year 3,000,-000,000 pounds of tea, 220,000,000 pounds of coffee and cocoa, 25,000,000 pounds of opium, 200,000,000 pounds of hashish, and 865,000,-

000 pounds of tobacco are consumed. Now add the quantity of arsenic and alcoholic liquors used, and the figures open into a wilderness. Strychnine has been pressed into service, and is used in very large doses. The Polynesians intoxicate themselves with a liquor prepared from pepper (*Piperinebrians vel methysticum*). The Kamchatkans use the *Agaricus muscarius;* and many eastern nations chew betel-nut. China is now greatly reducing the amount of opium used by its inhabitants, and without doubt the new Harrison anti-narcotic law, which went into effect in the United States March 1, 1915, will for a time lessen the amount of opium and other narcotic drugs consumed by Americans. In both countries, however, there will be great danger of an increased consumption of alcohol in every form.

Much has been written of late upon the opium-addiction of physicians and nurses. Why the apothecary is not in even greater danger of forming the habit I cannot understand. Opium and many other drugs, as cocaine and hashish, are always at his command. He has but to step into the little room in the rear of his shop where the deadly poisons are kept, to find whatever his soul craves. Dr. Crothers, in his " Morphinism and Narcomania from Other Drugs," says: " Some recent statistics indicate that the medical profession furnishes a large proportion of cases. In France and Germany, among the morphine cases known, the physicians are most prominent.

In a study of 3244 physicians in the United States, ten per cent were estimated as either secret or open users of the drug." Statistics like these certainly present a very distressing picture for the consideration of the thousands of invalids who must trust some physician, in the hope, at least, that he may be a temperate and conscientious practitioner.

Dr. Lambert, in a paper on " The Intoxication Impulse," said:

" There is no question but that the reasons for excessive drinking in youth are different from those of the later twenties and early thirties, and still different from those of the forties and later life. In early manhood excessive drinking is an attempt to celebrate the joy of life . . . while the man who has reached middle life or passed it seeks intoxication or the narcotic effect of alcohol. He deliberately drinks, not because he is with his friends, but because he wishes to forget himself, his friends, and existence itself. The vast majority that drink, however, be their age what it may, drink for the narcotic effect. They wish to obliterate something which they do not like to face or cannot face in consciousness.

" Women in only a small number of cases drink to excess; the vast majority of those who drink drink to obliterate something they do not like to face in consciousness. Often, moreover, after struggling against a desire to drink and bring on forgetfulness, they will, in their desperation and weariness, drink that they may forget the struggle

and cease to remember both the dreaded memory
and their struggle to forget it.

" There is a large class of men whose individual problems drive them to narcotic forgetfulness.
They are persons of sensitive natures; men who
from their early youth have harbored feelings that
have been hurt by being misunderstood, have been
hurt by feeling that in some way they were not the
same as their average boyish companions, and
therefore inferior."

Cocaine and heroin are able to give for the
time self-confidence as well as oblivion. In the
early days the Peruvian Indians used cocaine.
They chewed the leaves of the plant which contains the drug. It greatly increased their power
of endurance, and enabled them to go upon the
war-path many hours without sleep or rest.
Here we have after every line the sound of the
waves of the River of Oblivion. Men desire to
escape from themselves, from their past, from
their present, and from their anticipation of the
future. St. Augustine said long centuries ago:
" Men are restless, and never can they find rest
until they find it in God." There alone is peace,
calmness and repose. Men would forget for a
time defeat, failure, and inferiority. They would
forget the success of others and the want of appreciation under which they themselves have
writhed. I confess I do not understand the feeling here presented. It is a great thing to live
in one's art, and in it to live one's own life.

Why may we not trust our own estimate of our own worth?

Men and women of artistic and literary life,— musicians, artists, authors, actors, and sometimes statesmen,— seem to feel a special need for one kind of stimulant or another. In certain cases an agent having an opposite effect is demanded, and the overtaxed brain finds temporary relief in a drug having a sedative influence and capable of allaying nervous irritation. This may be seen by running the eye over the following list of persons given to the use of alcohol: David Hume, Thomas Moore, Robert Burns, Edgar A. Poe, Joseph Addison, Richard Chenevix Trench, Thomas Hood, Leo X, Turlough O'Carolan, Thomas Paine, Daniel Webster, Peter Paul Rubens, Benjamin Disraeli, William E. Gladstone, Benjamin Charles Incledon, Edmund Kean, and Johann Wolfgang von Goethe. Some of these used alcohol to excess and were injured thereby. Could they have used it to the degree called for by the special demands of their mental and physical systems, they might have been helped; but it seems to be given to comparatively few to employ stimulants with anything like moderation. It is, therefore, as a rule better that most men should find their help in other directions. Still, not all in the foregoing list misused drink. Some, and the list might have been greatly enlarged, used wine and other intoxicants without harm to themselves. I am not so sure that their example was harmless to others, but of that I may not judge.

The following persons resorted to tobacco: Walter Raleigh, Alfred Tennyson, John Keats, Thomas Carlyle, Leo XIII, Napoleon I, Isaac Newton, and Robert Louis Stevenson. These are, of course, but a few of the many distinguished men who believed themselves benefited by the use of tobacco. Fewer persons have been hurt by the weed than by alcohol and drugs, but then it must be remembered that there is in tobacco very much less of that oblivion for which men seek than can be extracted from comparatively small amounts of alcohol or opium.

Here are the names of six men who were habitual users of opium; it will be seen at a glance that they were, all of them, men of a peculiar cast of mind: Thomas De Quincey, Samuel Taylor Coleridge, Dante Gabriel Rossetti, John Philip Kemble, John Randolph, and Robert Hall. With the single exception of Randolph, the above-named men were all gifted with a vivid and powerful imagination. Three of them were authors. Hall, though a distinguished clergyman, was a man of remarkable literary finish. Read his miscellaneous works and Foster's " Essay on the Character of Dr. Robert Hall " if you are not already acquainted with his beautiful English, which always charms the reader. All six of the men named were men of great intensity. William Wilberforce was a confirmed user of opium, but he was in most of his characteristics unlike the others here grouped. Alexander Pope found his intellectual help and strength in strong coffee. Alexander Wedderburn was in the habit of applying blisters to his person.

The hunger for immortality is by no means universal. There are in this world millions of men and women who not only do not want to live forever, but who long for that very extinction which we so dread whenever the dark thought of its possibility clouds the mind. And that thought, so unwelcome, against which we contend, comes soon or late to well-nigh every thoughtful person. In England and America as well as in distant India there are those who hope for annihilation and who look forward to it with expectancy. I do not see what is to restrain such persons (if they are not Brahmans or Buddhists) from suicide when physical or mental distress renders the world for them unattractive. Why endure the hopeless pain of a disease like cancer if death ends all? The deterrent influence that operates upon minds developed under the force of Christian teaching is, in most cases where self-murder suggests itself, the fear that death does not end all. It is this that "makes us rather bear those ills we have than fly to others that we know not of." Yet of course there are those who, maddened by anguish or impelled by a firm conviction that death is followed by annihilation, scruple not to slay themselves.

Most men can in time bring themselves to believe anything. The philosopher who every morning and evening said aloud to himself, " *Post mortem nihil est, ipsaque mors nihil,*" in time came to believe the Latin words, and, having a severe tooth-ache, shot himself. The last words of Harriet Martineau, the learned translator of the works of Auguste Comte, were: " I have had a noble share of life, and I do not ask for any other life. I see no reason why the existence of Harriet Martineau should be perpetuated." She looked forward to the River of Oblivion with inward satisfaction. She had had all she wanted of this life, and, complacency filling her soul, she proceeded to cast aside the squeezed orange. It did not occur to her to inquire whether millions of her fellow creatures had enjoyed even so much as a teaspoonful of the juice from the orange of which she had had her fill. One may suck all the juice out of life and chew and swallow pulp and rind as well, and be made only the more selfish thereby. Professor Clifford rejoiced in the belief that death meant for all the sorrow, trouble, and sin of this life the peace of dreamless and endless slumber. I knew well the late Moncure D. Conway, the able biographer of Thomas Paine, and I am sure, from many conversations held with him at the Authors' Club in New York and elsewhere, that death meant to him precisely what it did to Professor Clifford. He had no desire for another life.

Nirvana, stripped of all adventitious surroundings, is nothing but extinction of being. Mr. Alger has pointed out, in his " Critical History of the Doctrine of Future Life," that seven theories of the soul's destination are known to theological science. They are annihilation, reabsorption, resurrection, conveyance, recurrence, migration, and transition. There seem to be or to have been advocates of each of these theories. Annihilation comes first in the list, and has in the East many who hold firmly to it. Strange as it may seem to us who dwell under a different sky and are trained to cherish a contrary faith, the Nirvana of the far East is to Oriental minds precisely what a Buddhist writer calls it, " the abyss of peace, starless and never-ending rest." The weariness of life which overhangs the Oriental world and creates a dense pessimism that persists even in the presence of youth, health, and wealth, is a thing well-nigh unknown in our Christian civilization. And yet in some places in our own land it is beginning to appear. I fear it will increase as our civilization becomes older. World-weariness, life-weariness, and pessimism brood over the sleeping East with its ancient and changeless civilization. Doubtless the religious uncertainty of the age in which we live has something to do with the low estimate of life we see around us. With a decadent civilization comes an increase of insanity. Without Christianity the moral trend of the world is downward. In other words, take from us the hope of another world, and the world we now have degenerates. Doubtless Buddha has been a source of comfort to millions of souls, but the East that embraced his doctrine is dreaming still, and dreaming often most unholy dreams. She will change only when the living Christ comes to dwell within her heart.

Max Müller has pointed out, in his " Chips from a German Workshop," the fact that a keen sense of human misery is the starting point in the philosophy of both Brahmanism and Buddhism. But the solution of the dark mystery of evil is not the same in both religious systems. The Brahman, admitting that the creation of the world, and so of every man in it, was an accident to be overcome, holds that the unhappy consequences of it are to be neutralized through absorption of the human soul into the universal Spirit, or Brahma. The Buddhist, on the contrary, holding with his neighbor, the Brahman, that creation was a sad mistake and that life is a calamity, does not see his way out of the difficulty through absorption into the universal Spirit, but holds that Nirvana can be reached only after centuries of transmigrating, and that Nirvana, when reached, will be found to be not absorption, but absolute extinction, of being. Nirvana is freedom from birth and death, and all that these contain. It is freedom from transmigration that prolongs man's existence by extending it through countless circles of animal and even plant life. It is one of the great doctrines of the East that man is punished for an evil life by being born over and over again into inferior forms of existence. A wicked man may after death reappear in the world as a loathsome serpent or a despised insect. Man ascends " an infinite ladder of redemption," through births and deaths without number, until at last, after millions of centuries, the wriggling worm is endowed again with human consciousness, and, standing erect beneath the stars, it calls itself a man. Now comes the supreme opportunity. If as a man he does right, the doors of Nirvana open. He enters through those doors and passes into nothingness. He is now blown out as a flame is extinguished by the evening breeze. His weary spirit fades away in darkness and oblivion. His transmigrating days and all other days are over forever.

To Eastern philosophy consciousness is a thing to be dreaded. Inanimate nature is in some ways more to be desired than man's estate, which is cursed by perpetual change. Life and change are two great evils. Change means, after this life, transmigration with its humiliation and distress. Life is to be extinguished. But suicide will not extinguish it, for death only brings man into the field of transmigration. The man slays himself, and at once he may become a ser-

pent, a fish, or a bug, and as such he is no less
a living creature than when he was a man.  Not
death, but Nirvana, is the ultimate good and the
great liberator.

The consequences of our good or evil deeds
are mystically embodied in what is called our
Karma.  This follows us from life to life,
through our many transmigrations, and deter-
mines what these shall be.  It lifts us in the direction of heaven and Nirvana, or pushes us toward hell and perpetual change.  Karma is the
entire sum of what we have done, whether good
or bad, and is in a measure under our control.
The Buddhist's heaven is not a finality.  We
cannot remain in its divine enclosure forever.
After a time we must depart from its glory and
begin again the dismal round of transmigration.
Nothing endures but Nirvana.  Extinction of
being or annihilation is the supreme and only
real good.  To that the Buddhist aspires.  All
his philosophy cries to him:

" Be worthy of death; and so learn to live
That every incarnation of thy soul,
In other realms, and worlds, and firmaments,
Shall be more pure and high."

A distinguished Hindoo writer said of Nirvana,
" It is freedom from all sorrow.  It is nothing,
and yet, nevertheless, it is that for which we all
strive."  To the Buddhist the words of the poet
are true in every line:

" Cessation is true rest,
And sleep for them opprest;
And not to be were best.

" Annihilation is
A better state than this,
Better than woe or bliss.

" The name is dread; the thing
Is death without its sting,
An overshadowing."

The doctrine of transmigration offers few attractions to the western mind, and yet it is not without its brighter side. No doubt it has failed of exalting the life of man, but it has certainly improved the condition of the lower animals. There is little cruelty in India. One does not like to maltreat the dog that may be his father, nor will he slay the reptile that may be his mother.

" Crush not the feeble, inoffensive worm:
Thy sister's spirit wears that humble form.
Why should thy cruel arrow smite yon bird?
In him thy brother's plaintive song is heard.
Let not thy anger on thy dog descend;
That faithful animal was once thy friend."

Mr. Alger says, in his book before referred to, " The etymological force of the word Nirvana is extinction." He goes on to say: " When the fire is extinguished, the substance of the flame continues to exist under other forms; " and so he thinks that after all the word may have contained the thought of immortality. I very much doubt whether the originators of the doctrine of transmigration and of the sister doctrine of Nirvana knew anything of the indestructibleness of matter. When they saw the flame expire, they thought it annihilated. I believe the early Buddhists regarded Nirvana as extinction of personality.

The Brahman held to an opinion very different from that of the Buddhist. The former believed in the existence of a Universal Spirit who created all things, and he looked forward to absorption into the Divine Person as the highest possible good. The latter believe in no God of any kind, and they anticipate personal extinction as the blessed end of all the transmigrations through which the pilgrim-soul must pass. Both hold to the doctrine of transmigration, but the Brahman regards all his different births as a fixed necessity, ending at last in oneness with God. In the final absorption the Brahman parts from his personal and human consciousness, and becomes Brahma. He exchanges his human consciousness for the divine consciousness. He is able to say, " I am Brahma." He is of the substance of God.

The feeling is beautifully expressed in a Hindu song which has been thus translated into English by a missionary:

" The snowflake that glistens at noon on Kilasa,
    Dissolved by the sunbeam, descends to the plain;

There mingling with Gunga, it flows to the ocean,
And lost in its waters, returns not again.

"On the rose-leaf at morning bright glistens the
dewdrop
That in vapor exhaled falls in nourishing rain;
Then in rills back to Gunga through green fields
meanders,
Till onward it flows to the ocean again.

"A snowflake still whitens the peak of Kilasa,
But the snowflake of yesterday flows to the main;
At dawning a dewdrop still hangs on the rose-leaf,
But the dewdrop of yesterday comes not again.

"The soul that is freed from the bondage of nature
Escapes from illusions of joy and of pain;
And pure as the flame that is lost in the sunshine,
It comes not,— it goes not,— it comes not again."

Of course absorption into the person of God
is a doctrine by no means confined to the far
East. In all lands and ages it has been variously
expressed, and it is ever at the foundation of
mysticism in whatever shape. It may be discovered in Latin and Greek authors, and in early
and even modern Christian writers. To all the
soul sometimes appears to be

"A silver stream
Breaking with laughter from the lake divine
Whence all things flow."

Lethe is not far removed from Nirvana. The
same necessity and deep desire created both.

Among the rivers of the underworld no stream can compare with the calm and refreshing waters of the River of Oblivion, flowing through quiet shores fringed with drowsy poppies and the crimson cups of fragrant roses.

" Music," it has been said, " is sweetest near or over rivers, where the echo thereof is best rebounded by the water." The sad, sweet music of humanity sounds forever over the River of Oblivion. Its echoes float, now tenderly, and anon with fierce and rebellious fury, as the case may be with the man from whose heart come all those feelings, regrets, and desires that lend variety to the deathless harmony. For those who sorrow forgetfulness has its own delight. The waters that ripple in " the dancing tide " are cool and refreshing.

From old age we sometimes catch our first vision of the river. The harassing and tormenting passions die, one by one. The ache and smart of life disappear. We enjoy less, but it is true also that we suffer less. In youth and midlife we know the bitterness of a sorrowful heart. Care shifts its burden to our shoulders. We are burned by the raging fever of love. Age soothes our sorrow, lifts the burden, and whispers to love, " No more." We grow old and forget. And then we are ourselves forgotten.